EARTHLY IMMORTALITIES

EARTHLY IMMORTALITIES

How the Dead Live On
in the Lives of Others

PETER MOORE

REAKTION BOOKS

To George Laurence and Muriel

IN PIAM MEMORIAM

Published by
REAKTION BOOKS LTD
Unit 32, Waterside
44–48 Wharf Road
London N1 7UX, UK
www.reaktionbooks.co.uk

First published 2019
Copyright © Peter Moore 2019

Printed and bound in Great Britain
by T. J. International, Padstow, Cornwall

A catalogue record for this book is available from the British Library

ISBN 978 1 78914 058 3

CONTENTS

PREFACE

The idea of writing this book suggested itself while I was writing another, a book on the subject of post-mortem survival.[1] In the course of writing this earlier book, it became clear to me that two quite distinct conceptions of immortality have been of concern to humankind – two distinct conceptions which nevertheless intersect in various ways. On the one hand is the idea that we continue our existence in another world after ending our life in this one. This I call 'otherworldly immortality'. On the other, those who have died can be seen as 'living on' in this world, through what they have said or done or materially left behind them. It is this second kind of post-mortem survival, which I loosely define as 'earthly immortality', which forms the main subject of the present book.

One has only to glance through publishers' catalogues and academic journals to see that intellectual interest in the broad area of death and dying is very much alive and kicking, so to speak. This interest embraces a variety of topics mediated through a whole spectrum of disciplines. How people deal with and reflect upon death and dying is an issue for religion, philosophy, psychology, psychiatry, medicine, anthropology, sociology, history and literary studies. Where the question of an afterlife arises, it is not surprising that it is ideas about some kind of 'otherworldly immortality' that command the most attention. Somewhat thinner on the ground are studies that explicitly address the question of an earthly immortality. Among the books that have dealt with this theme in recent decades, special mention should be made of Zygmunt Bauman's *Mortality, Immortality and Other Life Strategies* (1992), Stephen R. L. Clark's *How to Live Forever: Science*

Fiction and Philosophy (1995), Andrew Bennett's *Romantic Poets and the Culture of Posterity* (1999), Robert Harrison's *The Dominion of the Dead* (2003), Sandra Gilbert's *Death's Door* (2006), Samuel Scheffler's *Death and the Afterlife* (2013) and Thomas W. Laqueur's *The Work of the Dead* (2015). These fine works of scholarship, along with many of the other books and articles cited in the References or listed in the Bibliography, encouraged me to think there was room for a more general account of ideas about earthly immortality, one which would allow broader reflection on the nature and value of such immortality and on its relationship to conceptions of otherworldly immortality.

The central focus of the book is on how the ideas, activities and personalities of those who have died, in their continuing influence upon the lives of later generations, can be said to constitute an earthly afterlife for the dead. But attention is also given to some important subsidiary themes relating to mortality and posterity. One of these is the idea that people might be able to live on by not dying in the first place. This idea, originally confined to legend and fantasy, has in modern times come to be regarded by some as a real possibility within the grasp of the cybernetic and medical sciences. Nor is the idea of achieving an immortality of earthly existence absent from at least some religious traditions. The most obvious candidates here are versions of the doctrines of resurrection and reincarnation. But do either of these doctrines really promise what would-be earthly immortalists are seeking?

A second theme concerns the way in which people have learned, or at least sought, to come to terms with their mortality by eschewing any hope or even desire for immortality. Prominent here is the idea that it is not mortality that is the problem, but rather the immortality for which we not only hopelessly but mistakenly yearn. On this view, happiness and fulfilment in life come from viewing one's present earthly existence as something complete in itself. At its most positive, it is the view that human mortality is a blessing rather than a curse, and that whatever meaning our lives may have, or may acquire, is to be found within and not beyond the limits of our mortal existence. Such views are nevertheless open to challenge.

A third subsidiary theme concerns the attitudes people have to the world that will one day continue to exist without them, and also the attitudes they may have to the prospect of a future world in which all human life has become extinct. To what extent does the meaning we find in our present lives depend upon our assumption that there will always be new generations to continue the human adventure? And even if human life is likely one day to disappear from the Earth, might there yet be responsibilities which we, along with future generations, would have towards a coming world without us?

INTRODUCTION

'Tis immortality decyphers man,
And opens all the myst'ries of his make.
Without it, half his instincts are a riddle;
Without it, all his virtues are a dream.
EDWARD YOUNG[1]

I

What usually comes to mind when we think about the possibility of post-mortem survival is personal survival of bodily death in an otherworldly afterlife. A belief in this kind of afterlife continues to inform the hopes, and in some cases fears, of millions of people around the world. This is not the only possible kind of afterlife, however. The dead can also be the subjects of an earthly afterlife. They can be seen as maintaining their earthly identities, and even some kind of 'real presence', in the memories of the living, in the lives of their progeny, in their creative and other achievements, in their physical possessions, and even in their bodily remains. My purpose in this book is to identify the varieties of earthly afterlife; to see how such afterlives are engendered, cultivated and celebrated; and to examine how ideas about earthly afterlives relate to ideas about otherworldly afterlives.

An instructive parallel to the idea of an earthly afterlife is found in the phenomenon of the 'literary afterlife' (and also of the 'iconographic afterlife' and the 'musical afterlife'). In its more general usage, the term 'literary afterlife' describes how ideas, texts and events, as well as characters both real and fictional, are kept alive within the literary traditions of a culture. Thus one can talk about, for example, the 'literary afterlife' of the Vietnam War, of King Arthur's Camelot or of Darwin's *On the Origin of Species*. In the more specific sense relevant here, however, the term applies where fictional characters originating with one author reappear, in later texts or in different media, in the work of others. They will not necessarily appear under their original names or with their original identities intact. Thus fictional characters (or events, or places) may 'live on' not just through a continuing interest in their original stories, but through their reappearance in new forms or contexts, literary or non-literary. The 'afterlives' of Classical and biblical characters in the visual, literary and musical arts provide obvious examples here.[2] In more recent times one can cite characters such as Bram Stoker's Count Dracula or Ian Fleming's James Bond, both of whom have lived on more vigorously after their authors' deaths than they did beforehand, mainly through the medium of cinema. In some cases, moreover, characters manage to 'escape' their fictional confines and come to be treated as real historical figures. Many people have visited Baker Street in London to see where 'Sherlock Holmes' once lived. A literary afterlife can also form part of an earthly afterlife. For example, the various characters in Shakespeare's plays are a principle means whereby Shakespeare's own earthly afterlife is manifested. The 'immortality' of these characters is also Shakespeare's 'immortality'.[3]

Yet an afterlife – of whatever kind – does not necessarily entail an eternal or immortal state of existence. An earthly afterlife, like the ordinary life that precedes it, must eventually come to an end, even if it lasts until the end of the world. As for 'immortality', in many contexts this term is used rather loosely to refer not to an eternal or unchanging state of existence, whether here on Earth or in a next world, but rather to a life which although ended for a particular individual is now preserved, potentially indefinitely, in the minds of the living. But whereas an 'earthly immortality' in any literal sense names an ideal or aspiration rather than a realizable attainment, a longer or shorter 'earthly afterlife' of some kind is not only a realistic prospect but for many people an inevitable one.

II

The reality, or prospect, of some kind of earthly afterlife for the dead can be a powerful consolation for the bereaved, not least when the existence of an otherworldly afterlife is doubted or denied. Quite apart from this, many people consider an earthly afterlife worthy of cultivation and celebration in its own right – and even as something superior to any kind of otherworldly afterlife. Whatever their value in relation to otherworldly survival, moreover, the earthly afterlives of the dead undoubtedly play an important role in the development of our individual and historical identities.

History speaks to the living through the dead. According to Edward Shils, essential to the survival of every social group is a collective consciousness based on a legacy of human memories. These memories, received and reinterpreted by each generation, make up a cumulative and normative tradition, 'which links the generations of the dead with the generations of the living in the constitution of a society', functioning as 'a guarantor of order and civilization'.[4] In this way the dead – the named and the nameless alike – continue to make their mark in history. 'It is this chain of memory and of the tradition which assimilates it that enables societies to go on reproducing themselves while also changing.'[5] But in this continuous relationship between the living and the dead through human history, not all commentators have accorded priority to the living. According to Auguste Comte, for example,

> the social existence of man really consists much more in the continuous succession of generations than in the solidarity of the existing generation. The living are always, by the necessity of the case – and the more so the more we advance in time – under the government of the dead. Such is the fundamental law of human order.[6]

Not all commentators have taken such a benign view of the influence of the dead on the living, however. As Karl Marx famously states,

> Men make their own history, but they do not make it as they please; they do not make it under self-selected circumstances, but under circumstances existing already, given and transmitted from the past. The tradition of all dead generations weighs like a nightmare on the brains of the living.[7]

Our attitudes to the ideas and achievements of past generations may be positive or negative, or simply neutral, but there can be no doubting their pervasive influence upon our own lives. At a more personal level, our own identities are profoundly shaped by our memories of, and attachment to, those now dead. It is we ourselves, here and now, who are living the earthly immortality of countless earlier individuals long or recently dead. Our own earthly afterlives may be only a future condition or possibility, but we are already part of the earthly afterlives of others. Our present lives are part of their posterity; and their immortality is part of our own. This is brought out in Alice Meynell's poem 'A Song of Derivations', which opens as follows:

> I come from nothing; but from where
> Come the undying thoughts I bear?
> Down, through long links of death and birth,
> From the past poets of the earth,
> My immortality is there.[8]

Meynell is referring specifically to poets and to poetry, but what she says surely applies to every field of human interest and endeavour. Immortality is also understood here not so much as an eternal existence of some kind, whether earthly or otherworldly, but rather as a quality of human experience already accessible within a finite lifetime.

The earthly afterlives of the dead undoubtedly provide as powerful a means of maintaining some kind of relationship with them as does any form of otherworldly survival, and in some respects a more powerful one (since an earthly afterlife is an open book as an otherworldly one is not). Praise and respect for the dead are maintained by acknowledging and engaging with their earthly legacies. Likewise, when we talk of the dead being dishonoured or even harmed, we refer – at least in the first instance – to something done or not done in relation to their earthly legacy: misrepresentation of what they did or said, neglect or belittlement of their achievements, abuse or destruction of their bodily remains, and so on. Whether or not the dead continue to exist in another world, they certainly continue to have a presence within this one.

III

In most contexts, earthly and otherworldly afterlives are neither incompatible nor in competition with one another. Bereaved people who take comfort from believing that their loved ones continue to exist in another world are rarely indifferent to the prospect of these loved ones also living on through their earthly legacy. Again, earthly commemorations of the dead are typically informed by references to their otherworldly survival, just as their otherworldly survival is likely to be described in earthly terms – either because it is believed to be literally earth-like or because earthly metaphors are deemed the only meaningful way of describing a life hereafter. In many traditions, moreover, the quality and even possibility of a post-mortem existence is held to depend upon the proper burial and commemoration of a person's mortal remains. Some afterlife conceptions actually blur the distinction between the otherworldly and the earthly, by locating the surviving person within the confines of the present world. Prominent examples here are certain versions of the doctrines of resurrection and reincarnation.

In many cultures, moreover, the present world and the otherworld are not regarded as mutually exclusive realms of existence. Thus it is widely believed, or simply assumed, that the souls or spirits of the dead will continue to have a role in earthly affairs, and even to be accessible to the living at certain times or under certain circumstances. Beliefs about the earthly presence and influence of the dead, whether true or false, will thus contribute to the overall earthly afterlife of deceased persons. The Christian cult of saints provides a clear example not just of the presumed continuity between this world and the otherworld, but of the posthumous activity of the dead in the construction of their earthly afterlives. Hagiographies can, accordingly, be viewed as texts which both celebrate a saint's exemplary life on Earth and encourage the living to seek spiritual or material benefits from that saint's continuing activity on Earth. In other contexts, of course, the presumed influence or activities of the dead may be viewed as troublesome, or even as malign, and this experience too will colour the overall narrative of a person's earthly afterlife. In all of this, however, the fact remains that the earthly afterlives of the dead are experienced not by the dead themselves but only by the living. What the surviving dead themselves would continue to experience, whether in this world or in what for them would be the next world, is a topic beyond the scope of the present enquiry.

Despite their often close connections, therefore, the fundamental differences between an earthly and an otherworldly afterlife cannot be forgotten. An otherworldly afterlife typically implies the substantive survival of the self: persons remain self-conscious subjects with continuing identities in a new mode of existence.[9] In an earthly afterlife, by contrast, the dead are substantively absent. They do not 'inhabit' their own earthly afterlives, we might say.[10] It is quite another question, of course, whether the dead, if they do survive in an otherworldly afterlife, could also be aware of their earthly legacies. But if they were aware of them, this could only be as part of their otherworldly afterlives. On

Earth itself, the earthly afterlives of the dead are experienced only by the living, and indeed depend for their continuation exclusively upon the interests and activities of the living. Yet this does not mean that people cannot anticipate the nature of their prospective earthly afterlife while they are still alive. The things for which one will be remembered are in most cases well in place long before one dies. Thus the living can face death with the satisfaction (or regret) of knowing how others are likely to go on remembering them, upholding their values, furthering their projects, and so on. More to the point, while time and opportunity remain, they can take steps to make their lives memorable and worthy of respect.[11]

The second fundamental difference between earthly and otherworldly afterlives is in respect of temporality. An otherworldly afterlife is typically understood as the realization, or attainment, of an eternal mode of existence – one which, while not necessarily unchanging in itself, is not threatened by the destructive change to which all earthly things are subject. Earthly afterlives, by contrast, are subject to exactly the same processes that led to the death of their subjects in the first place. One question here is what exactly is meant by an eternal mode of existence. According to the philosopher John McTaggart, the word 'eternity' has at least three distinct uses: 'to denote unending time, to denote the timelessness of truths, and to denote the timelessness of existences'. He considers the first of these to be an improper usage, despite its being the most popular one.[12] A distinction can also be drawn between the eternal and the sempiternal, the former being ascribed to any entity having 'the complete possession all at once of illimitable life' (Boethius) and the latter to any entity having limitless duration in time.[13] There is a certain amount of what might be called metaphysical snobbery among philosophers and theologians in regard to time, with timelessness typically considered superior to the merely everlasting. Given that the ordinary human experience of time is already puzzling enough, it would seem rash to assume that the surviving dead (who presumably do not by dying cease being human) would stop existing in time or stop experiencing time, or that a timeless existence, whatever this might mean, would necessarily be superior to a 'timeful' one. If time does indeed continue for the dead, one might reasonably expect it to be experienced as richly as it is on Earth, even if some of the ways in which it is experienced are likely to be inconceivable to the living.

Given the fundamental difference between an earthly and an otherworldly afterlife, one might well question whether the same set of terms should be used to describe both, and even why one should want to compare them in the first place. No form of earthly afterlife, however extensive, could last forever, and no form of earthly afterlife could possibly satisfy one's hope or expectation of surviving death as a self-conscious subject. Christopher Cherry, one of the very few philosophers to have examined the logic of seeking 'surrogates' for post-mortem survival, comments that 'to suppose that there are acceptable surrogates for survival is to hold consciousness staggeringly cheaply.' In any case, there is a very simple answer to the question of whether mortal beings can do anything to satisfy their desire to go on living: 'Absolutely nothing. My consciousness cannot be deputed; even if my servants can do my living for me they cannot *be alive* in my stead.'[14] What is equally true is that surviving in an otherworldly afterlife could do nothing either to create or to obstruct an earthly afterlife. No form of otherworldly survival could guarantee that one would have an earthly afterlife, let alone the kind of earthly afterlife one might desire. Likewise, if it were one's preference not to be the subject of an earthly afterlife, no form of otherworldly survival could guarantee this either.

In any case, recognizing both forms of survival as distinct types of an 'afterlife' carries with it no implication of any equivalence between the two, still less of either of them being an acceptable substitute for the other.[15] Earthly and otherworldly afterlives constitute two logically quite independent kinds of survival. The point of comparing them is not to see whether one might stand in for the other, but rather to examine the relationship between them in the beliefs and behaviour of people who are confronting death and its aftermath. There are, for example, compensatory relationships between the two kinds of afterlife. The prospect, or at least hope, of a deceased individual having a certain kind of earthly afterlife can be consoling both for the bereaved and for the individual in question while still alive. By the same token, the hope or prospect of an otherworldly afterlife can be consoling for those who believe that a loved one will have no earthly afterlife to speak of, or will be the subject of an unjust earthly afterlife. On the other hand, those whose lives are firmly oriented towards otherworldly realities may be indifferent as to whether or not they are remembered on Earth after their death. Moreover, as I am suggesting in this book, being personally remembered and celebrated after death ('posthumous personhood') is not the only form an earthly afterlife can take: the lives of the dead will continue to have effects in the world long after the names and identities of their authors have been forgotten ('anonymous immortality').

These ideas are poignantly expressed by R. S. Thomas in a poem celebrating the lives of humble country clergymen.[16] These venerable figures, buried alongside their simple parishioners, left 'no books / memorials to their lonely thought'. Even the 'sublime words' they wrote 'On men's hearts and in the minds / Of Young children' were too soon forgotten. But it is not altogether clear what Thomas means at the end of the poem by suggesting that God 'will correct this'. What is it exactly that needs correction? Does Thomas mean that no such correction would be required had these clergymen left lasting memorials to their lives and thoughts in the form of books? Or does he mean that those without substantial earthly afterlives will be compensated for this deficit in an otherworldly afterlife? Surely any deficit in an earthly afterlife could only be made good on Earth itself. It is difficult to see why a godly clergyman's transition from earthly obscurity into heavenly glory should require the language of 'correction' rather than, say, the more traditional language of 'reward'.

IV

Strictly speaking, an otherworldly survival would no more entail permanent survival than would an earthly survival. In other words, post-mortem survival by no means guarantees what is generally defined as immortality. In some eschatologies, post-mortem survival is only temporary, or is conditional upon some ritual or moral factor,[17] or is exclusive to a particular (usually elite) group. Souls are not invariably understood to be naturally immortal entities, and in some mythologies even the gods themselves have limited lifespans.[18] Generally speaking, however, an otherworldly survival is associated with the attainment or realization of an everlasting or an eternal mode of existence; that is, with some form of immortality in the stricter sense.

Is there, then, any justification for using the term 'immortality' in relation to an earthly as well as an otherworldly afterlife? To do so depends upon accepting that the term has looser as well as stricter applications. The *Oxford English Dictionary* gives two meanings. The first is: 'The quality or condition of being immortal; exemption from death or annihilation; endless life or existence; eternity; perpetuity.'

And the second: 'The condition of being celebrated through all time; enduring fame or remembrance.'[19] It should be noted that this second definition suggests that relatively few people would be subjects of an earthly immortality. But there is no reason why the term should not be used more generously to include any deceased person whose memory is kept alive, for whatever reason, by any number of the living, whether large or small.

Support for a looser, or more generous, application of the term 'immortality' may be found in the fact that for most people the ideal type of earthly afterlife would be one that lasted indefinitely – in theory as long as there were human beings anywhere in existence. This ideal is most likely to be one modelled on conceptions of otherworldly immortality. What people anticipating an otherworldly afterlife ideally wish for is immortality in the strict sense. By analogy, what people anticipating an earthly afterlife ideally wish for is an afterlife that will last indefinitely. Artists, inventors and statesmen alike, if they want their achievements to survive at all, would ideally want them to survive for as long as possible. Had Hitler's 'thousand-year Reich' actually survived for this long, his successors would no doubt have wished to renew the lease for a further such period. All conceptions of survival, one might say, aspire to the condition of immortality.

Further support for a looser usage of the term 'immortality' can be found in the notion that what is most important about a person's life resides in what a person has done for, or shown to, others – that is, in what can be called a person's life-work, 'the work which is the object or activity of a person's whole life' (*OED*). For example, we may think of Shakespeare as having achieved immortality through his literary works. These works are what we value about Shakespeare and are virtually all that we know about Shakespeare anyway; when we refer to 'Shakespeare', we are usually referring to the works, not the man. Given a choice between the indefinite earthly survival of Shakespeare the man (arguably a somewhat grotesque possibility) and the indefinite survival of his works, most people (including, quite possibly, Shakespeare himself) would have little hesitation in opting for the works over the man. Preserved and valued, these works are thought to have an enduring and even 'timeless' quality that mortal individuals do not and cannot have. It could be argued, therefore, that we need a word like 'immortality', if not this very term, to describe the way in which an author's works escape the mortal limitations of the author's biological and historical life. One writer identifies what he calls the 'immortality effect': 'Writers, artists, philosophers, and other manufacturers of cultural artefacts have a perennial fascination with the immortality effect, the ability of a poem, novel, statue, painting, photograph, symphony, or philosophical work to survive beyond the death of its originating individual.'[20] The same points hold true in the case of those whose life-work is, for example, medical discovery (Alexander Fleming), charitable work (Thomas John Barnardo) or national leadership (Kemal Ataturk).

Something more needs to be said about the relationship between immortality and eternity. The former term tends to share the ambiguity of the latter one. Eternity, a key element in at least some conceptions of immortality, connotes not merely a perpetual existence of some kind, but rather a particular quality of existence, or mode of experience, that lifts it above mere perpetuity. William Blake writes about holding 'eternity in an hour', and T. S. Eliot about history being 'a pattern of timeless moments'. In a similar way, we may perceive an eternal or timeless quality in the works of these poets themselves. T. Campbell Finlayson, a nineteenth-century critic of spiritualism, notes similar ambiguities in the usage of the term 'immortality':

> Surely it is conceivable that a human soul may survive death, and yet not necessarily live on for ever and ever. Its continued existence must depend on the will of God. And again, it is conceivable that a human soul might be immortal – in the sense of living on for ever – and yet might never have what is distinctively called 'eternal life' – the true spiritual life of fellowship with God.[21]

This author not only distinguishes between surviving death for a limited period and living on perpetually after death, but discriminates between a merely temporal living on forever and an 'eternal' or 'spiritual' mode of doing so. That the term 'eternal' is subject to usages as loose if not looser than the term 'immortal', however, is shown in such expressions as being 'eternally grateful' to someone or describing something as being to one's 'eternal shame'.

The word 'eternal', strictly speaking, implies that whoever or whatever is so described has neither a beginning (birth) nor an end (death), whereas the root meaning of the word 'immortal' is 'undying' or 'immune from death', which leaves open several possibilities – that a being could be created immortal, that an originally mortal being might yet become immortal, or even that a once immortal being may cease to be immortal. After all, one's immunity from dying might, like one's immunity from anything else, be subject to conditions and hence to alteration.[22] Moreover, at least in the case of human beings, neither otherworldly nor earthly immortality can be attained without the subject first dying, at least physically. In the case of otherworldly immortality, of course, it is the existence of an undying soul which justifies the term 'immortality' (though theologies are divided on the question whether the soul is created immortal or is immortal because eternal). In the case of earthly immortality, it is the undying name or fame that justifies the term, and it is only with the death of the living subject that the immortality of words and deeds takes over.[23] An 'immortal' need not be one who cannot die; it is enough to be one who, against all norms and expectations, goes on living. To be an immortal in this lesser, conditional sense does not rule out one's eventually dying, or one's being subject to death under certain conditions. But of course, such conditional immortality can also be read as a confirmation of mortality the long way round. A classic example is that of the Greek hero Achilles, whose mother, the goddess Thetis, in one version of the myth, tries to ensure his immortality by feeding him ambrosia, the food of the gods, and then burning away his mortal parts. Unfortunately, in holding him over the fire she failed to treat one small part of him – his heel – that would later receive a fatal wound. Perhaps, therefore, it would be useful to distinguish between 'immortals' and 'eternals', reserving the latter term for those elite immortals who are both unborn and intrinsically immune to death. In some systems, of course, the one and only member of this class is God.

The root meaning of the term 'immortal' – one who does not or cannot die – points us to a further and in one sense more straightforward strategy for human immortality: not dying in the first place. For, nowadays, the prospect of artificially prolonging human life well beyond its seemingly natural limits is being taken increasingly seriously in some quarters. The artificial techniques in question – be they medical, genetic or cybernetic – seek to make all questions of an afterlife redundant. If we can go on living, either as we currently exist or in some enhanced form of existence, then we can stop being anxious as to whether or not we survive death, and likewise cease being concerned about what our earthly legacy might be once we are gone.

Extended lives on Earth, just like earthly afterlives, will not escape the ravages of time, although there are some who propose the possibility of extending human life indefinitely, or rather of transposing human consciousness into a form no longer subject to the illness and ageing that eventually lead to death. Part of the rationale of the movement known as 'transhumanism' is to create a new kind of humanity, free of the constraints and discontents of mortality. Running through all of this is the sense of 'overcoming' or even 'cheating' death, since without the relevant intervention, death would surely have 'claimed' the human lives in question. To this extent, then, a physicalist variety of earthly immortality, achieved by 'staying on' in person rather than vicariously, would also count as a survival of death. It is simply a pre-mortem rather than a post-mortem form of survival.

V

In light of the above considerations, I shall, in good conscience, use the generic term 'earthly immortality' on the one hand to refer to any form of earthly afterlife defined by a persisting legacy of some kind, and on the other to refer to any earthly life substantially if not indefinitely extended by artificial means. This looser or more generous use of the term 'immortality' not only conforms to the second of the two dictionary definitions cited earlier, but follows the practice of many other authors, whose own choice of terminology is therefore worth briefly reviewing here. One classicist, discussing ideas of immortality in Plato, makes a distinction between 'immortality in time' and 'immortality in eternity'.[24] This distinction, which corresponds fairly closely to my own distinction between earthly and otherworldly immortality, is based upon two different senses of 'soul' in ancient Greek thought – the idea of the soul as the life force and the idea of the soul as an immaterial entity released when the body dies. Other terms used to refer to what I call earthly immortality include 'social immortality' (contrasted with personal immortality), 'subjective immortality' (contrasted with objective immortality) and 'symbolic immortality' (contrasted with literal immortality). Each term has its advantages and disadvantages.

The term 'social immortality' emphasizes the crucial fact that the earthly legacy of a deceased person depends upon a continuing society of living persons. A person can only become and remain famous (or infamous) after death if there are others who recognize and celebrate (or deplore) whatever acts or achievements have made that person famous (or infamous). According to the social psychologists Rolf and Elsa von Eckartsberg, our social immortality depends on our place within a community of extended family and friends:

> This cast of characters of our existence survives our death. The survival community is launched at the funeral of the deceased. While the dead person is lowered into the ground, the person's spirit is raised in the speech and imagination of the survivors. A spiritual rebirth occurs. To the deceased person a new state of being, a new life: social immortality is bestowed in and through our collective commemoration ... Personal immortality for oneself may well be impossible, but social immortality, continued life in the consciousness and speech of others, is not.[25]

Despite its usefulness, however, the term 'social immortality' is too narrow to represent every form of what I have chosen to call 'earthly immortality'. Not every form of earthly immortality has a social dimension, as we shall see. Nor, where earthly immortality does depend on social recognition, is this recognition necessarily its key feature. Finally, the use of the term 'social' for earthly immortality could be taken to imply that otherworldly immortality, by contrast, would be an individual rather than a social survival, which the various conceptions of it in the relevant religious literature show is far from being the case. The term 'social immortality' is better reserved for describing collective rather than individual forms of earthly immortality, one whose subjects are groups or societies, or perhaps even the human race as a whole.

The term 'subjective immortality' highlights the fact that deceased individuals achieve earthly immortality by living on in the minds, or subjectivity, of others. Such an idea was an important strand in Auguste Comte's 'religion of humanity'.[26] Comte seems to have taken this idea of living on in the minds of others quite literally, believing that 'intellect and emotion ... may pass into another brain so as to be fused with the results attained by that other brain itself, supposing the two beings to be in sufficient harmony'.[27] The idea finds its analogue in some forms of otherworldly immortality – for example in the process theology of Charles Hartshorne, who argues that our individuality and achievements are preserved eternally in the mind and life of God.[28] The term 'subjective immortality' implies a contrast with an 'objective immortality', which is indeed used to refer to the traditional idea of the immortality of the soul in another world. The problem with this pair of terms is that they could equally well be used the other way around, so that 'subjective immortality' would refer to the soul's continuing self-awareness in an otherworldly afterlife, while an 'objective immortality' would refer to the persisting effects of a deceased person's life within the objective or external world (that is, it would refer to a deceased subject's earthly afterlife).

The term 'symbolic immortality' was coined by psychologist Robert J. Lifton to describe the ways in which human beings seek to transcend their inevitable finitude, and the sense of meaninglessness or despair this can engender, by acknowledging and contributing to the continuity of human life and culture.[29] The term 'symbolic immortality' tends to be all-consuming, however. To those who are sceptical about an otherworldly afterlife, any kind of immortality one might imagine, or to which one might aspire, will be symbolic rather than literal. Thus the quest for spiritual transcendence, represented in religious contexts as the quest for a literal form of immortality, will be understood as but another mode of symbolic immortality. Nor need a symbolic form of immortality be an enduring condition of some kind. One of the modes of symbolic immortality Lifton identifies is the ecstatic transcendence of time and self which can be experienced in spiritual rapture or drug-induced euphoria. It is clear that, for Lifton, symbolic immortality is ultimately a gesture – a gesture of escape from our sense of ephemeral individuality. The fact remains, however, that many people aspire to forms of earthly immortality that are seen as more than temporary escapes and far from being 'merely' symbolic. For example, those who seek to guarantee the persistence of family name or blood line think of this as a real and not merely a symbolic form of earthly immortality.

VI

Having clarified the main themes of this book, and some of its key terminology, it will be useful briefly to summarize the topics dealt with in each chapter. In Chapter One, 'Minding Mortality', I examine a range of both positive and negative attitudes towards death and dying. The human tendency to deny death, or at least one's own death, has been exaggerated in some quarters, and in any case such denial is generally trumped by the human ability to neutralize the effect upon us of death or the thought of death, or at least to accommodate ourselves to its inevitability. Various strategies of accommodation and neutralization are reviewed.

As regards attitudes to an afterlife of some kind, the main distinction lies between those who expect, or hope for, an otherworldly immortality of some kind, and those who believe that death spells our complete extinction. But there are important distinctions within each of these camps, since to accept the truth of something does not mean welcoming it. Just as among sceptics there are many who regret the non-existence of an afterlife (as they see it), so among believers in post-mortem survival there are some who would rather not survive. Those who are divided on the question of survival, however, are more likely to agree on the value of the more tangible possibilities of an earthly immortality.

In Chapter Two, 'Staying On', I consider some of the ways in which people have imagined solving the problem of mortality by not dying in the first place. For most of human history this has been confined to myths or legends about solitary human individuals blessed, or cursed, with immortality. For philosophers and writers of fiction, the fantasy of earthly immortality has provided a fruitful way of thinking about human identity and the meaning of life. In recent decades, however, some people have dared to think that what was once merely promised by magic or religion might one day actually be delivered by science – the possibility, if not of a terrestrial immortality in the strict sense, then at least of a much extended existence on Earth. This might be achieved through genetic engineering or even through the cybernetic uploading or replication of human consciousness. This is, in particular, the practical ambition of the movement known as transhumanism, according to which mortality, rather than being accepted as a defining characteristic of humanity, is seen as one last ailment to be overcome through human knowledge and ingenuity.

This chapter develops the theme of survival through earthly continuance by exploring the idea that, rather than simply extending their present lives, individuals might return to an earthly existence after their present lives come to an end. This idea of 'staying on' by way of 'coming back' is found mainly in religious rather than secular contexts, its chief expressions being the doctrines of resurrection and reincarnation. As we shall see, however, only the most literalist versions of these doctrines could begin to meet the criterion of a subject resuming a familiar earthly existence. Resurrected and reincarnated persons are generally seen as beginning new lives rather than resuming old ones, and the new life is not necessarily seen as taking place in the same world in which the old one was lived. The extended if not indefinite means of earthly continuance promoted by transhumanism – medical, genetic or cybernetic – could be seen as secular analogues of resurrection and reincarnation.

In Chapter Three, 'Posthumous Personhood', I examine ways in which the identities of the dead are preserved and cherished in forms of earthly survival which depend upon the memories, interests and interventions of others. There is, to begin with, the ancient and widespread idea that persons survive through the preservation of their names and in acts and artefacts of memorialization. Such name-based immortality also occurs when deceased individuals continue to exist as 'legal persons', with powers and interests in the world they no longer inhabit as living persons. A more secure form of earthly immortality, also involving the power of the name, depends upon having descendants. In this way one's name, and even one's physical and mental characteristics, are reasserted through successive generations. For many, however, the highest form of posthumous personhood is the immortality of being remembered, and commemorated, for having achieved or created something, one's name and one's accomplishment ideally becoming interchangeable.

Chapter Four, 'Anonymous Immortality', examines the various ways in which the dead can be said to live on through the continuing effects of their words and actions independently of their being remembered as particular individuals. Many ideas, inventions, artefacts and works of art have authors whose names and identities are now obscure if not completely forgotten; and yet these individuals can still be regarded as 'living on' in or through the things they have done or created. To put it more abstractly, the past itself is immortal and can never be undone. Everyone who has ever existed will have made a unique contribution, however small, within the ongoing life of the world, and the elements composing the minds and bodies of everyone who has ever existed will never cease being part of this world and indeed of the universe as a whole.

While the idea of an anonymous immortality might seem like a contradiction in terms, people clearly do find consolation in the thought that the things they have done, and the ways they have influenced others, will survive long after their own authorship or agency ceases to be acknowledged. This form of earthly immortality might well be described as the purest form of earthly immortality, being free of any taint of self-regard or self-glorification. Nor is it difficult to argue that all forms of earthly immortality tend towards anonymity anyway.

Chapter Five, 'Doing without an Afterlife?', examines ways in which people have sought to reconcile themselves to their own and others' mortality in terms of mortality itself. Thus there are those who reject the aspiration to any kind of afterlife, earthly or otherworldly, as an unnecessary burden for human beings living their lives to the full in the here and now. If our human nature is defined by our mortality, hankering after some kind of immortality is as futile as it is undignified. The one life we do enjoy is, so to speak, its own reward, and it cannot be fulfilled, understood or justified other than within its own unique terms and finite boundaries. Even the desire for an earthly immortality may evince a failure to accept, and enjoy, the unique and finite status of one's present life. Thus human mortality, far from being regretted, can be celebrated as a virtue in its own right. On this view, our mortality, far from constraining us, in reality liberates us.

It can be argued, however, that what those inclined to 'celebrate' human mortality are doing amounts to little more than making a virtue out of a necessity – I have to die, therefore I should be glad to die. The human desire for immortality seems the stronger instinct and its pursuit arguably the nobler enterprise. It is difficult to accept that any rational being not completely overwhelmed by suffering would ever want to cease existing. It is certainly difficult to see the desire for an abundance of life as more unhealthy than the desire for oblivion.

Chapter Six, 'Death and the End of the World', examines three distinct though overlapping senses in which death can be said to bring about the end of the world. First, we experience the ending of a world when those who are close to us die, and even with the death of some well-known person whom we did not know personally. It can give rise to the strong albeit irrational idea that it is strange, and even wrong, that the world should go on as normal after this death. Second, those who are actually dying, or who are facing or contemplating death, also experience, or anticipate, the ending of a world, since to be alive is to inhabit a unique and particular world of which one is, as it were, both captain and crew. We know, of course, that the world as an objective entity will continue after we have gone, but our own particular awareness and appropriation of this world will disappear with our death. Third, there is the possibility that a future human generation may, through some catastrophe, face death collectively rather than individually, aware that in a relatively short time no one will be left to continue the adventure of the human race. In theory there could even be a very last man or woman left alone to face humanity's impending extinction.

The possibility that a future generation will face death collectively rather than individually, knowing that humanity is about to vanish from the face of the Earth, raises a topic rarely addressed in discussions about death and dying: that of the status and value of the world independently of our own presence within it. This is the subject of Chapter Seven, 'What of the World without Us?'. The Earth, with its long history, is the necessary backdrop to any traditional eschatology, but its place in more secular visions of the end of the world also needs to be considered. What value, if any, can the world and its other living inhabitants be said to have independently of our own habitation of it and use of its various resources? What attitudes, and indeed what responsibilities, should one have towards a planet from which all humans may or will one day disappear? What should we think and do about all the physical artefacts and terrestrial interventions the human race will have left in its wake? Should we, in connection with this latter question, bear in mind the possibility that other intelligent beings exist in the universe?

Chapter Eight, 'This World is Not Enough', brings together the various strands of argument presented in the preceding chapters. Arguably, the gap between earthly and otherworldly conceptions of immortality is narrower than we might suppose, since it is easy to see ideas and images of a 'next world' as projections and idealizations of life in this world. In this respect, traditional religious eschatologies can be as earthbound and as self-serving as any of the forms of earthly immortality. On the other hand, it can be argued, whatever nobler instincts and aspirations find expression in these otherworldly eschatologies also inform many of the conceptions of an earthly immortality. These conceptions may derive much of their force and meaning from deep-seated instincts which seek fulfilment in an otherworldly immortality. It is thus possible to see the varieties of earthly immortality not merely as imitations, but more positively as intimations, of the otherworldly forms of immortality which earlier generations and many people still today have desired, both for themselves and for others.

The title of this final chapter could be read as an epigraph for the book as a whole. As such, it implies that those who, in the face of mortality, desire worldly continuance – either in the sense of not dying or in the sense of living on vicariously in the lives of others – will never find the idea of a this-worldly survival fully satisfactory in comparison with that other kind of immortality, an otherworldly immortality. 'This world is not enough' thus offers a significant variation on a motto which, in its earlier uses, expressed pride and ambition rather than humility or self-denial. The Latin motto *non sufficit orbis* (the world is not enough) was used by the empire-building Spanish king Philip II,[30] as well as by other monarchs.[31] A possible source was the apocryphal epitaph widely believed to have been inscribed on Alexander's tomb: *sufficit huic tumulus, cui non suffecerit orbis* (this tomb must suffice for one for whom the whole world was not enough). Its ultimate if not direct, source, however, was a satire by the Roman writer Juvenal, mocking rather than celebrating Alexander's worldly ambitions:

One globe is all too little for the youth of Pella [Alexander's birthplace]; he chafes uneasily within the narrow limits of the world, as though he were cooped up within the rocks of Gyara or the diminutive Seriphos; but yet when once he shall have entered the city fortified by the potter's art [Babylon, where he died], a sarcophagus will suffice him! Death alone proclaims how small are our poor human bodies![32]

ONE

MINDING MORTALITY

Down, down, down into the darkness of the grave
Gently they go, the beautiful, the tender, the kind;
Quietly they go, the intelligent, the witty, the brave.
I know. But I do not approve. And I am not resigned.
EDNA ST VINCENT MILLAY, 'Dirge without Music' (1928)

I

'Minding mortality' can be understood in two rather different ways. It can mean that we regret the fact that we must die, that we do not 'approve' of this fact, that we are not 'resigned' to it – in short, that we mind dying. But 'minding mortality' can also refer to how we manage, or try to manage, the fact of our mortality; how we accommodate, or try to accommodate, this fact within our lives.[1] One way of minding mortality in this second sense is to be ever 'mindful' of death, remaining aware of death as the ever-encroaching boundary of our lives. By keeping mortality in mind, we may become less fearful of death, less likely to meet death with anger or denial. Moreover to be fully mindful of mortality is also to be alert to questions about immortality. Whether or not some kind of afterlife awaits us, and if so what kind of afterlife this might be, are questions that cannot easily be brushed aside. In this first chapter I look at some of the ways, both negative and positive, in which we 'mind' both mortality and immortality.

For most people, of course, 'minding mortality' cannot and should not be a full-time occupation. Just as it is natural for human beings to cling to life and to avoid death, so is it natural, and indeed healthy, to avoid thinking about death and dying most of the time. When we do think about it, this is often because death itself, or the threat of death, has confronted us rather than we it. As Emily Dickinson puts it, in one of her best-known poems,

Because I could not stop for Death –
He kindly stopped for me –

The Carriage held but just Ourselves –
And Immortality.[2]

Her poem is striking because she is writing about death by writing about her own death. One's own death is, in actuality, the one death that one cannot observe from the outside, as it were, as well as the one death we are motivated to think about as little as possible. But the idea of being some kind of 'spectral' observer of, or commentator on, one's own death follows a well-established literary convention.[3] Moreover, 'since no poet can write of death from an immediate experience of it, the imagining of death necessarily involves images not directly belonging to it.'[4]

Not surprisingly, we think most about death, including our own death, when someone close to us dies. Then we are faced with the complex emotions and socially modulated responses involved in grief and mourning, which are perhaps the principal forms of minding mortality. It is not easy to draw any clear distinction between grief and mourning, but perhaps one could say that whereas grief belongs more to the first of the two senses of 'minding death' I differentiated earlier, mourning belongs more to the second. Since Freud, psychologists and others have talked about the 'work of mourning'. One might equally well talk about mourning as part of the 'management' or 'minding' of grief. In this context, however, 'minding mortality' is liable to be more about coping with the loss created by a particular death than about reflecting on death or dying as such. Dickinson personifies Death as a polite and considerate gentleman, calling by in a carriage. More often, our image of death is unpleasant and our emotional response to the idea or experience of it negative and extreme. Fear, anger and denial are the responses most often in question here, commonly overshadowing the gentler responses of sorrow, regret and resignation.

Fear and anxiety, and more rarely terror, are the most natural and most primitive of these negative responses to death. It is also the most personal, in the sense that one can only really fear one's own death, in the same way that one can only suffer the pain of one's own toothache, no matter how sympathetic others are to you or you to others in a similar position. To clarify more precisely what it is that one fears in fearing death, however, requires us to recognize a further distinction – the distinction between death and dying. 'It's not that I'm afraid to die,' says a character in a play by Woody Allen, 'I just don't want to be there when it happens.'[5] What this character actually means here is that dying is exactly what he is afraid of, and that what he is not afraid of is being dead. He is afraid of the experience of dying, but not (or so he claims) of the fact of his mortality, not of death itself. But the terms 'death' and 'dying' tend to be used interchangeably: we are sometimes referring to dying when we talk about death, and sometimes referring to death when we talk about dying. As the quip in Allen's play demonstrates, we use the verb 'to die' not only to refer to the actual experience of dying but when we are talking about the prospect or inevitability of death. Yet death and dying, although properly distinguishable, are not as neatly separable as some might imagine. Those who declare that it is not death that they fear, but dying, may be telling us only a half-truth. We might suspect the same of people who say that it is not the prospect of marriage itself that makes them nervous, but only the business of getting married.

Bearing in mind the distinction between death and dying, and depending on the context, we can understand the fear of death as a fear of losing one's life, or as a fear of the pain and suffering experienced in the course of dying, or as a fear of what might or might not come after death. The first of these fears, fear of losing one's life, can be viewed more positively as the desire, or struggle, to go on living. In itself, this has nothing to do with death. Nor in one sense does a fear of the process of dying, since dying is, of course, still a part of the experience of living.[6] The French essayist Michel de Montaigne, who thought about death a good deal, came to see dying as 'only a few bad moments at the end of life'.[7] This also makes fear of dying – as distinct from the fear of death – of little or no philosophical interest. Fear of what may or may not follow death is more complex, and philosophically far more interesting, since it is a specifically metaphysical or religious fear. It might be the fear of what awaits one in the next world, or an uncertainty as to whether or not there is a next world, or a dread of no longer existing.

The Epicureans famously considered it to be as irrational to fear one's non-existence after death as to be troubled by one's non-existence before birth.[8] Many who go along with this reasoning will hesitate to take the further step of regarding one's eventual extinction as a good thing. 'Despise not death, but welcome it, for Nature wills it like all else,' advises Marcus Aurelius.

For dissolution is but one of the processes of Nature, associated with thy life's various seasons, such as to be young, to be old, to wax to our prime and to reach it, to grow teeth and beard and gray hairs, to beget, conceive and bring forth. A man then that has reasoned the matter out should not take up towards death the attitude of indifference, eagerness, or scorn, but await it as one of the processes of Nature.[9]

But while Epicureans and Stoics might affect and even achieve serenity in the face of death, the dread expressed by other 'extinctionists' (as we might call them) is real enough and cannot easily be dismissed. In his poem 'Aubade' Philip Larkin describes as 'specious' the argument that dying materialists cannot be afraid of an imminent nothingness, since it is precisely the idea of the nothingness that generates the fear. Certainly the 'furnace fear' he feels as an atheist seems quite as terrifying as the fear of hellfire expressed by some religious believers. Each day 'unresting death' is that much closer, and with it 'the dread / Of dying and being dead'. One's mind, contemplating this imminent nothingness, 'blanks at the glare', not through regret or remorse for one's failures in life, but at the 'total emptiness', the 'sure extinction', in which we shall be lost forever. This is what the fear of death is all about. '. . . Not to be here, / Not to be anywhere, / And soon; nothing more terrible, nothing more true.'[10]

In this poem Larkin fears death, but he fears it more in sorrow than in anger. Anger, however, is also an emotion commonly evoked by death and dying. The death that we 'mind', in the sense of being angry about it, can be our own death, the death of another or even death as such. Fear of death, or at least fear of dying, can be seen as an instinctive response which in many cases actually prevents death. Anger, where it is not a disguised form of fear, is a response more associated with the inevitability of death, and with the realization of one's impotence to do anything about it. To be angry about death is to take death more personally, even to see it as something unjust or malign. Death is the enemy of life, the negation of all human interests and ambitions, and hence something to be resisted at all costs. It is this view which is so movingly expressed by Dylan Thomas when he exhorts his father, and thereby all of us, not to 'go gentle into that good night', but on the contrary to 'rage, rage against the dying of the light'. His poem is less about how one should die, or approach death, than about human mortality itself. It expresses frustration and power-lessness in face of death's inevitability.[11] The poem is both angry and elegiac; like Millay's poem 'Dirge without Music', it is as much a hymn to life as a complaint against death. It acknowledges the long tradition of hypostasizing Death as the enemy, but also evokes the view, just as widely represented, that what matters most in dying is how one dies. How one dies sets the seal upon one's life as a whole, whether in rela-tion to one's prospective otherworldly afterlife or in relation to one's earthly afterlife. In many traditions, one's final moments in this life are thought to have a decisive effect upon one's condition in the next. One's final moments may also set the ball rolling, so to speak, on the nature of one's earthly afterlife. Some of the most important memories people have of the dead concern the manner in which they died, including the report or recollection of what they said on their deathbed.[12]

The third of the negative responses to death mentioned earlier is denial. It has become something of a cliché to say that people, at least in the Western world, tend to be in denial of death, or that death has replaced sex as society's taboo subject.[13] This view has been encouraged by a 'five stages' model of dying which was to become almost canon-ical in some quarters – a model which was subsequently mapped onto the experience of bereavement too.[14] Denial is the first of these stages, followed by anger, bargaining, depression and acceptance. That most people are in denial of death, however, is a sweeping claim far too readily accepted. Likewise it is too readily assumed that those actually dying must be going through a period of denial. Much depends, of course, on what exactly is meant by denial, and on what exactly people are supposed to be denying.

What looks like a classic expression of the denial of death occurs in Leo Tolstoy's novella *The Death of Ivan Ilych* (1886). In this story, the dying Ivan readily accepts the proposition that all men are mortal, yet finds it hard to apply it to his own case. 'In the depth of his heart he knew he was dying, but not only was he not accustomed to the thought, he simply did not and could not grasp it.'

> The syllogism he had learnt from Kiesewetter's Logic: 'Caius is a man, men are mortal, therefore Caius is mortal,' had always seemed to him correct as applied to Caius, but certainly not as applied to himself. That Caius – man in the abstract – was mortal, was perfectly correct, but he was not Caius, not an

abstract man, but a creature quite, quite separate from all others. He had been little Vanya, with a mamma and a papa, with Mitya and Volodya, with the toys, a coachman and a nurse, afterwards with Katenka and with all the joys, griefs, and delights of childhood, boyhood, and youth. What did Caius know of the smell of that striped leather ball Vanya had been so fond of? Had Caius kissed his mother's hand like that, and did the silk of her dress rustle so for Caius? Had he rioted like that at school when the pastry was bad? Had Caius been in love like that? Could Caius preside at a session as he did? 'Caius really was mortal, and it was right for him to die; but for me, little Vanya, Ivan Ilych, with all my thoughts and emotions, it's altogether a different matter. It cannot be that I ought to die. That would be too terrible.'[15]

A careful reading of Tolstoy's narrative shows us that what Ivan's internal monologue expresses is a fear of death, an unwillingness to die and even a sense of the injustice of having to die – all of which is predicated precisely on Ivan's awareness of death rather than his denial of it.

This is not to say that denial of some sort is not part of the natural response to death and dying, which is why it is important to understand exactly what is meant by denial and where the denial is focused. What should be noted is that the denial is always about a particular individual, oneself or another, never about death as such. In the case of an individual's death, the so-called 'denial' is closer to disbelief, but an emotional rather than an intellectual disbelief. When a loved one dies, one might say 'I just can't believe that she's gone', which of course depends on knowledge of the fact that she has gone. When it comes to denying one's own death – whether as an inevitable future event or because one actually is dying – one might do well to recall those folktales about a group of fools who think that one of their number must be missing because each of them, in counting up the group, omits to count himself. Sigmund Freud pointed out that it is 'impossible to imagine our own death; and whenever we attempt to do so we can perceive that we are in fact still present as spectators'. He does not see this as simply an epistemological artefact – a consequence of being oneself rather than seeing oneself, so to speak. Instead he affirms 'that at bottom no one believes in his own death, or, to put the same thing in another way, that in the unconscious every one of us is convinced of his own immortality.'[16] We might respond to this by saying that at bottom we do believe in our own death, but find it easy to keep this fact and its implications at a distance most of the time. This is not exactly denial. We have much less difficulty in thinking about other people's deaths. But another possible explanation for being convinced of our own immortality is that such a conviction, rather than being evidence of some deep-seated psychological evasion, springs from the fact that we are indeed immortal, and that we cannot but sense it, however inchoately.

According to the psychologist Ernest Becker, our fear of death leads us to a denial of death which we reinforce by identifying with cultural symbols and social systems which transcend our finite lives and thus serve as a buffer against our fears about our extinction as individuals. By identifying with these symbols and systems (political, religious and so on) and the values implicit within them, we build up our self-esteem and find meaning in a world otherwise rendered meaningless and worthless by our individual and collective mortality.[17] In short, 'man transcends death via culture.'

> Man transcends death not only by continuing to feed his appetites, but especially by finding a meaning for his life, some kind of larger scheme into which he fits: he may believe he has fulfilled God's purpose, or done his duty to his ancestors or family, or achieved something which has enriched mankind. This is how man assures the expansive meaning of his life in the face of the real limitations of his body; the 'immortal self' can take very spiritual forms, and spirituality is not a simple reflex of hunger and fear. It is an expression of the will to live, the burning desire of the creature to count, to make a difference on the planet because he has lived, has emerged on it, and has worked, suffered, and died.[18]

But to look to a denial of death as the determining factor in the genesis and development of human culture seems contrary to both instinct and evidence. A theory of human behaviour based on the pleasure principle and (in the face of death) an attitude of *carpe diem*, and a theory of culture based on the social morality of a gregarious species and the aesthetic instincts of its individual members, would seem to beg fewer questions.

Becker's ideas about the creative function of the denial of death became the basis of what is known, in psychology circles, as 'Terror Management Theory' (TMT), the 'terror' being the fear and anxiety caused by the prospect of death.[19] This theory is driven by the 'mortality salience' hypothesis, according to which thoughts or images of death, whether spontaneously arising or experimentally induced, lead people to construct or reaffirm cultural symbols and systems (religious or secular) such as deflect or diminish one's death-related anxieties. The theory appears to vastly exaggerate the extent and intensity of the fears and anxieties associated with death. People may be fearful and anxious about death and dying, sometimes extremely so, but to describe this as 'terror' represents at least an inaccurate use of English if not an over-interpretation of the empirical evidence. Moreover, as critics of the theory have pointed out, death-related anxieties would, if anything, enhance the instinct for self-preservation (whose key role in human life is a basic premise of the theory), whereas a psychological mechanism favouring the suppression or reduction of one's fear of death is more likely to compromise one's chances of survival, and such a mechanism is unlikely to have been reinforced through the innumerable generations of human evolution.[20]

When people talk about the denial of death, one might suggest that what they are really referring to is an unwillingness or refusal to think through the implications of one's (usually quite readily acknowledged) mortality. Only something deniable can be denied; the undeniable can only be refused. In this respect the denial of death is not quite like, say, the denial of climate change, where the facts themselves are still thought to be in dispute. Reasons can always be found for not thinking or doing much (or anything) about climate change – the relevant scientific data is unclear, it may never happen, it won't affect me (or my generation), future generations will manage somehow, it's too late anyway, and so on. This will not do in the case of death. There is no gainsaying the fact of human mortality. People do not live their lives oblivious to this fact, but in most cases they do live their lives without thinking very much about it, if not taking steps to avoid thinking about it. Living one's life always thinking about the fact that it will end would be rather like spending most of one's holiday worrying about the journey home, or letting one's enjoyment of a film, play or concert performance be spoiled by the nagging thought that it will soon come to an end (which is not, of course, the same as wondering how it will end – this sometimes being part of the enjoyment).

Merely dwelling on death and dying is not in itself likely to reduce negative reactions such as fear, anger or denial (in the sense of refusal). Nor do such responses allow people to get past death itself. Rather they delay any serious thinking about the meaning of death or about what may or may not come after it. Moreover, it is easy enough to become obsessively fearful of death or indeed morbidly fascinated by it. But if we put off thinking about it until it comes upon us, we shall, like Everyman in the medieval morality play of that name, find ourselves unprepared. 'O Death,' says Everyman, 'thou comest when I had thee least in mind!'[21] He then asks Death if he might, literally, buy more time. (This line alone justifies one in thinking the play no less relevant today than it was in the fifteenth century.) The question for all of us, therefore, is how we can best mind – in the sense of best manage – our mortality *in media via*.

The idea of managing something implies the exercise of control over something (as in 'I am the manager of a large firm'), but also coping with something difficult (as in 'I managed to get to the station on time'). So it is with our management of death. For Everyman, such management is 'crisis management' occasioned by his own negligence. Fortunately, in this particular play, all turns out well. Everyman, under the supervision of the rather neutral figure of Death, knuckles down to the task of preparing for death and for life after death.

The minding, or managing, of the actual experience of dying – in the senses both of coping and of controlling – is concentrated in what may be called the 'deathbed experience'. This experience involves at least two parties – those who are dying and those who are caring for, or at least attending, the dying.[22] The deathbed has always been a site of various struggles – physical, emotional, moral, religious, legal and medical. For the dying, dying can be hard work, physiologically and psychologically. This is quite apart from any struggles of a spiritual kind. For the living, the dying present a number of difficult choices – how much the dying are told, whether about their condition or about other matters away from the deathbed; what medication to prescribe and when; or what interventions to make in the best interests of the patient and in line with the law. Shai Lavi, asking how and why dying became such a problem, traces the modern crisis of dying to 'the medicalization of the deathbed'.

Associated with this phenomenon are the hastening of death and the prolongation of life. Both reflect a new way of experiencing dying and a new will to master death, shared by physician and patient. Thus, the question of freedom at the deathbed is not about how much or how little choice the terminal patient has, but rather how dying became a matter of choice in the first place.

Dying persons, no less than pregnant women, were now regarded as 'patients'. Through the nineteenth and twentieth centuries, the increasing confidence of the medical professionals variously to ease the process of dying, or advance or delay the event of death itself, meant that priests and the like tended to be pushed into the background:

> the old ministers of hope, as harbingers of death, were kept away from the deathbed. But as modern medicine clearly could not offer the promise of an otherworldly salvation, physicians opted for a more tangible and limited hope: not the promise of a world to come, but a this-worldly guarantee that as long as life persisted, something could always be done for the dying patient.[23]

The increasing skills and responsibilities exercised by medical professionals in the 'minding' of dying have encouraged new goals and values in some of the non-medical care given to the dying. It is as if the experience of terminal illness and dying has become a last opportunity for people to 'live well', a final stage of life to be celebrated, enhanced or extended for as long as possible before what for many people, on both sides of the deathbed so to speak, is the 'big sleep'. No one, presumably, has yet had the nerve to send, or to market, a new category of 'End of Life' greetings cards, but such items would be a perfect expression of some of the attitudes now current.

II

According to the seventeenth-century French writer François de La Rochefoucauld, death, like the sun, cannot be outstared.[24] The only direct approach to death is achieved by dying – although many of the dying lose consciousness before the moment of death.[25] Minding or managing death is best approached indirectly, at an angle we might say, as when looking at the sun. In fact we have no other option, as Kenneth Burke explains:

> So far as this world of our positive experience is concerned, death can only be an idea, not something known by us as we know our bodily sensations. In fact, its ideality is probably one element that recommends it to the use of poets, whose trade it is to deal exclusively in symbols. And since so much modern effort is expended upon the spreading and preventing of death, or upon the use of death as a rhetoric of threat, the essential ideality of the term is disguised by the overwhelming material reality of the conditions in which it is involved. Moreover, since no poet can write of death from an immediate experience of it, the imagining of death necessarily involves images not directly belonging to it. It lies beyond the realm of images – or at least beyond the realm of such images as the living body knows.[26]

We can of course directly confront the material reality and bodily consequences of death, and such confrontation has in fact been a principal form of minding mortality in many cultures. In European culture, there was from Classical into Christian times the long literary and iconographic tradition of *ars moriendi*, the Art of Dying.[27] On the other side of the world, the Buddhist tradition had developed elaborate techniques of detached mindfulness (*sati*) to probe the nature and implications of the truth of impermanence. One particular set of exercises, the cemetery meditations, focuses explicitly on the physical processes of human decomposition (*maranasati*). The meditator is instructed to visit charnel grounds to contemplate corpses in various states and stages of decay, and to create vivid mental images of such corpses through visualization techniques. Nine progressive stages of decomposition are differentiated. Here are the summaries given of the sixth of these meditations:

> And, further, O bhikkhus [monks], if a bhikkhu, in whatever way, sees a body thrown in the charnel ground and reduced to bones gone loose, scattered in all directions – a bone of the hand, a bone of the foot, a shin bone, a thigh bone, the pelvis, spine and skull, each in a different place – he thinks of his

own body thus: 'This body of mine, too, is of the same nature as that body, is going to be like that body, and has not got past the condition of becoming like that body.'[28]

Such deliberate focusing on the processes of death may strike the outsider as excessively morbid, but it should be emphasized that it differs fundamentally from the self-indulgent kind of representations associated with the darker side of Romanticism – the kind we find in, for example, John Keats's 'Isabella' (1818):

> Who hath not loiter'd in a green church-yard,
> And let his spirit, like a demon-mole,
> Work through the clayey soil and gravel hard,
> To see skull, coffin'd bones, and funeral stole;
> Pitying each form that hungry Death hath marr'd,
> And filling it once more with human soul?[29]

This is certainly a 'minding' of mortality, but one that is closer to the first than to the second of the two senses I distinguished at the start of this chapter.

We grapple best with ideas about death, as with other kinds of idea, when these are given tangible expression. What one who seeks to manage death can do, therefore, is to try to give shape to the abstract mystery of death by representing it in images, stories, symbols and rituals which help one to face up to it, think about it, prepare for it, or consider what if anything might follow it. Some representations try to capture the mystery or contradictions of death, while others concentrate on a particular 'face' of death, or promote a particular interpretation of it or attitude towards it. These representations variously serve to explain or justify death, ward it off, propitiate it, negotiate with it, accept it or even venerate it. Death is often personified, on the one hand as an enemy, opponent or even a monster, and on the other hand as a friend,[30] teacher, saint or god.

It is in myth especially that we find attempts to make sense of, if not to justify, human mortality. Many cultures have myths about the origins of death and the purpose of death. Some myths refer to a time when human beings were immortal, or at least to a time when death had not yet been discovered. In some cases death is brought into the world by a simple blunder. In other cases it comes as a punishment. In some stories death is a curse, in others a blessing. A classic example of an aetiological myth of death is the second of the two creation accounts in Genesis, where Adam and Eve lose their presumed immortality through choosing to eat the fruit of the tree of knowledge. Implicit in this and other myths, however, is the idea that the lost immortality can be recovered, albeit in a very different form. Other myths about death, however, are concerned not with the origins of death but with what comes afterwards, with eschatology and the state of the dead.

In many myths the world of the dead is presided over by a god of death. The fact that many such gods have functions or attributes relating to other areas of human life – such as fertility, wealth, desire or knowledge – attests to a recognition that death is not wholly negative, but is on the contrary a necessary and even positive feature of creation. The most positive link is that between death and rebirth. This is seen both in nature and in human experience. What is more, many rituals of initiation are based on the idea of a symbolic death and rebirth.[31] The well-known Greek myth of Persephone's annual return to Earth after her abduction by Pluto, commonly understood to represent nature's annual cycle of death and regeneration, may have more specific associations with a female initiation ritual.[32] In the Hindu Katha Upanishad, the Brahmin boy Nachiketa is sent to the underworld where he meets Yama, the God of Death. Yama tests Nachiketa by offering him various worldly goods, which he refuses, eventually receiving the greatest gift of all: knowledge of the deathless state that lies beyond the cycle of birth and death. Here Yama's role is more that of teacher of the living than ruler of the dead.

Like many other gods of the dead, Pluto and Yama also have their sinister side, but this does not predominate in the representations just described. In some cases, however, the dark or gruesome side of death is emphasized and dramatized. Both the Greek and the Hebrew underworlds, Hades and Sheol, are in some texts described as voracious monsters, swallowing up the living indiscriminately.[33] The Hindu goddess Kali, one of the representations of the Mother Goddess in her fierce aspect, is depicted with a garland of skulls around her neck and a skirt decorated with severed hands, while holding aloft a severed head. She takes her name from Kala, Time, whose all-devouring nature she personifies. But the gruesome trophies she displays also function as symbols of the possibility of her devotees' liberation from the cycle of birth and death.[34]

Some representations based on the gruesome aspects of death, however, function more straightforwardly as cases of memento mori, reminders of the ever-present possibility of death. One of the most ubiquitous images is that of a skeleton or emaciated corpse. In European culture, such figures have close links with the medieval theme of the Dance of Death. But there are also links with other themes. The familiar scythe-bearing figure of the Grim Reaper, typically represented as a skeleton or as an old man, owes much to the mythology and iconography of Time (Saturn, Chronos). In the celebrations which mark the Mexican Day of the Dead (closely associated with All Souls' Day), skeleton costumes and sculptures, and sweets in the form of skulls and bones, form an integral part of the festivities, proximity to such images being one way of coming to terms with death.[35] Mexican culture has also produced one of the most extraordinary creations in humanity's long dialogue with death: the cult of the skeleton 'saint', Santa Muerte.[36]

Because death is a natural phenomenon and even a gift or blessing, we find many benign representations of death in art and literature. It is hardly surprising that, especially for the poor and oppressed, death is sometimes welcomed as a saviour. In Baudelaire's poem 'La Mort des pauvres' (The Death of the Poor), Death is hypostasized in various ways, even as an entity more positive than Life itself:

> It is Death, indeed, that consoles and keeps life going;
> Death is the goal of life, Death the sole hope
> Which, like an elixir, raises and intoxicates us,
> Giving us the heart to live on another day . . .[37]

Nor is it surprising, given the suffering associated with dying, that death is so often represented as a sympathetic friend or as a helpful messenger; the angel of death may be a sombre figure, but is rarely a horrific one. Baudelaire likens death to an elixir, but death is more usually imagined in opposite terms, namely as a sleep of some kind. The association of death with sleep, or with something akin to sleep, is a widespread and an ancient one. In Greek mythology, for example, Death (Thanatos) is the brother of Sleep (Hypnos) – twin sons of the Goddess Night (Nyx).[38] Comparisons between death and sleep, based on their obvious natural similarities, have become a familiar way of removing the fear of death, if not of actually beautifying it. Baudelaire's poem presents the sleep of death as a kind of spell woven by Death personified as an angel: 'It is an Angel, whose fingers magically weave/ Sleep and the gift of ecstatic dreams,/ Who makes a bed for the poor and naked.' The poem concludes by looking beyond the experience of death and dying to the world beyond, Death now being represented through positive imagery of a more impersonal kind: 'It is the glory of the gods, the mystic granary,/ The poor man's purse and ancient fatherland,/ The doorway opening onto unknown Heavens!'

Mention should also be made of the figure of the psychopomp, the conductor of souls from this world to the next. A personification of the process of dying rather than of death itself, the psychopomp may take the form of a god, angel or animal. Hermes is one example, the archangel Michael another. Emily Dickinson's polite gentleman calling by in his carriage is but a psychopomp in modern dress.

These reifications of death help to keep in focus truths too difficult to grasp or too easy to lose sight of when kept in the abstract. On the other hand, some representations of death can stimulate the very negative responses which prevent one from coming to terms with it. 'Men fear death as children fear to go in the dark,' says Francis Bacon in his essay on the subject, adding that 'as that natural fear in children is increased with tales, so is the other.'[39] That some representations can also lead one badly astray is nicely illustrated in Geoffrey Chaucer's 'Pardoner's Tale'. In this darkly comic homiletic, a trio of drunken youths, incensed at the news that a friend of theirs is a recent victim of the plague, are taken with the idea that death is literally some kind of serial killer. So minded, they vow to track down and kill 'this traitor Death'. In the course of looking for this non-existent individual, they are directed (by an aged man who longs for death) to a heap of gold coins, their greed to possess which erases all thoughts of killing death. The efforts of each of the trio to cheat his companions out of their share of the gold, however, lead inexorably to all three of them dying. The gold has proved, at least for the audience of this tale, a far better symbol of death than any more traditional representation.

III

From minding death we now pass to minding the afterlife. In doing so, we must bear in mind both senses of minding – the sense of objecting to and the sense of managing an afterlife – although it is with the latter that I shall be mainly concerned. This book is about the idea of an earthly rather than an otherworldly afterlife. But there are instructive parallels between the ways otherworldly and earthly afterlives are minded, as well as various connections between the two kinds of afterlife which cannot be ignored.

An otherworldly afterlife is what large numbers of people, probably still the global majority, expect for themselves and others after death. These constitute the world's 'confident believers'. Those within this category who fear that their afterlife may not be the kind of afterlife they would want can be called 'anxious believers'. Fear of hellfire, of purgatorial suffering, or of rebirth in an unhappy realm of existence are fears still widely held. Another category comprises those who strongly doubt, if not positively reject, the possibility of any form of afterlife, but who regret the non-existence of an afterlife (or at least of a certain kind of afterlife). These are the 'reluctant sceptics'. Some of these will also qualify as 'anxious' or 'fearful' sceptics, in so far as (irrationally or otherwise) they dread the thought of their expected extinction.

A further group to be acknowledged, a sizeable minority perhaps grown more sizeable in recent decades, is made up of those persons who are positively reconciled to the lack of any kind of afterlife, and who may well consider the idea of an afterlife not just an impossibility but an unworthy aspiration anyway. These are the 'confident sceptics'. Finally, distinct from those who are resigned to, or even happy with, the non-existence of an otherworldly afterlife is a small minority of persons who, despite not desiring an afterlife, are nevertheless inclined to believe that the existence of an afterlife is quite likely, if not highly probable. These are the 'reluctant believers', for whom annihilation is not the worst thing that can happen. One might nominate as their patron saint the Cambridge philosopher C. D. Broad, whose evaluation of the alleged evidence for post-mortem survival led him to state that he 'would be slightly more annoyed than surprised' to find himself still existing after death.[40]

Now it could be said that the afterlife expectations of most 'confident' and 'anxious' believers are managed for them, usually within the confines of a particular religious tradition. This is also likely to be true of the expectations of the 'confident sceptics', since the traditions of religious scepticism are no less institutionalized than those of religious belief. The extent to which people are willing or able to engage critically or creatively with their religious heritage varies considerably, however. One should be careful not to underestimate the extent to which even conventional believers are likely to adapt traditional ideas to their own particular attitudes and circumstances.

One way in which afterlife beliefs are managed (and, some would say, brought into being in the first place) is through the conception of an afterworld created in the image of our own world. This is already to blur somewhat the distinction between an otherworldly and an earthly afterlife. For some, a life after death is only conceivable, or tolerable, if it is thought to be a continuation, by other means, of one's familiar earthly existence. Alternatively, an otherworldly afterlife may be represented as an idealized version of earthly life. The conception of a world other than but similar to this world can provide a comforting way of thinking of the dead as not wholly departed from the living. Again, where earthly immortality is thought of as a social immortality, it is likely that the conception of a future human society bearing witness to the work and influence of those now dead will be modelled on the kind of heavenly or earthly paradise described in some religious narratives. George Eliot, an enthusiastic supporter of Auguste Comte's 'religion of humanity', with its vision of a future society incorporating the memory and influence of generations of the illustrious dead, expresses the hope in her poem 'O May I Join the Choir Invisible' (1867) that her own earthly afterlife will be as a contributor to this society:

> O may I join the choir invisible
> Of those immortal dead who live again
> In minds made better by their presence: live
> In pulses stirred to generosity,
> In deeds of daring rectitude, in scorn
> For miserable aims that end with self,
> In thoughts sublime that pierce the night like stars,
> And with their mild persistence urge man's search
> To vaster issues.

What otherworldly and earthly afterlives also have in common is that they require appropriate care and attention both before and after death. The preparation before death is largely the responsibility of the individual who will die. Clearly it is part of most religious thinking, in so far as a religion is regarded as a soteriology,[41] that the nature of one's post-mortem existence will have some relation to the way one has lived one's earthly life. In some religions it is properly performed rituals or the appropriate veneration of a deity which secure one a place in the afterworld, or which lead a person into one kind of afterlife rather than another. In other religions, the crucial factors are ethical (in the broadest sense) rather than ritual or cultic. For some people, or for some traditions, the nature of the afterlife is simply beyond human purview and control. In some eschatologies, the afterlife is a realm or condition to which all are destined regardless of individual status or earthly character. This is true, for example, of the gloomy underworlds described in many ancient Near Eastern texts. The same is true of the non-sectarian heaven of modern popular religion.

As regards the maintenance of an otherworldly afterlife, it is only the living who are able do what is necessary or desirable. Care or responsibility for the dead begins but by no means end with the funeral rites, and the funeral rites themselves may be only the beginning of a long sequence of rituals directed towards the care of the dead, and in some cases towards protection from the dead. An absence of funeral rites, or their incomplete or mismanaged execution, may compromise the state of the dead, or prevent the dead from completing the journey from this world to the next. In many traditions, the well-being of the dead depends on the continuing prayers and activities of the living, such as visits to the burial place to feed or venerate the dead. All of this is well illustrated in the Hindu tradition, where the funeral rites and subsequent rituals are all about 'managing' both a death and an after-life. Thus the deceased is cremated in a certain way in order to ensure a proper detachment from the body, and offerings are made both to the deceased and to the gods to ensure safe passage to the next world, and to prevent the deceased from getting stranded in this world as an unhappy ghost. In a larger context, these rites are part of an ongoing relationship between the living and the dead in which the dead play their part by helping the living.

Preparing for an otherworldly afterlife, and maintaining an other-worldly afterlife, have their counterparts in the case of an earthly afterlife. The living can do much both to secure and to shape how they will be remembered after death, how their achievements will be recognized and how their life-work will be continued. Just as people make provision for their death by specifying the kind of funeral they want, so do they stipulate, by means of wills and other devices, how their projects and interests are to be furthered after their death. For many people, however, their most substantial contribution to their earthly afterlife will be constituted by the family members they leave behind them. The production of progeny not only constitutes a form of earthly afterlife in itself; it is a necessary condition for other forms of earthly afterlife.

On the hypothesis of post-mortem survival, it is possible that the dead might also be able to intervene in the world in a way that affects their own earthly afterlife. We might think here of the ghost of Hamlet's father, whose spectral intervention and speech to Hamlet changes not only his own earthly legacy, but that of other characters too. The correction of an unjust reputation beyond the grave is a common theme in folklore and folktale especially.

It is the living, obviously, who take chief responsibility for the earthly afterlives of the dead. What the dead have done to secure their own earthly afterlives is enhanced or controlled, and in some cases frustrated or sabotaged, by what the living do or fail to do subsequently. Their more formal responsibilities include the announcement of the death, the organizing of funeral and disposal, the settlement of the estate, the distribution of the deceased's possessions, the furthering of cherished plans or projects, and so forth. At the same time it should be noted that these activities can also be, intentionally or otherwise, a means of 'signing off' a person's life, a closing of the accounts, so to speak, on a life now ended. Such activities certainly allow those closest to the deceased to present a suitably 'edited' version of the life now ended. For instance, crucial documents (such as letters or diaries) can be withheld or destroyed – sometimes on the initiative of family members, sometimes in conformity with the wishes of the deceased. Such editing can have a dramatic effect on the nature, and longevity, of an earthly afterlife. Moreover, the discovery of new facts about a deceased person's life can change an individual from a hero to a villain, or vice versa.[42]

Perhaps the most tangible and least ambiguous of the means whereby the living initiate and maintain the earthly afterlives of the dead is through memorialization, which includes acts and artefacts of public or private commemoration such as are familiar in every culture. As the terms 'memorialization' and 'commemoration' themselves remind us, however, even the most lasting of monuments and institutions depend for their recognition and continuance upon the memories of the living, just as these memories in turn depend upon a community, large or small, within which these memories are communicated and transmitted (via oral transmission, written records, artefacts, customs and institutions). To the extent that the memories of the dead are preserved and celebrated, their earthly afterlives are maintained; to the extent that such memories fade, and the various items which nourish or stimulate memories are lost or neglected, earthly afterlives will decline.

For a simple illustration of how tenuously the earthly afterlives of the dead may depend upon physical monuments, we can compare the observations of two near-contemporary figures writing in the seventeenth century. The first is Thomas Browne (1605–1682), for whom the discovery of a group of Roman urns provoked a long disquisition on the themes of mortality and immortality. Browne, sceptical of all ambitions to earthly immortality, ironically imputes mismanagement of their earthly afterlives to those whose unearthed bodily remains carried no identification:

> But who were the proprietaries of these bones, or what bodies these ashes made up, were a question above Antiquarism . . .
> Had they made as good provision for their names, as they have done for their Reliques, they had not so grosly erred in the art of perpetuation. But to subsist in bones, and to be but Pyramidally extant, is a fallacy in duration. Vain ashes, which in the oblivion of names, persons, times, and sexes, have found unto themselves, a fruitlesse continuation, and only arise unto late posterity, as Emblemes of mortall vanities.[43]

The second figure is John Weever (1576–1632), the author of a book recording church monuments in which he is more respectful than Browne of the idea of earthly immortality. For Weever, like Browne, the due remembrance of the dead will often depend upon just the kind of inscription found lacking in the case of Browne's Roman urns:

> Having seen, judicious reader, how carefully, in other kingdoms, the monuments of the dead are preserved, and their inscriptions or epitaphs registered in their church-books; . . . And also knowing withall how barbarously within these his majesty's dominions, they are (to the shame of our time) broken down, and utterly almost all ruinated, their brasen inscriptions erazed, torn away, and pilfered; by which inhuman, deformidable act,

the honorable memory of many virtuous and noble persons deceased, is extinguished, and the true understanding of divers families in these realms (who have descended of these worthy persons aforesaid) is so darkened, as the true course of their inheritance is thereby partly interrupted: grieving at this unsufferable injury, offered as well to the living as the dead, out of the respect I bore to venerable antiquity, and the due regard to continue the rememberance of the defunct to future posterity; I determined with myself to collect such memorials of the deceased, as were remaining as yet undefaced; as also to revive the memories of eminent worthy persons entombed or interred, either in parish, or in abbey churches; howsoever some of their sepulchres are at this day no where to be discerned; neither their bones and ashy remains in any place to be gathered.[44]

What Weever is doing in recording these monuments, apart from the antiquarian interest, is proving that we are not just passive witnesses to the earthly afterlives of others but capable of their active maintenance.

The parallels between earthly and otherworldly afterlives relate not just to the way in which these afterlives are secured, maintained or restored, but to the fact that there are in both cases different kinds of afterlife to be taken into account. Ideas about a shadowy life in the underworld, a dual destiny of heaven and hell, resurrection, mystical absorption into a greater unity and so on, all have their analogues in the case of earthly afterlives. Thus many of the dead who have disappeared from living human memory continue a shadowy afterlife in documents, inscriptions, bodily remains and so on, which may or may not attract the attention of archaeologists, historians and others. Just as Odysseus visiting Hades gave temporary voice to the shadowy souls there, so can the historian or archaeologist give voice to the largely forgotten dead among the living.

Relatively few among the dead enjoy a heaven of fame or suffer a hell of infamy for their earthly works and deeds. Fewer still may enjoy a glorious resurrection when their possessions, bodies or even identities are recovered after centuries of oblivion – as in the case of the Egyptian pharaoh Tutankhamun, for example. For the vast majority of the dead, however, an earthly afterlife as a known or identifiable individual is soon over, and yet the effect or influence of what they did or said is carried forward in the minds, bodies and institutions of a future humanity. All earthly afterlives fade gradually into anonymity. Even the most famous people known to present generations will one day be totally forgotten. But for as long as the relevant memories, records, monuments, artefacts and bodily remains persist, the earthly afterlives of the dead can be sustained, extended or indeed revived. As Robert Graves observes, it requires little magic to bring the dead back to life:

> Few are wholly dead:
> Blow on a dead man's embers
> And a live flame will start.[45]

The real subject of this poem, of course, is the ease with which those who seek to revive the dead – biographers, actors and others – can all too easily find their own lives being taken over in the process. If this is to be counted as a form of earthly immortality, it must also be viewed as a rather unhealthy one.

But the way in which the dead 'live on' within the personal histories of the living can have more positive manifestations. Denise Levertov, in her poem 'The Change',[46] describes how the lamented dead can cease to be the 'terrible weight of their absence' and become instead a kind of stabilizing presence, uniting with those who mourn them. Their 'weight' is now a fruitful burden for the living, one that guides and steadies their course. Rather than being pictured as elsewhere and as other, the dead inhabit, however briefly, a living person's very subjectivity. The dead are no longer separate, no longer to be seen. On the contrary,

> It's they who see: they displace,
> for seconds, for minutes, maybe longer,
> the mourner's gaze with their own.

TWO

STAYING ON

I don't want to achieve immortality through my work; I want to achieve immortality through not dying. I don't want to live on in the hearts of my countrymen; I want to live on in my apartment.
WOODY ALLEN[1]

I

'Everything ends.' So runs the tagline for *Six Feet Under*, a television series about a family firm of undertakers which at the end of the final episode shows how each of its (hitherto surviving) main characters will meet their end.[2] The typically human response to the truth that everything ends is to not think too much about what this means for oneself, and to carry on as if life will never end while knowing of course that it surely will.[3] As the television series demonstrates, undertakers are no different from the rest of us in thinking like this. At the same time, there are many people who either hope or fear, if they do not firmly believe, that although everything earthly comes to an end, another world awaits them where life in some form goes on forever.

But there are also those who take a more radical approach to the fact that everything ends, which is to imagine how the inevitable end of our life might be deferred, perhaps indefinitely, in which case the question of what might or might not happen after death can also be deferred, perhaps indefinitely. For them, the best way of dealing with death is not to die in the first place. The idea that one's earthly life might be indefinitely prolonged or periodically renewed – that one might 'stay on' in an earthly existence or even 'come back' to one after dying – is the subject of this second chapter.

For most of human history, the idea of 'staying on' in an earthly existence has been mainly the stuff of legend, fantasy and science fiction, although the idea does occur in religious contexts too. More recently, however, some scientists and those who call themselves 'transhumanists' have seriously proposed the feasibility of extending human life well beyond the currently normal human lifespan – if not indefinitely. Transhumanists like to cite the ideas of the French Enlightenment philosopher the Marquis de Condorcet (1743–1794), who is treated almost as one of their founding fathers. Condorcet was an early champion of the idea of an unlimited human progress based on scientific knowledge, believing that human beings had every reason for thinking that 'nature has set no limit to our hopes'. In particular, he foresaw a time when social reform and medical science would eliminate the poverty and disease responsible for premature death, and speculated about an indefinite extension of the human lifespan:

> Would it be absurd at this point to imagine that this amelioration of the human species must be regarded as susceptible of indefinite progress, that a time will come when death will be only a result of unusual accidents or the slower and slower deterioration of vital forces, and even that the average interval between birth and this deterioration will have no assignable limit? Human beings will certainly not become immortal, but can there not be an indefinite increase in the interval between the beginning of life and the average point at which existence becomes difficult for them naturally, without illness or accident?[4]

Although such earthly 'immortality' might more realistically be termed 'hyperlongevity', the latter possibility raises questions similar to those that would apply to human beings who were able to live forever. Chief among these is whether beings nature has 'designed' to be mortal could cope with living an indefinitely extended life, let alone a truly immortal one. It might be thought that the longer one went on living, the more dreadful would become the prospect of one's eventual mortality: as the decades – or indeed centuries – went by, one might feel that one had more and more to lose. But some would argue the contrary: that as the years rolled by, life would become increasingly wearisome, and – depending on one's particular circumstances – increasingly lonely. Eventually one might start longing for death. Whether those whose immortality was part of their nature could ever find life tedious or lonely is another question. Much would depend on one's bodily as well as one's mental state. Because not dying does not in itself entail the end of ageing, a life of hyperlongevity could become a living hell in comparison with the experiences of those who suffer the weaknesses and indignities of old age within a normal lifespan.

According to the looser use of the term employed in this book, 'immortality' can mean living on indefinitely as well as being intrinsically immune to dying. An immortal in the strict sense would be one who could not die rather than simply one who went on living (and who might eventually die). A hyperlongevite (if such a barbarous term be permitted) would presumably have to die eventually.[5] Indeed, such a one might be murdered, or killed in a road accident or fall victim to fatal disease or environmental catastrophe. Or a hyperlongevite might give up on longevity, choosing to die 'prematurely'. Hyperlongevism could take different forms. One's lifespan might be miraculously extended, or extended through artificial means. Alternatively, one might be periodically restored to the vitality of youth through some gift or technique of rejuvenation.

How earthly immortality in the form of 'staying on' might come about, and whether it would be considered a desirable or an undesirable state for a human being, are questions explored in a wide range of legendary, literary and dramatic sources. Arguably the fictional genre yielding the richest material for it is that of science fiction, of both the literary and the cinematic kind.[6] In these sources, earthly immortality is sometimes a condition imposed, or granted, by supernatural beings, and sometimes the result of human ingenuity. Yet the distinction between a magical or supernatural cause of earthly immortality and a natural or scientific one is not always easy to apply, since what is magical or supernatural to some people will by others be regarded as purely natural. In modern times, moreover, there is much scientific speculation about the possibility of artificially extending human life through genetic or cybernetic means.

II

Narratives describing an earthly immortality granted or imposed by the gods generally serve to demonstrate the advantage of human mortality rather than to celebrate the benefits of becoming immortal. This is especially so where earthly immortality is imposed as a punishment for some transgression. Even those immortalities which ostensibly represent a reward or gift are by their very nature double-edged, the subtext being that humans will never find earthly immortality a comfortable fit. In one of the world's earliest surviving narratives, the *Gilgamesh* epic (dated to around 1700 BCE), the eponymous royal hero sets out on a long and hazardous journey to find Utnapishtim, a man to whom, in an earlier age, the gods had granted immortality after he (and his wife) had survived the great deluge in which the rest of his generation had been destroyed. Gilgamesh finds him a rather sad figure, anything but full of the joys of immortality. His response to Gilgamesh's quest for eternal life is a gloomy one:

> The handsome young man, the lovely young woman –
> in their prime, death comes and drags them away.
> Though no one has seen death's face or heard
> death's voice, suddenly, savagely, death
> destroys us, all of us, old or young.
> And yet we build houses, make contracts, brothers
> divide their inheritance, conflicts occur –
> as though this human life lasted forever.
> The river rises, flows over its banks
> and carries us all away, like mayflies
> floating downstream: they stare at the sun,
> then all at once there is nothing.[7]

Utnapishtim's immortality was a reluctant gift of the gods; and Gilgamesh realizes that it is not something that mere mortals can choose for themselves. More as a test than a real offer, Utnapishtim suggests to Gilgamesh that if he can resist sleep for six days and seven nights, he might yet gain immortality. But the exhausted Gilgamesh almost immediately falls into a deep sleep, that analogue of death itself, thereby proving himself all too human. Utnapishtim does reveal to Gilgamesh the whereabouts of a submarine plant that at least confers rejuvenation. Having managed to secure this valuable 'consolation prize', however, Gilgamesh immediately loses it again: it is stolen by a snake while he is bathing.[8] Gilgamesh returns to his kingdom reconciled to the fact that the only form of immortality available to mortals is that provided by earthly fame, and sets about making himself famous for all time by building the great walls of his city, Uruk. Given that his story is still current, one must acknowledge that his bid for this kind of earthly immortality has been successful.

In other legendary or mythic narratives, we meet characters whose immortality has been imposed upon them as a punishment of some kind. One of the oldest of these is the legend of the 'Wandering Jew', named in some sources as Ahasuerus, a Jerusalem shoemaker who made the mistake of taunting Jesus as he paused to rest on his way to crucifixion, which event he also witnesses.[9] Telling Jesus to hurry along, Ahasuerus receives the chilling reply: 'I go, but you shall stay'; and from this moment on, Ahasuerus is doomed to wander the Earth until the Second Coming. He is very likely the prototype of later wanderers such as Coleridge's Ancient Mariner and Wagner's Flying Dutchman.[10] For these figures, typically represented as aged rather than youthful figures, longevity is a burden, one that can be relieved only at the end of time or when they meet another human able to redeem them. Despite their special status, however, these figures do not lose their essentially human characteristics, and the agony of their lives answers in decidedly negative terms the paradoxical question: 'What would it be like for a mortal to live as an immortal?'

But would the experience of immortality be any different if, rather than being a punishment, or even a gift, from a divine being, it were an achievement of human beings themselves, obtained on their own terms and directed to their own purposes? This would not be immortality in the strict sense, which goes against the very logic of being born and growing up as a human being. True immortals, such as gods or angels, are depicted as ageless or at least unageing beings. According to authorities such as the thirteenth-century theologian Bonaventure, angels are not eternal beings (like God) but aeviternal beings – that is, beings as old as creation itself.[11] Presumably even their experience of time would differ from the experience of those who simply lived on indefinitely. But human beings might be capable of creating for themselves the looser form of immortality I have called hyperlongevity, where dying is indefinitely postponed. If so, the ideal kind of hyperlongevity a human being might hope for would presumably be that of remaining at the prime of life, enjoying a perpetual state of mature youthfulness.

It is important to reiterate the point made earlier that the mere prolongation of life would not in itself entail remaining youthful. Instructive here is the story of Tithonus, a Trojan hero beloved by Eos (Aurora), goddess of dawn. When Eos begged Zeus to make Tithonus immortal, she forgot also to ask that he be granted perpetual youth. For

Tithonus, therefore, immortality meant getting older and older without ever dying. In Tennyson's poem of this name, Tithonus laments his tragic exile from the natural cycle of life and death:

> The woods decay, the woods decay and fall,
> The vapours weep their burthen to the ground,
> Man comes and tills the field and lies beneath,
> And after many a summer dies the swan.
> Me only cruel immortality
> Consumes . . . [12]

This poem gave Aldous Huxley the title of his satirical novel *After Many a Summer* (1939), which features a thanatophobic Californian multimillionaire and art collector, Jo Stoyte, who is financing the research into longevity conducted by his personal physician, Dr Obispo. Meanwhile an archivist also employed by Stoyte, Jeremy Pordage, has discovered some notebooks of an eighteenth-century English ancestor, the Earl of Gonister, who was himself in search of biological immortality. By consuming the raw viscera of carp (a fish known for its extreme longevity) the Earl had succeeded in restoring his youth, at the age of 81 fathering three children with his former housekeeper. To avoid scandal, he and his new family moved into the cellars, where on a visit to England Pordage and Dr Obispo discover they still dwell. Immortal (or undying) they may be, but in the intervening years they have in fact devolved into ape-like degenerates, their hyperlongevity thereby purchased at a terrible price.[13] Huxley's description of the sorry state of these hyper-geriatric creatures continues a literary thread going back to the Roman satirist Juvenal,[14] and more recently exemplified in Jonathan Swift's *Gulliver's Travels*, which includes a visit to the land of Luggnagg, where Gulliver meets the repulsively immortal Struldbrugs.[15] Much to the amusement of Dr Obispo, Stoyte decides to adopt the diet of carp pioneered by his ancestor, thus demonstrating that an immortality of the flesh, even if achievable, is just another worldly possession standing in the way of the selfless and fleshless immortality that lies beyond the mortal.

But even those who succeed in becoming immune to ageing, or to the effects of ageing, or who are able to ward these off indefinitely through some rejuvenating elixir, may nevertheless eventually long for death. Bernard Williams's discussion of what he calls the 'tedium of

immortality' takes as its starting point the situation of the main character in a play by Karel Čapek (1922) and an opera by Leoš Janáček
based upon it (1925) called *The Makropulos Case*.[16] This character, an
opera singer who currently goes by the name of Emilia Marty, has
had her ageing arrested for over three hundred years thanks to a secret
alchemical formula discovered in the sixteenth century by her father,
Hieronymus Makropulos, the private physician to Emperor Rudolf ii.
The emperor, eager to benefit from the formula, commands Makropulos
to test it out first on his own daughter, Elina. Over the years, as she
youthfully lives on, Elina has to reinvent herself and deceive others,
adopting a succession of aliases using names with the initials 'E. M.'
Although victim rather than the author of her longevity, Elina has
nevertheless been exploiting her condition. When after more than
three centuries the process of ageing starts to manifest again, Elina
succeeds in getting hold of the document containing the secret formula that would give her another period of youthfulness, but at the
last minute she renounces the plan, declaring that it's 'a great mistake
to live so long', that an endlessly renewed life robs life of its meaning:

> But in me life has come to a standstill, O Jesù Christe, I cannot
> go on. How dreadful this loneliness! In the end it's the same,
> Kristina, singing and silence. There's no joy in goodness, there
> is no joy in evil. Joyless the earth, joyless the sky! When you
> know that then your soul dies within you.[17]

She hands the formula to the young singer Kristina, whose lover she
had stolen; but, before anyone can stop her, the wise Kristina burns
the document.

Arguments for the tedium of immortality inevitably take their
cue from the tedium of mortality – that is, from the tedium already
experienced in mortal lives of ordinary length. Such arguments may
be unconvincing to those who rarely or never experience the tedium
of mortality, and would not apply at all if a renewed or extended life
offered experiences or opportunities distinctively different from those
known hitherto.

The narrative arts are particularly well suited to representing the
difficulties and dilemmas faced by one blessed, or burdened, with seeming immortality or at least with extreme longevity (the difference in
this context is immaterial). But *The Makropulos Case* (play and opera

alike) focuses mainly on the 'endgame' of Elina's personal drama within a small circle of friends and acquaintances. The broader implications of hyperlongevity are explored in more detail in other narratives. In Matt Haig's novel *How to Stop Time* (2017), the protagonist Tom Hazard is a hyperlongevite rather than a true immortal, one of a very small number of human beings who age at such a slow rate that their lives span several centuries. In the film *The Age of Adaline* (2015), directed by Lee Toland Krieger, the eponymous protagonist is uniquely immortal; following a freak accident that transforms her metabolism, she has been stuck at the biological age of 29 for almost a century. Both characters find it periodically necessary to change their identity, residence and employment in order to avoid the curiosity, and dangers, that would inevitably attend public recognition of their condition. Adaline's predicament is not simply or even mainly the result of being stuck at a certain age; it comes mostly from the fact that she is alone in this situation. Tom has to contend with additional dangers posed by the existence of several others who share his condition. Commenting on Adaline's condition, the film's omniscient narrator states that several decades later the metabolic anomaly which had brought Adaline's biological clock to a stop would become a scientific discovery – suggesting a future in which people would, wisely or unwisely, embrace the chance of earthly immortality thereby made possible.[18]

I have shown how in much religion, myth and legend, and often in fantasy fiction too, human immortality tends to be presented as a burden, even where it is not specifically a punishment. To balance the rather grim catalogue of human misfortune detailed above, therefore, it is worth stressing that there are also traditions in which earthly immortality is regarded as a worthy and wholly benign aspiration, even where it is regarded as a means towards an otherworldly goal. The most prominent example here is Chinese Taoism, where the virtues of earthly longevity and immortality are very clearly affirmed. The texts abound with references to rejuvenating or immortalizing 'elixirs of life', closely similar to those found in Western alchemy. Taoism, however, comprises various strands, often interwoven with non-Taoist ideas. Scholars tend to differentiate 'philosophical' from 'religious' Taoism, or 'religious' from 'magical' Taoism, although in the context of the lived history of Taoism these distinctions are somewhat artificial. It is possible, however, to identify one strand of Taoism concerned with the quest for what Joseph Needham calls 'material immortality', this quest being pursued through various combinations of alchemy, medicine, magic and meditation.[19] This strand of Taoism is sometimes called 'Xian Taoism', the *xian* (or *hsien*) being a type of earthly immortal, of whom the tradition cites both legendary and historical examples. By virtue of their attributes and achievements, however, these immortals tend inevitably to be regarded as supernatural beings, which somewhat undercuts their status as human beings who have attained immortality. Moreover, the attainment of earthly immortality, or at least of hyperlongevity, is often presented not as an ultimate goal but a stage preceding an ascent to heaven, where the true immortals dwell. The true sage is described by Zhuangzi (Chuang-tzu) as resembling

> a quail at rest, a little fledgling at its meal, a bird in flight who leaves no trail behind. When the world has the Way [Tao], he joins in the chorus with all other things. When the world is without the Way, he nurses his Virtue and retires in leisure. And after a thousand years, should he weary of the world, he will leave it and ascend to the immortals, riding on those white clouds all the way up to the village of God.[20]

Thus the Taoist language of earthly immortality is in many contexts a rhetorical device for talking about, or preparing for, some form of immortality transcending mere earthly continuance. One might even see it as comparable to some versions of the idea of resurrection in Christianity, where a renewed physical existence on Earth is but a prelude to an eternal existence in heaven. Even so, the sources leave little doubt that both within and outside the Taoist tradition there existed a real interest in a literal, earthly immortality as well as various practices associated with this. The quest for earthly immortality, restricted to a small elite of qualified practitioners, is an extreme manifestation of the more widespread Chinese pursuit of rejuvenation and longevity. This pursuit is typically more secular than religious, reflecting the Chinese emphasis on living life to the full here and now.

III

Speculations as to the sort of life a human immortal or hyperlongevite might lead generally involve extrapolating from ordinary mortal lives. But it can also be instructive to consider those forms of immortality enjoyed, or suffered, by beings who, while similar to humans, either never were or no longer are human. I shall take, as three examples, the case of angels, the case of vampires and the case of androids.

Angels have a long and complex pedigree in the history of religions, appearing in a variety of forms. Here I consider only those angels who are either asserted or imagined to be similar to human beings. Although naturally immortal, angels have sufficient in common with human beings to warrant meaningful comparisons between them. For one thing, angels manifest themselves to, and interact with, human beings, and in one well-known biblical episode even wrestle with them (Genesis 32:22–32). In the Bible and other sources the wingless angels who visit Earth appear indistinguishable from human beings (see, for example, the story of the three angels who visited Lot in Genesis 19). Nor is it universally assumed that angels must be the superior creatures. In the Quran, only Iblis (Satan) among the angels refuses to prostrate himself before the newly created Adam as God's superior creation – superior because man worships God despite the limitations and temptations of his earthly nature. Angels, or at least angels under a certain image, have come to be regarded as a benchmark for what is best in human nature: wisdom, beauty, love and so on. Benjamin Disraeli, in a speech delivered at the Oxford Diocesan Conference in 1864, provoked laughter among the audience by suggesting that Darwin's theory of evolution asked us to decide whether man was ape or angel, famously (and to great applause) declaring himself to be 'on the side of the angels'. Many people, however, have come to accept that humanity's position midway between the angels and the animals is the key to both the glory and the predicament of our species. 'Angel' as a human term of endearment or judgement suggests that the best humans come close to being angels and might even aspire actually to becoming such. No less interesting is the idea, movingly represented in Wim Wenders's film *Wings of Desire* (1987), that angels might well envy aspects of human life and hence aspire to 'fall' into a mortal body in order to enjoy the kind of physical sensations inaccessible to them as immaterial and intellectual beings. George Berkeley, for one, would have regarded this as a bad choice:

We are dazzled, indeed, with the glory and grandeur of things here below, because we know no better. But, I am apt to think, if we knew what it was to be an angel for one hour, we should return to this world, though it were to sit on the brightest throne in it, with vastly more loathing and reluctance than we would now descend into a loathsome dungeon or sepulchre.[21]

The vampire presents us with a rather different and altogether more sinister 'thought experiment' in human immortality. In broad folkloric terms, the vampire is a particular type, and a particularly unpleasant type, of supernatural revenant: an animated corpse that leaves its grave, physically or in the form of a spirit double of some kind, to harass and in some cases feed upon the living, its victims themselves joining the ranks of the undead. 'Revenant' is a convenient generic term covering all forms of post-mortem reappearance of the dead. The most commonly reported revenants are the various kinds of ghost or apparition, which (however explained) generally present themselves as incorporeal entities intersecting, but not interacting with, the materiality of the physical world. But there are also physical revenants, in the form of the 'undead': corpses of deceased persons animated or reanimated either by their own earthbound souls or by a possessing demon or spirit of some other kind. Vampires, understood as corpses who (or which) prey upon the blood or life force of the living, belong in the latter category, even where the vampire visits its victims through a ghost or double while its corpse remains in the grave. All vampires are 'undead' but not all 'undead' are vampires (in this particular sense).

Here I shall refer specifically to modern, literary vampires, which while rooted in eastern European folklore are fundamentally the invention of Romanticism and the Gothic literary tradition, prominent examples being found in works by Théophile Gautier, Sheridan Le Fanu and Bram Stoker, the authors, respectively, of *La Morte amoureuse* (1836), *Carmilla* (1872) and *Dracula* (1897). The modern vampire is not a revenant but rather a human being who, whether through accident or design, has attained a kind of earthly immortality which must be lived secretively and in fear of destruction by ordinary mortals. Whereas the folkloric vampire is sub-human, the modern vampire is, if anything, super-human, albeit at the cost of being in exile from the rest of the world. Unlike so many other commentators on the vampire and its literary incarnations, Mary Hallab resists facile interpretations in terms of repressed sexual desire or fear of the Other, seeing our fascination with the idea of the vampire as a means of engaging with the idea of immortality. The vampire – as lover, hero, outcast or free-spirited individual – is an embodiment of 'the human desire for knowledge, transcendence, and control over this life and the next'.[22]

The vampire has purchased immortality at a terrible price. As one who is neither alive nor dead, but rather one of the living dead, the vampire is doomed to 'prey on life for ever but not possess it'.[23] In Bram Stoker's seminal work *Dracula*, the vampirologist Van Helsing explains what happens when an individual becomes one of the 'undead':

> When they become such, there comes with the change the curse of immortality; they cannot die, but must go on age after age adding new victims and multiplying the evils of the world; for all that die from the preying of the Un-dead become themselves Un-dead, and prey on their kind. And so the circle goes on ever widening, like as the ripples from a stone thrown in the water.[24]

The vampire, however, is an immortal only in the weaker sense that unlike ordinary mortals, he or she will not necessarily die – or more accurately (since the vampire is already dead – 'undead' rather than alive) will not necessarily be destroyed. For even if the vampire is lucky enough, unlike Count Dracula himself, perpetually to escape the efforts of vampire hunters like Van Helsing (not to mention such traditional natural dangers as fire or sunlight) for the rest of human history, there is never any guarantee of perpetual survival, since vampires are locked into a symbiosis with the unreliable (and to vampires threatening) world of the mortal humans on whom they prey. Some vampire narratives, however, present the vampire as a tormented figure, a still human individual trapped in or possessed by vampirism. At the very end of Stoker's novel, when Count Dracula is at last destroyed and crumbles to dust, his erstwhile victim Mina Harker records these words in her description of the event: 'I shall be glad as long as I live that even in that moment of final dissolution, there was in the face a look of peace, such as I never could have imagined might have rested there.'[25]

Post-Romantic vampires, by contrast, rarely cease being human. They are more knowing, and more world-weary, than their fierce and solitary Gothic predecessors. They tend to be portrayed as sensitive and highly self-aware figures, often part of an elite community of fellow vampires. But their greater humanity only makes their relationship with their own special kind of immortality that much more nuanced.

As we see in Anne Rice's novels, vampires may well question their own and others' relationship with the immortality they now enjoy:

> How many vampires do you think have the stamina for immortality? They have the most dismal notions of immortality to begin with. For in becoming immortal they want all the forms of their life to be fixed as they are and incorruptible: carriages made in the same dependable fashion, clothing of the cut which suited their prime, men attired and speaking in the manner they have always understood and valued. When, in fact, all things change except the vampire himself; everything except the vampire is subject to constant corruption and distortion. Soon, with an inflexible mind, and often even with the most flexible mind, this immortality becomes a penitential sentence in a madhouse of figures and forms that are hopelessly unintelligible and without value. One evening a vampire rises and realizes what he has feared perhaps for decades, that he simply wants no more of life at any cost. That whatever style or fashion or shape of existence made immortality attractive to him has been swept off the face of the earth.[26]

The predicament of the vampire illustrates how the quest for immortality may destroy the very basis on which such a quest was predicated – namely, one's humanity.

The third case for imaginative thinking about immortality is that of the humanoid robot or 'android'. It illustrates another possibility: that of creating from scratch an immortal or potentially immortal being modelled on a human being but not hampered by human mortality. A *locus classicus* for this idea is Philip K. Dick's novel *Do Androids Dream of Electric Sheep?* (1968), the basis of the feature film *Blade Runner* (1982). In this story, androids are manufactured to serve various military, industrial and social functions, some of them becoming so human-like that they are, to all but a few experts, indistinguishable from humans – except of course that they never grow older. Programmed with false memories to accommodate them within human society, some of these 'replicants' become so sophisticated that they become autonomous, creatively adept at passing themselves off as human. Some of them, perhaps, are not even aware that they are not human – which raises the parallel possibility that some people who are accepted as humans are in reality androids.[27]

There are various questions about the relationship of such artificial humans to the real humans who have created them. What, in a post-religious context, would be the essential difference between the two? Would it be as simple as the difference between, say, a mechanical heart and an organically natural heart? Would, or could, androids have rights – or at least would there be codes of conduct governing the ways in which humans treated them? How, in any case, would a future society in which androids played any significant role regulate interactions between humans and androids?[28] In 2016 the European Parliament's Committee on Legal Affairs issued a draft report, 'with recommendations to the Commission on Civil Law Rules on Robotics', following a debate in which MEPs called for the adoption of rules to govern how humans should interact with artificial intelligence and robots. In particular, this report called for a consideration of what impact on human dignity there might be 'if and when robots replace human care and companionship', and of what questions about human dignity could arise 'in the context of "repairing" or enhancing human beings'. The report observes that

> ultimately there is a possibility that within the space of a few decades AI could surpass human intellectual capacity in a manner which, if not prepared for, could pose a challenge to humanity's capacity to control its own creation and, consequently, perhaps also to its capacity to be in charge of its own destiny and to ensure the survival of the species.[29]

In Philip K. Dick's novel, the main protagonist is Rick Deckard, a professional bounty hunter hired to 'retire' rogue androids. Rick has started a relationship with an advanced android named Rachael. She is aware of being an android but admits to having fellow feeling for Pris, one of the female androids on Rick's hit list.

> . . . 'You know what I have? Toward this Pris android?'
> 'Empathy,' he said.
> 'Something like that. Identification; there goes I. My God; maybe that's what'll happen. In the confusion you'll retire me, not her. And she can go back to Seattle and live my life. I never felt this way before. We are machines, stamped out like bottle caps. It's an illusion that I – I personally – really exist; I'm just representative of a type.' She shuddered.[30]

Rachael also reflects on the inability of her kind to bear children.

> 'Is it a loss?' Rachael repeated. 'I don't really know; I have no way to tell. How does it feel to have a child? How does it feel to be born, for that matter? We're not born; we don't grow up; instead of dying from illness or old age we wear out like ants. Ants again; that's what we are. Not you; I mean me. Chitinous reflex-machines who aren't really alive.' She twisted her head to one side, said loudly, 'I'm not alive! You're not going to bed with a woman. Don't be disappointed; okay? Have you ever made love to an android before?'
>
> 'No,' he said, taking off his shirt and tie.
>
> 'I understand – they tell me – it's convincing if you don't think too much about it. But if you think too much, if you reflect on what you're doing – then you can't go on.'[31]

There are of course many people who, in accordance with current reductionist anthropologies, might want to say similar things about human beings themselves; but however reductionist their view of humans, they might nevertheless be inclined to say something *differently* reductionist about androids! I return to the case of androids later, and more specifically to the question of whether android technology could provide a vehicle for mortal humans to achieve some kind of personal earthly immortality.

IV

It is not inherently impossible that human immortals or hyperlongevites would, with or without technological support, continue to find their lives fulfilling and enjoyable as the centuries went by, but neither is it impossible that a vastly extended earthly existence, particularly if all or most other people continued to live normal lifespans, might well be accompanied by unforeseen social, psychological and even physical difficulties. At worst, staying on indefinitely could turn out to resemble more a living death than a life lived beyond the reach of death. Perhaps, therefore, a better way of achieving or manifesting earthly continuance would be by 'coming back' from death rather than simply 'staying on' without dying; dying, far from being the obstacle to earthly immortality, might turn out to be the unlikely key to its achievement.

Coming back from death to another earthly existence is an idea most closely associated with resurrection and reincarnation. These are specifically religious doctrines, or at least doctrines elaborated mainly within religious contexts. The general tendency of religious teaching is to look beyond ephemeral worldly existence to an eternal otherworldly destiny. In some versions of resurrection, however, this otherworldly destiny, or at least the prelude to it, has been pictured in terms of a renewed earthly existence. In doctrines of reincarnation, on the other hand, repeated earthly existences are part of the ephemeral world from which, ultimately, liberation is sought. Even so, what many of those who believe in reincarnation desire is a next life which will be happier (or at least not unhappier) than their present life. The question here is whether the lives of resurrected or reincarnated persons could – within any version of these doctrines – properly be described as cases of 'staying on' within an earthly existence.

In religious contexts the term 'resurrection' – literally a rising up or standing up – refers (like its equivalents in other languages) to a revival from death through divine agency. The term is used to identify two kinds of event: on the one hand cases of individual persons being raised from the dead in the course of history, and on the other hand an eschatological event – that is, an event that occurs at the end of history and embraces (potentially at least) the whole of humanity.

In both the Old and New Testaments several examples occur of individuals being resurrected in the non-eschatological sense. Some of these cases, it is worth noting, are of younger people whose deaths, both then and now, would be regarded as 'untimely'. In some cases – and especially in those of Lazarus and Jesus himself – the resurrection of a particular individual is seen as a prophetic sign of the general resurrection. Nowadays some of the individual resurrections from the dead narrated in religious texts might well be reinterpreted as resuscitations from comatose or catatonic states; Jesus himself describes Jairus's daughter as 'only sleeping'. The salient point, however, is that even those who had literally been resurrected from the dead would have returned not to an earthly immortality but to a resumption of their original lives in their familiar bodies. All would face the prospect of dying again. Their 'coming back' would not be a prelude to 'staying on'.

The eschatological idea of resurrection first emerged in Zoroastrian eschatology, whence it entered the Jewish, Christian and Islamic traditions. It is this second sense of resurrection that is mainly of interest here, since it specifically relates to the idea of immortality. It is one thing to be brought back to a mortal life again, quite another to be brought back to an immortal one. It is to the latter that several of the Old Testament prophets refer. Thus Isaiah declares that 'Your dead shall live; their bodies shall rise. You who dwell in the dust, awake and sing for joy! For your dew is a dew of light, and the earth will give birth to the dead' (26:19). And Daniel states that 'many of those who sleep in the dust of the earth shall awake, some to everlasting life, and some to shame and everlasting contempt' (12:2). This eschatological resurrection entails not simply the reanimation of recently deceased individuals, but the recreation of living bodies from components long decayed and dispersed.

St Augustine, like many other theologians, insists that it will be the self-same body that has died that will rise from its grave (or from its scattered components) to become a new, transformed but still physical body:

> As for bodies that have been consumed by wild beasts, or by fire, or those parts that have disintegrated into dust and ashes, or those parts that have dissolved into moisture, or have evaporated into the air, it is unthinkable that the Creator should lack the power to revive them all and restore them to life.[32]

In marked contrast to descriptions such as this are those which present resurrection bodies as quite different from our ephemeral fleshly bodies and as located elsewhere than on Earth. The most important example occurs in St Paul's First Letter to the Corinthians, which describes how at the resurrection the earthly body will be transformed into a celestial or spiritual body. 'The body is sown in corruption; it is raised in incorruption. It is sown in dishonour, it is raised in glory. It is sown in weakness, it is raised in power. It is sown a natural body, it is raised a spiritual body' (15:42–4). This spiritual body is ontologically continuous with the corruptible earthly body, and resurrected persons at least resemble their old earthly selves in still being embodied. But their embodiment is of a different order, and pertains to a celestial rather than an earthly existence. The Pauline view of resurrection is not about reconstituted or reanimated earthly bodies coming out of tombs and resuming some kind of an earthly life. And even texts in which the language of resurrection remains resolutely physical or material can be interpreted as figuratively referring to the resurrection as a celestial event.

For resurrected persons to qualify as the subjects of an earthly immortality, two conditions would have to be fulfilled. To begin with, the body in or as which a person is resurrected would have to be, if not a version of the body in which they had died, then at least a body capable of interacting with this same world. Second, the world they did in fact inhabit would have to be Earth itself, or at least a world historically continuous with this Earth. While some texts insist that the new resurrection body would be physically identical or at least similar to the old body, what chiefly matters is that this body be a physical body located on this material Earth. That the particular form of the body is of secondary importance can be shown by considering two hypothetical cases of 'staying on' – the case of a person whose cryonically preserved head has been successfully grafted onto a donor body and the case of a person whose mind or memory has been 'uploaded' to a completely artificial body of some kind at (or just prior to) the death of their original, biological body. It seems reasonable to predict that, for these individuals themselves (and for any observers who might be called upon to comment), what would confirm the conclusion that they had succeeded in 'staying on' would not be the particular form of their new physical or artificial body but the fact that the world in which these 'resurrected' persons found themselves, and with which they interacted through their new bodies, should be the same world as the world in which they had died (or undergone their suspension).

In so far as the resurrection is regarded as an objective event within earthly history and the resurrection life that follows it a fully earthly existence, resurrected persons might well qualify as subjects of some form of earthly immortality. There is nothing logically wrong with the idea of a divine being resurrecting human beings to a purely earthly immortality or hyperlongevity – after all, it is hardly more of a miracle than the original one of being created out of nothing. In apocalyptic Judaism, the expectation seems to have been that in the new Messianic kingdom ushered in by the resurrection the resurrected would live on eternally in an earthly existence. In most traditions, however, the earthly resurrection life is destined to last only for a set period (most commonly a thousand years), after which earthly history would come to an end and an otherworldly immortality supervene. A thousand years of earthly existence might at least be said to constitute an enviably long period of hyperlongevity, but the real question is whether, in any of these resurrection scenarios, the resurrection life would unambiguously qualify as an earthly rather than a celestial one. Indeed, what many believers may expect or imagine the immortality of the resurrection life to be is some kind of continuation, albeit much-improved, of their earthly lives. If so, they understand the eschatological kind of resurrection to be little more than a de luxe version of the non-eschatological kind – in other words, to be an immortality that perpetuates rather than ends or transcends history.

The lack of eschatological ambition shown by those who understand the resurrection of the dead to be a reprisal of earthly existence is echoed, perhaps, in the rather limited expectations some people have of reincarnation. This doctrine is found in many cultures, but is most commonly associated with the religions of India and the Far East, where it has undergone its most detailed and systematic development. Unlike the resurrection life, which represents either the ultimate or penultimate state of existence in monotheistic eschatology, a reincarnated life is merely another episode in an indefinite chain of lives – a chain which can be broken only by selfless detachment from the world. Were these different incarnations exclusively earthly ones, then one might be tempted to say that the successive lives of a reincarnating person constituted a serial form of earthly immortality for that person. There are, however, two difficulties with this suggestion.

The first difficulty is that this present world is not the only possible location for reincarnating beings. There are many different worlds within which beings are reborn. In the Buddhist view, a human rebirth is a rare and valuable occurrence, worth treating almost as a unique opportunity, since it is only on Earth that there is enough suffering to awaken the desire for liberation from the cycle of birth and death (*samsara*) and enough comfort to enable one to pursue this goal. In the other spheres of rebirth, which vary between blissful heavenly worlds and hellish worlds full of pain, one will only be distracted from such striving. If one were able to move simply from one earthly existence to another then reincarnation might indeed be regarded as tantamount to a serial form of earthly immortality, or at least hyperlongevity. On a grander scale, given that the earthly sphere is only one of many worlds, the entire course of one's reincarnations might be described as manifesting a samsaric rather than an earthly immortality – albeit an immortality which serious religious practitioners are devoted to ending. Certainly for many ordinary believers the hope is for a happy rebirth, whether on Earth or in some pleasant heavenly realm. But even if reincarnation were to this extent a means to overcoming death, it would not function as a way of transcending it, since to be born again means having to die again.

But none of this takes into account a second and greater difficulty for the idea of reincarnation as a means or manifestation of 'staying on' in an earthly (or samsaric) existence. This is the difficulty of specifying the identity of the one who is reincarnated. Clearly, unless some real connection existed between earlier and later reincarnated individuals, it would not make sense to use the language of rebirth or reincarnation in the first place. In the Hindu and Platonic traditions, reincarnation is understood as the transmigration of an unchanging soul or person through many lives. In the *Bhagavad Gita* it is stated that the reincarnating self leaves behind its old bodies and enters new ones in the same way as a man casts off his worn-out clothes and puts on new ones.[33] The question here is how to differentiate the transmigrating entity from the empirical details of each separate life in which it is incarnated. The Buddhist tradition, using the language of re-becoming rather than that of reincarnation, holds the more radical view that there is no permanent soul or person surviving unchanged through the succession of lives; rather do these successive lives, as a stream of becoming, themselves constitute the ever-changing person.

When an individual desires an earthly immortality, what is desired is precisely a 'staying on' or – in the present context – a 'coming back' as that same individual, not a desire that someone else should do so in one's place. In neither the Buddhist nor the Hindu view of reincarnation, however, can souls or persons re-become or reincarnate as the self-same *individuals* they were in a previous life, since individuals are defined by the boundaries of the unique and particular lives of which they are both products and producers. Consider the hypothetical claim that Napoleon was a reincarnation of Cleopatra. What this claim implies is that the person formerly individuated as Cleopatra was subsequently (with or without intervening lives) individuated as Napoleon. Cleopatra as a finite historical individual with interests in the future of Egypt, her dynastic succession, her own fame and legacy and so on, would have long ceased to exist. To say that Napoleon was 'really' Cleopatra would be as absurd as saying that Cleopatra was 'really' Napoleon. What Hindu thinkers might variously say is that Cleopatra and Napoleon are, or are incarnations of, the same soul, not that they were the same individual. What a Buddhist thinker might say is that the individual known as Cleopatra was part cause of, or an earlier stage in, the psycho-empirical stream of personhood subsequently individuated as Napoleon.

The dilemmas created by the prospect of a reincarnated person actually seeking to pick up the threads of a previous life are nicely illustrated in the comedy film about reincarnation *Chances Are* (dir. Emile Ardolino, 1989). In this film, the protagonist dies (as Louie) in an accident, leaving behind his newly pregnant wife. Allowed by the celestial authorities to return to Earth, he rushes off before receiving the statutory antimemory injection. After reaching manhood (as Alex), he meets 'his' (that is, Louie's) wife, daughter and best friend from the previous life. He and his 'daughter' experience an immediate mutual attraction, but when memories of his previous life start kicking in, he rebuffs the attentions of his 'daughter' while just about convincing his 'wife' that he really is, or was, her husband. Eventually a head injury and an injection from a visiting heavenly official erase all memories of his previous life. This leaves him free to resume his romance with the daughter, while his 'wife', no longer trapped by the memories of her dead husband, marries the husband's best friend, who has for years been in love with her.

The film's humorous tagline raises important questions about the logic of reincarnation: 'Alex has a lifetime of wonderful memories. Unfortunately they're not his!' One individual cannot actually have another individual's memories, or rather one cannot have them and straightforwardly call them 'one's own'. What one might say is that the 'memories' belong neither to Louie nor to Alex, but rather to the person of whom both Louie and Alex are temporary individuations. Memory is an important criterion of identity, though it is hard to resist the argument that memory presupposes rather than constitutes identity. In *Chances Are*, once Alex's memories of his previous life vanish, all problems seem to be resolved, and yet by the film's own logic he might still be said to be having an affair with his own (that is, Louie's) daughter, despite having now forgotten that she had been his daughter.

People do in fact claim to have memories of past lives, some of the most persuasive cases being those of children who, usually quite artlessly, talk and behave as if they remember a previous life. They may identify or be identified by others who were 'their' former relatives or associates, and even have bodily marks corresponding to traumas suffered by their deceased 'predecessor'.[34] Whatever their evidential value, however, the one thing these cases could never establish is that an individual with memories of a past life is the same individual as the subject of that past life. Indeed it is worth noting that until their past-life memories fade away, which they usually do relatively quickly, these children are not fully at ease as the new individuals they are in their present life. Theoretically, a case could be made for seeing reincarnation as an earthly immortality lived 'in instalments', with successive individuals recognizing their predecessors as earlier versions of themselves, albeit aware that, as individuals, they themselves will not survive. In practice, however, the doctrine represents a doubtful option for those intent upon 'staying on', predicated as it is upon the annihilation rather than perpetuation of the individual. Serious consideration of the implications of rebirth or reincarnation is more likely to direct attention to the value of the immortality that comes from breaking free from, rather than staying within, the cycle of birth and death.

One cannot leave the theme of 'staying on' by 'coming back' without mentioning an idea about earthly immortality which in its radical simplicity trumps any version of resurrection or reincarnation. This is Friedrich Nietzsche's notion of 'eternal recurrence', according to which we all live exactly the same lives over and over again, just as the history of the universe as a whole is perpetually repeated. Although there is some evidence that Nietzsche intended this 'myth' as an objective (albeit unfalsifiable) cosmological doctrine, its main significance in his thought is as an existential strategy or even ethical imperative which allows one to face personal suffering in an indifferent universe.

Nietzsche imagines a demon stealing up to one in one's loneliest moment and saying:

> This life as you now live it and have lived it, you will have to live once more and innumerable times more; and there will be nothing new in it, but every pain and every joy and every thought and sigh and everything unutterably small or great in your life will have to return to you, all in the same succession and sequence – even this spider and this moonlight between the trees, and even this moment and I myself. The eternal hourglass of existence is turned upside down again and again, and you with it, speck of dust![35]

According to Nietzsche, one can only respond to this proposition 'with either total despair or total exhilaration, and certainly not with indifference. It challenges one to accept that the only way to justify one's life and to find meaning in it is to accept it in its entirety, and in every detail, the mark of this ability being expressed in the desire that it be eternally repeated.' It is easy enough to see why one might wish the joys and pleasures of one's life to be eternally repeated, but why should one wish the same of one's anxieties and sufferings? The answer is not that one has to take the bad with the good in a universe where even the slightest change would alter everything. Rather it is that by willing our life to be exactly as it is, we give it a meaning it would otherwise lack, and by willing its sufferings as well as its joys – indeed, especially by willing its sufferings – we show that we are no longer the passive victims of an indifferent if not hostile universe.[36] It is a creative form of *amor fati*. There are similarities here with how Albert Camus interprets the myth of Sisyphus, the king whom Zeus punished by having him endlessly repeat the task of pushing a rock up a steep hill only to see it roll all the way down again. 'One must,' says Camus, 'imagine Sisyphus happy.'[37]

Camus pointed to the absurdity of every life, just as Nietzsche pointed to the essentially tragic nature of life. It can therefore be argued that in embracing, as he did, a life of suffering, 'Nietzsche was able to see that a life of intense pain and suffering is perhaps the only life it really makes sense to want to live again.'[38] By contrast, a life one regarded as happy and fulfilled is exactly the kind of life one would not need or even want to go on repeating again and again. What seems to be important about Nietzsche's vision of recurrence is not the recurrence as such, but rather the demonstration, through a willingness to own one's life down to its smallest details, that one is not the passive or helpless victim of fate but rather in charge of one's own destiny.

V

In magical and supernatural narratives, earthly immortality is a rare gift of the gods, or else is a curse or punishment of some kind. In specifically religious contexts, where we find the doctrines of resurrection and reincarnation, earthly immortality is usually a prelude to some form of non-earthly immortality. In the context of science and technology, however, the quest for earthly immortality is sought within the confines of Earth itself and relies exclusively on the deployment of human resources. The 'scientific' quest for immortality generally implies not simply a rejection of magical or religious solutions to the problem of human mortality, but a critique of magic and religion as ways of thinking which inhibit humankind from achieving its fullest potential. 'Death is an imposition on the human race, and no longer acceptable. Men and women have all but lost their ability to accommodate themselves to personal extinction; they must now proceed physically to overcome it. In short, to kill death; to put an end to mortality as a certain consequence of being born.'[39]

Medical science and technology have already succeeded in mitigating or slowing down the processes of ageing, and more and more of the conditions and diseases responsible for the ending of human life have also been countered. In the process, medical science has become increasingly familiar with the aetiology of disease and the mechanisms of degeneration, giving rise to hopes that one day it will be able not merely to ensure a full and healthy life for all human beings but substantially to extend the boundary of what is considered a normal lifespan.

And there are yet bolder remedies for mortality (or surrogates for immortality) on the horizon. Some people, confident that medical science will eventually be able to halt and even reverse the effects of ageing, have elected to have their body (and in some cases, rather more optimistically, their head or even just their brain) cryonically preserved until a time arrives when their body might be restored to healthy life or their head or brain matched with a new physical or perhaps artificial body. Cryonics is a particular application of the more general science of cryogenics, a branch of physics which investigates the effects on various materials of extremely low temperatures achieved through the use of liquefied gases. The *OED* defines cryonics as the 'practice or technique of cryogenically preserving a person's body with the aim of reviving it in the future'. To eliminate or minimize tissue damage, the sooner organic matter is frozen the better. Cryogenically preserved bodies need to be frozen immediately upon death, to be stored in a suitable facility until such a time as a remedy for the cause of death has been discovered. Where euthanasia is permitted, subjects suffering from terminal conditions might elect to have their bodies frozen prior to death.

According to the *OED*, the term 'cryonics' first appeared in an advertisement placed in the science fiction magazine *Galaxy*: 'Immortality is within your grasp. The Cryonics Society of New York Inc. is the leading non-profit organization in the field of cryogenic interment.' Similar ideas were already current. For example, Robert Heinlein in several of his novels uses the idea of what he calls 'cold-rest' or 'cold-sleep' as a technique for surviving interstellar travel – although, as with any form of suspended animation, the subjects are not actually dead, but indeed 'only sleeping'.[40] From one point of view cryonics describes an existing scientific achievement; from another it represents an act of faith in the unlimited potential of future scientific discovery. It is easy enough to freeze bodies to the required low temperature – the first such body was frozen in 1965 – but impossible as yet to unfreeze them intact (that is, without fatal tissue damage). And even if scientists did know how to unfreeze bodies without damage, the hoped-for medical advances capable of curing the diseases from which their subjects died, or were going to die, have not yet been made. For the moment, cryonics as a method of life-extension, let alone as a door to a more substantial earthly immortality, remains firmly within the realm of science fiction. So far it can only be regarded as an elaborate – and expensive – mode of bodily interment.

While the means whereby a cryonically preserved body would be stored and subsequently reanimated might seem like a parody of resurrection, its effect would be closer to that of reincarnation, since the new world within which the subject would be revived would be a continuation of the subject's original world.[41] Again, although the social and psychological effects of the reanimation of a cryonically preserved body would not differ essentially from the effects of awakening from coma or suspended animation, the essential difference is that frozen subjects will have been organically dead, and in particular brain dead, for the whole period of their cryonic suspension. Naturally, various psychological, social and ethical objections, as well as the obvious technical ones, have been raised against the idea of cryonic suspension. The project of cryonic suspension and reanimation is regarded by most experts as either too fantastic, or too socially or ethically problematic, for serious consideration. Yet by no means all of those with enough knowledge of the subject to have a worthwhile opinion on it have dismissed or ridiculed the idea. One of these argues 'that insofar as the alternatives to cryonics are burial or cremation, and thus certain, irreversible death, even small chances for success can be sufficient to make opting for cryonics a rational choice.'[42] According to another, who regards a version of Pascal's Wager[43] as the strongest argument in favour of using cryonic suspension, 'it might be imprudent not to use the technology, given the relatively minor expense involved and the potential payoff.'

> We have seen that many of the arguments against cryonic storage fail on their own terms, or because of the peculiar way in which successful reanimation would change our very conception of death: in essence, successful cryonics would be a form of life-support that delays, rather than returns the user from, death. It is true that there is only one convincing argument in favour of cryonics. But the point is that this positive argument is so very strong, both practically and ethically, that it trumps all the self-interested arguments against cryonics, and the ethical objections are not strong enough to prohibit the practice. At worst, cryonics offers a slim chance of living for a few more years. At best, it offers a slim chance of living forever. Ultimately, the Cryonic Wager is overwhelmingly attractive for the rational humanist, even without the prospect of eternal life.[44]

Another approach to artificial immortality is suggested by the science of cloning. Producing progeny who will in turn produce progeny is for many people the best surrogate for their own individual immortality, and the science of cloning might be considered a way of ensuring that one's progeny maintained valued family traits or were of the desired gender. Reproducing progeny who were clones of oneself, however, would be regarded by most people as a step too far.[45] It is bad enough, one might think, that parents should want their naturally generated children to follow the pattern of their own lives. It is worth noting, however, that cloning has already been used in the service of surrogate immortality. A British couple, devastated by the death of their dog Dylan, employed the services of a South Korean company specializing in dog cloning to create twin puppies from Dylan's DNA. The technique involves implanting DNA from the original animal into a dog egg with its nucleus removed. This egg, after receiving electric shocks to trigger cell division, is then implanted into a surrogate female. The resultant animals are likely physically to resemble the original dog and to have a similar 'personality'. Despite the mythology surrounding the use of the term 'clone', however, a cloned animal and the original animal can never be identical:

The DNA in the chromosomes of every cell may be identical, but the dead animal and the clone had different egg donors. They would have gestated in different wombs. And, because they were born at different times, they are unlikely to have identical rearing experiences, which also define character. So the product puppy, however loveable, and however like in appearance, will be a different animal. There are some things in life you can't have twice.[46]

If cloned dogs are unlikely to be identical to their originals, then cloned humans are still more unlikely to be so. More importantly, however, in neither case will the clone be identical *with* its original. A cloned version of Woody Allen (or a sequence of such clones) taking over his apartment is unlikely to satisfy the original Allen's desire for earthly immortality.

Whereas medical intervention, cryonic preservation and cloning stress the importance of bodily life and bodily continuity, there are other approaches to earthly immortality or its surrogates which focus rather on the mental data that define a human being. The cybernetic equivalent of cloning is the development of what has come to be known as 'digital' or 'virtual' immortality. In one sense this is no more than the continuation by other means of more traditional forms of conservation and memorialization. But 'cybernetic cloning' also opens up the possibility of creating replicas or simulacra of deceased persons which maintain the presence of these persons in far more vivid ways, even to the extent of enabling deceased persons to continue contributing to the life of society. Likewise, the living might find great consolation in knowing that some kind of copy of themselves will 'stay on' to represent them after they have died.

These ideas are no longer confined to popular culture and science fiction. They are also taken seriously by scientific institutions and other bodies. In 2007 the USA's National Science Foundation awarded half a million dollars to universities in Orlando and Chicago to fund research into how artificial intelligence, archiving and computer imaging might be used 'to create convincing, digital versions of real people, a possible first step toward virtual immortality'. The goal, according to Jason Leigh of the University of Chicago's Electronic Visualization Laboratory, 'is to combine artificial intelligence with the latest advanced graphics and video game-type technology to enable us to create historical archives of people beyond what can be achieved using traditional technologies such as text, audio, and video footage'.[47] This technology promises possibilities going well beyond merely new ways of archiving the past or memorializing the dead. As one article in an online periodical somewhat artlessly puts it, 'Maybe you can't live forever, but there's no reason why your virtual counterpart can't.'[48] This prospect raises as many questions about the psychology and sociology of investing in this possibility as it does about the status of a 'virtual counterpart'.

There are those who seriously foresee the possibility of 'uploading' into a computer the contents of one's mind or brain, so that after one's death one could be said to be 'living on' at least as a mental entity. How this uploading is understood varies. Those who regard the brain itself as 'merely' a sophisticated computer, and the mind as its output, seem to believe that consciousness itself can, in theory if not yet in practice, be transposed from its present biological context into an artificial environment of some kind. Others are equally ambitious about the possibility of *replicating* the effects or appearance of consciousness and personality, while eschewing any claim to have duplicated, transposed or recreated consciousness or personality itself. The 'mind' and 'personality' of a chess grandmaster might be 'immortalized' by being uploaded into a computer which could then play games with other chess experts, some of whom it might well beat. The grandmaster too might have derived great satisfaction from knowing that his chess skills would continue to be deployed indefinitely into the future, despite the fact that he would not be there in person to enjoy the experience. Similarly, a computer programmed to 'speak' with the voice of a recently deceased grandparent 'who' could discuss his or her life and times with grandchildren and great-grandchildren might be a pleasing enough compromise with mortality for grandparent and grandchildren alike. Even if such computerized individuals were to pass the 'Turing Test', however, few people would describe them as surviving personalities.[49] But people could enjoy the experience of 'communicating' with the dead without deluding themselves into thinking that these dead were somehow still present as self-conscious personalities.

Just how convincing even a machine personality can be, however, is vividly illustrated by the on-board computer HAL in Stanley Kubrick's film *2001: A Space Odyssey* (1968). And the Cartesian illusion of autonomy created by an artificial intelligence lodged in a machine environment is likely to be further enhanced if that intelligence is given a convincing humanoid body of some kind. Strictly speaking, of course, this should add nothing to the case for its being a real person. In a similar way, the recorded roar of a lion coming from the mouth of an impressive looking artificial lion no more makes this lion a real lion than the same roar coming from a hi-fi speaker makes this hi-fi speaker a real lion. Thus the manufacture of humanoid robots, or androids, should not in itself narrow the gap between the living human and the non-living machine. Just as the computerized chess grandmaster is no more than a chess machine with attitude, so are these androids no more than non-clunky robots programmed to simulate, or mimic, various human functions and responses. If the simulation or mimicry were sophisticated enough to result in innovative responses, then these would be essentially no different from the randomizing and innovatory functions possible in computerized chess games. On the other hand, the psychology and sociology of the human–android encounter would inevitably be quite different from the psychology and sociology of interacting with a non-humanoid machine of some kind (through screen or speaker). Their very design would encourage a narrowing of the gap between treating them as if they were humans and treating them *as* humans. There would very likely be rules and customs, and even laws, governing the way people should use, treat and otherwise interact with androids, just as there are with any other complex and valuable human artefacts – for example, motor cars, oil rigs, chainsaws, medieval manuscripts and so on.[50]

Given the human tendency to anthropomorphize both animate and inanimate entities, however, there is bound to be some elision between treating androids as *if* they were real humans and treating them *as* real humans. Certainly it is possible that androids could eventually become sophisticated enough to be mistaken for real humans. This would mean not just passing the 'Turing Test', but also being superficially indistinguishable from real humans in appearance and behaviour. Most people, however, would accept that the difference between a real human being and an android is, in principle, no different from the difference between a human being and a waxwork image of a human being (or for that matter a statue, portrait, film, photograph or voice-recording of a human being). Even so, some theorists have argued that by virtue of its very complexity an android (or for that matter a non-humanoid artificial intelligence) either would already possess or could acquire a creative autonomy and even a self-consciousness that would render it comparable (if never fully identical to) a human being.[51]

This would be all very well for androids themselves, one might say; but what does this technology do for humans? One answer is that android replicas of once existing human beings could serve to keep alive their memories for the benefit and enjoyment of future generations. Thus one might imagine an android version of Einstein not only looking and speaking like the real Einstein but actually coming up with some new Einsteinian insight or theory. Even if complex androids had or could achieve the status of self-conscious and autonomous entities, however, the 'Einstein' android would not be the same person as Einstein himself was. No one could claim that the original Einstein had been resurrected to a new lease of earthly life.

Another answer to the question about the usefulness of androids to human beings is that individuals could, even in their own lifetimes, have a replica of themselves created which would continue to represent their lives and interests after their death. The fact that such virtual counterparts could be made ready before one's death, however, would surely demonstrate the error in thinking that after one's death this counterpart could be in any sense a continuation of oneself as a real person.

Neither of these two answers challenges human mortality itself. But there is a third and more radical answer that does. For android technology could play a part in life-extension programmes, by providing not only new bottles for old wine, so to speak, but new wine too. Repairing or enhancing defunct or diseased body parts with artificial components could be just the start of it. The brain too might conceivably be replaced with artificial materials, or the mind reloaded onto more durable platforms, in ways that preserved physical and functional continuity between the old person and the new. Such intervention could begin in the womb itself, if not before. Humans might themselves become androids, or at least the difference between these two categories might start to blur.

This is the kind of speculation – and programme – that is part of the broad movement known as transhumanism, which envisages science and technology taking control of human evolution in order to enhance and extend human capacities, the ultimate goal being to overcome human mortality. Transhumanism, according to one definition, is 'the intellectual and cultural movement that affirms the possibility and desirability of fundamentally improving the human condition through applied reason, especially by developing and making widely available technologies to eliminate aging and to greatly enhance human intellectual, physical, and psychological capacities.'[52]

The term 'transhumanism', first popularized by the biologist Julian Huxley,[53] is linked to another term, 'posthumanism', which refers to the vision of a humanity transformed by the full realization of its evolutionary and technological potential. Transhumanism, despite the prophetic zeal of its apologists, is essentially anti-religious in its outlook. Nor is its focus exclusively scientific and technological; it also has a philosophical, social and political agenda.[54] At its centre, however, is the promise of a world in which new developments in genetics, cybernetics, biotechnology, nanotechnology, gerontology, life-extension science and so on will have brought about new kinds of human being – beings in full control of their environment and capable of realizing their fullest potential. The aim of transhumanism is the creation of the posthuman person.

> Becoming posthuman means exceeding the limitations that define the less desirable aspects of the 'human condition'. Posthuman beings would no longer suffer from disease, aging, and inevitable death (but they are likely to face other challenges). They would have vastly greater physical capability and freedom of form – often referred to as 'morphological freedom'. Posthumans would also have much greater cognitive capabilities, and more refined emotions (more joy, less anger, or whatever changes each individual prefers). Transhumanists typically look to expand the range of possible future environments for posthuman life, including space colonization and the creation of rich virtual worlds.[55]

The transhumanist project, then, differs both in kind and scale from mere attempts either to improve human longevity or to ensure that the dead 'live on' in digital form or through 'virtual counterparts'. It proposes nothing less than that people will cease becoming dead in the first place, making whatever changes to human form and function that may be necessary in the process.

Inevitably the transhumanist project is susceptible to numerous criticisms, technological, ethical, social and psychological. The most radical criticism is that, far from saving humanity from mortality, the project is more likely to lead to the extinction than the apotheosis of humankind. Humankind would be replaced by what, in effect, would be a new species, no longer exclusively biological or perhaps no longer biological at all – and quite possibly no longer even human. Just as vampires are described as the 'undead', so might the posthumans succeeding the original humans be described as the 'unliving'.

VI

The desire for unlimited life on Earth can be seen in two ways – on the one hand as an expression of the natural desire for a long and hence indefinitely longer life, and on the other hand as a misplaced yearning for a transcendence that can only be found on the other side of mortality, so to speak. There is nothing illogical or even impossible about the idea of an indefinitely extended life on Earth, of living on for as long as Earth itself (or its colonies elsewhere) survive. But 'fixing' mortality, should this prove possible, would be only part of the problem. There would also be social, psychological, ethical and other issues to consider. Various arguments can be adduced in support of the thesis that earthly immortality would, in and of itself,[56] fail to satisfy those who hope for it or fantasize about it. Some of these arguments, it should be noted, have been directed to otherworldly immortality too, but here I am concerned with them only as they apply to earthly immortality. The main targets of these arguments are the tedium, loneliness or loss of a sense of life's meaning that immortal humans would suffer.

The argument that an extended life on Earth would necessarily engender boredom is generally unconvincing – whether it is a question of literally living on forever, of living on for several centuries or even simply of surviving a few extra decades. Some people manage to find life tedious after only a few decades. Others never find it so, however long they have lived; and there is no reason to suppose this would change if they went on living indefinitely. Of course there are circumstances one could imagine which would become tedious, but there is no reason to suppose that living forever would increase rather than reduce the likelihood of such circumstances arising or becoming permanent. A certain amount of tedium may well be a price worth paying for a potentially endless supply of non-tedious experiences. Think of the boredom endured by people queuing for hours to get tickets for a concert or sporting event. Nor is there reason to suppose that the predictability of one's survival day by day, week by week, and so on, would be mirrored by the predictability of one's circumstances. One can never step in the same river twice.[57] Bernard Williams's contention that an immortal person would run out of the 'categorial aims' that make life worth living is not difficult to challenge, and there are in any case simple desires (relating to a variety of pleasures and experiences, both physical and mental) whose satisfaction only encourages their return. Excess may well cause an appetite to 'sicken and so die', but no appetite remains surfeited forever.[58]

Arguments about the unsatisfactoriness of being immortal also raise important points about what might be called the 'sociology of immortality'. Life might well be difficult for the solitary immortal, stuck in a world where every new friend or partner would eventually yield to death. Many experiences, including presumably the experience of being immortal, are enhanced by the existence of others capable of having the same experiences. Arguably the best circumstance in which to be immortal would be where one was a member of a small group which shared this fundamental difference from the rest of humanity – a difference which might or might not go hand in hand with exploiting the rest of humanity. If, by contrast, everyone were immortal, then one of the very conditions that made immortality satisfactory would no longer obtain. There could be instructive parallels here with the difference between a small group of people being very wealthy and everybody being very wealthy – except that the notion of wealth is a relative one, so that it might no longer make sense (or no longer make the same sort of sense) to say that everybody was wealthy. Even if it did still make sense to say this, at least the social (including political) consequences of everybody being wealthy would be very different from those of a society in which only a few were.

The sociological consequences of a world in which all humans were immortal could be imagined in quite different ways. Would a society of immortals resemble the sort of wise and benign beings that Jonathan Swift's Gulliver looks forward to meeting when first told of such beings, or would it rather consist of beings like the repulsive and degenerate Struldbrugs he actually meets? One thing is fairly clear. The nature of a society in which humans no longer grew old and died would be very different from any society we now know or can even imagine. Much would depend on whether children continued to be born and to grow up, and also on whether (and how) human beings might continue to change, and even age, without ever dying. It is a fallacy to think that immortality, whether earthly or otherworldly, would necessarily imply stasis or perfection. It could well entail endless change and even a kind of perpetual progress.

The point about change and progress bears upon the claim that an endless human life would lack meaning, or more exactly that an immortal human subject would no longer be able to find meaning in life. That lives can only have meaning if they must one day come to an end seems little more than a prejudice. Death may indeed function as a boundary that gives shape and purpose to what one does, but its absence would not entail the lack of other important boundaries. The human immortal would continue to be constrained by the laws of nature, the cycles of life, the rules of games, the wishes of others and so on. It may further be argued that, for immortals, procrastination would be the order of the day: why do anything now, why even do it soon, when there is unlimited time ahead in which to do it? Here too the argument seems on a weak footing. From all the factors that impel or stimulate human action, one particular factor – the pressure of time – is selected from all the rest. People act not only because they have limited time, but for the inherent pleasure of the act, or to respond to the needs and wishes of others, and most basically of all because engaging in activities of various kinds is part and parcel of being human. For all we know these springs of action might well be enhanced for hyperlongevites or immortals. What seems undeniable is that many of those who are manifestly not immortal are procrastinators with far less reason for being so than our hypothetical immortals.

Two basic questions emerge from any conception or imagining of what earthly immortality might be like, whether for individuals or for an entire society. The first asks whether such a state is possible, the second whether it is desirable. These are questions that have fascinated or troubled those who were all too familiar with the reality of human mortality. Posthumans, were they ever to appear within human history, would be standing on the shoulders of countless generations of mortal predecessors. To this extent they would still carry the traces or memories of (past) human mortality. It is conceivable, of course, that a future society would be composed both of mortals and immortals, just as in Swift's country of Luggnagg. In this imaginary society whether a Luggnaggian is born mortal or immortal is a matter of chance.[59]

In a transhumanist society it would more likely be a matter of choice – in which case the matter of its desirability or otherwise becomes a burning existential question.

Here and now, however, and for the foreseeable future one supposes, the idea of an earthly immortality (and even of some more credible form of hyperlongevity) functions mainly as a vehicle for reviewing the advantages and disadvantages of our being solidly mortal. Traditionally, the only worldly remedy for the sting of mortality is to be found in a vicarious immortality based on one's surviving earthly legacy. The forms that such immortality might take are the subject of the next two chapters.

THREE

POSTHUMOUS PERSONHOOD

But strew his ashes to the wind
Whose sword or voice has served mankind, –
And is he dead, whose glorious mind
Lifts thine on high? –
To live in hearts we leave behind
Is not to die.

THOMAS CAMPBELL[1]

I

That deceased persons continue to live on in the hearts and minds of others is a familiar sentiment with which most people can readily identify. The same is true of the idea that a person's achievements will serve as their memorials after death. Such sentiments are commonly expressed in the course of offering consolation to the bereaved. What seems more in doubt is whether such persistence through memory and memorial amounts to anything substantial enough to be described as an earthly afterlife. The subjects of an earthly afterlife 'live on' by proxy, and the means through which they do so are themselves subject to decay. It is not easy to remain, or to become, a person posthumously.

Earthly and otherworldly afterlives constitute two quite different kinds of destiny, and as such are not really commensurable, even if in many contexts there are close links between them. Nevertheless, comparisons are often drawn between them, by some to demonstrate the vanity of earthly ambitions and by others to underline the illusory nature of religious hopes. Those who consider an earthly afterlife superior to any otherworldly one will emphasize the continuing 'presence' of the dead in their earthly legacy as against their disappearance into some otherworldly realm which, even if it exists, remains inaccessible to the living. The idea that those on Earth are better qualified as curators of the dead than any doubtful or distant deity in heaven is cousin to the view that it is better to worship God freely in natural surroundings than under the control of priests in special buildings. This is the main theme of the poem by Thomas Campbell from which the stanza heading this chapter is taken. In this poem the argument is the essentially Protestant one that the sacred cannot be confined within rituals, buildings or monuments. For the true believer, the entire Earth is hallowed ground. And just as the beauties and wonders of Nature give us the best insights into divine truth, so do the minds and hearts of the living provide the best vehicles for cherishing our memories of the dead.

Two important questions need to be asked here. First, what role does the idea of an earthly immortality have beyond the conventions of poetic elegy or the rhetoric of consolation? Second, to what extent do memories and memorials of the dead define an earthly afterlife for the bereaved rather than for the dead themselves? What makes the first of these questions pertinent is the undoubted fact that much of what the bereaved do following a person's death, from the signing of the death certificate onwards, serves to confirm the ending rather than the continuance of a life. Mourning itself is a process of coming to terms with the fact that a deceased person has gone from Earth forever. For all except those closest to the deceased, forgetting begins to compete with remembering as soon as the funeral and the immediate period of mourning are over.

What brings the second question into focus is the fact that bereaved persons themselves can be viewed as 'survivors'. At the end of an obituary, for example, we often read that such and such a person is 'survived by' this or that family member. To this extent the lives of the bereaved themselves, charged with the memories and legacies of the dead, can realistically be described as 'afterlives'. By the same token, however, the lives of these 'survivors' become the principal vehicles of the earthly afterlives of the dead. In the second stanza of Campbell's poem, it is said of the dead that 'in ourselves their souls exist, / A part of ours'. This suggests, perhaps, the idea of an earthly afterlife as a communion of two or more previously separate lives, which again offers a contrast with the idea of the solitary survival of the soul in some otherworldly realm.

However we answer these two questions, it is important to emphasize that the basis of any person's earthly afterlife, and thereby also its chief point of weakness, is memory. Shakespeare in one of his best-known sonnets (18) assures the beloved that she (and, by implication, he too) will live on in the 'eternal lines' of the poem he addresses to her. But the poem concludes on what is both a supremely confident and yet still conditional note:

> Nor shall Death brag thou wander'st in his shade,
> When in eternal lines to time thou grow'st;
> So long as men can breathe, or eyes can see,
> So long lives this, and this gives life to thee.

One possibility the poet does not consider, and within the performative rhetoric of the poem cannot consider, is that while people may go on breathing and reading into the indefinite future, the poem itself will be neglected, forgotten or even completely lost.

To explicate further the role of memory and culture in the preservation of an earthly afterlife, it is useful to differentiate between 'recollections', 'remainders' and 'reminders'. Recollections, in this context, can be defined as the personal memories living persons have of a deceased person. From one point of view, such memories can be a sufficient as well as a necessary condition of the deceased's having an earthly immortality. In Isabel Allende's novel *Eva Luna* (1987) we find a simple expression of this view, one that suggests the 'contractual' nature of our relationship with the dead through memory.

> 'There is no death, daughter. People die only when we forget them,' my mother explained shortly before she left me. 'If you can remember me, I will be with you always.'
> 'I will remember you,' I promised.[2]

We find a statement of essentially the same idea in the *Notebooks* of Samuel Butler: 'To die completely, a person must not only forget but be forgotten, and he who is not forgotten is not dead. This is as old as [Horace's] *non omnis moriar* [I shall not die completely] and a great deal older, but very few people realise it.'[3]

Memories can of course be self-sustaining, but in many cases they depend upon, or are triggered by, the diverse 'remainders' of a person's life. These remainders are the things which the dead leave behind them, or of which they take leave. Such remainders include not only such items as letters, diaries, photographs, recordings, personal possessions and the like, but other people, particular places and even empty spaces. In the musical drama *Les Misérables* (1980), based on Victor Hugo's famous novel (1862), the character Marius sings of the grief and pain caused by the absence of friends who have died fighting for the revolutionary cause. In the song 'Empty Chairs at Empty Tables', Marius imagines himself back at the café once frequented by his lively revolutionary friends who have now died. But what he now pictures is the emptiness of the place where these friends will never meet or sing again.[4]

Paradoxically, the absence of a loved one can itself be a kind of presence, or can create a vacuum within which a presence is imagined. Absence can create a sense that the now absent person is 'nowhere but everywhere', the slightest details of life triggering memories and imaginations of the deceased. This may be one explanation of the phenomenon reported by many bereaved persons, and particularly by survivors of long partnerships, of vividly sensing the presence of the deceased person. In some cases this may well qualify as some kind of psychic experience, especially where it is characterized by specifically apparitional, auditory or olfactory manifestations, and it may or may not also be associated with some kind of belief about the survival of the dead in an otherworldly afterlife. Where it is associated with the latter, it would constitute another example of the overlap between earthly and otherworldly conceptions of immortality. Regardless of such a connection, however, it represents one aspect of what I am defining as earthly immortality.

Where remainders trigger memories of the deceased, they function as reminders, either spontaneously or through being 'managed' in some way. For a very short period of time (in most cases) the primary and most powerful physical remainder-reminder will be a person's corpse. Thereafter the main physical remainder-reminders will be the physical possessions of the deceased; letters and diaries and other things created by the deceased; and above all the presence and features of the deceased's progeny – of which more later. Photographs of the deceased (including post-mortem photographs) can be regarded as special cases of remainder-reminders, being artefacts which exist on the borderline between remainder and reminder. Technically, photographs are remainders of a person, fragments of a person's photic existence, with a 'magical' or 'uncanny' link to the real person whose image is 'taken' by the photographer (a telling use of this verb). As Roland Barthes puts it, the person or thing photographed is the target, the referent, a kind of little simulacrum, any *eidolon* emitted by the object, which I should like to call the *Spectrum* of the Photograph, because this word retains, through its root, a relation to 'spectacle' and adds to it that rather terrible thing which is there in every photograph: the return of the dead.[5]

More generally, however, photographs are what might be called photically engineered reminders rather than photic remainders of persons and things, specifically created for the purpose of factual record, personal memento or aesthetic representation. Photographs, particularly portrait photographs, nevertheless remain ambivalent. Less obviously than such items as a lock of hair or an item of clothing, but no less potently, photographs combine both presence and absence. A photograph, according to Susan Sontag, 'is both a pseudo-presence and a token of absence'.[6] The same might be said of letters, diaries and other personal writings of the deceased.

Most people for most of history left little or nothing behind them in the written record; the substance of their lives was preserved, if at all, in the oral traditions of family, community and nation, although names and other basic information might also be preserved in public documents and on gravestones. Only within a literate minority did individuals establish an earthly afterlife through personal documents such as letters, portraits, diaries and memoirs. In recent years, however, increasing numbers of people have started to leave behind them not so much a paper trail as a set of digital footprints, both visual and verbal, created by the use of the Internet both as an information archive and as the world's principal medium of social communication. Much of this data accumulates unintentionally, or at least haphazardly. But there are also both individuals and commercial companies who seek deliberately to construct what are designed to become posthumous digital afterlives for the benefit of friends, families and succeeding generations.[7] Nor do the opportunities opened up by digital technology consist merely of new methods of passively preserving the activities and memories of the deceased. As suggested in the previous chapter, digital technology might also seem to offer the possibility of extending or developing the lives of deceased persons in such a way as to make them 'live on' actively, or to be interactively accessible to others, in some new digital format.[8] It can be doubted, of course, whether a person's ideas and memories could continue to represent that person once they were cut off from either the physical body or the social context in which they had been formed.[9] Even where a surrogate body of some kind accompanied the continuing stream of mental data, would the living find the resulting experiences in any way equivalent to interactions with the deceased themselves?

In the longer term, earthly afterlives are built up and sustained by reminders which are not remainders, but rather things which have been deliberately created or preserved in order to fix and stimulate memory – such things as tombs, shrines, statues, biographies, anecdotes, documentaries, commemorative events and 'living memorials'.[10] The direct memories which people have of the dead will obviously die out when these people themselves die, but memories can be recorded and passed on to subsequent generations in oral, written or digital form, so that what subsequent generations inherit will be 'memories of memories', at second hand, third hand and so on.[11]

The subjective chain of memory is fragile and easily broken, but objective remainders and reminders can function to support the chain of memory and even to restore it when it is broken. Memories, of course, are not neutral bits of information, unaltered traces or images of the past. Even as purely psychological phenomena, memories can be unreliable or indeed delusory. As a social phenomenon, memory is inevitably selective, usually 'edited' and sometimes plainly manufactured, following the agenda of its conveyors and its audiences alike. However carefully the deceased may have prepared their identity for posterity, the deceased's successors 'do not always view the deceased the way the deceased view themselves. Besides, survivors are many and are likely to have conflicting memories of the one who has passed away. And those memories will change as time goes by.'[12]

Some of these points about how crucially the character of a person's earthly immortality depends upon the memories and intentions of others within a continuing social, national and sometimes even international context can be illustrated by reference to the life, death and afterlife of the Roman orator, lawyer and consul Servius Sulpicius Rufus, who died in 43 BCE in the course of a mission as the Senate's ambassador to Mark Antony. Although his is hardly a household name nowadays, Servius Sulpicius continues to be the subject of an earthly afterlife partly through the accidents of history and partly through the deliberate efforts of his contemporaries to ensure him such an afterlife.

He himself left various writings that have been influential in the history of Western culture. These are mainly legal texts but also letters, including a very moving letter of condolence to his friend and mentor, the rather better known Marcus Tullius Cicero, following the death of the latter's daughter Tullia.[13] The document I have selected here, however, is not from Servius Sulpicius but from Cicero, one from the series of his orations known as the 'Philippics'.[14]

Servius, despite ill-health, had reluctantly agreed to the Senate's request that he make the journey, as its ambassador, to meet with Mark Antony, then defiantly opposing the will of the Senate. But his illness got the better of him and he died before being able to complete the mission. In his oration, Cicero proposes that Servius be honoured with a public funeral, a sepulchre and a statue, even though the latter honour was traditionally reserved for those whose blood had been shed in the service of the Republic. Cicero argued that it was the fact and not the manner of dying that counted, pointing out that the ancestors of Rome had 'thought fit that a monument should be erected to any man whose death was caused by an embassy, in order to tempt men in perilous wars to be the more bold in undertaking the office of an ambassador'. Such a monument would give such men 'an imperishable memory in exchange for this transitory life'. Here already we have the kernel of the idea of an earthly afterlife with a clearly social function. Cicero points out that an existing statue of a former ambassador, Cnaeus Octavius, was given 'as a recompense for his life' such as 'might ennoble his progeny for many years', and that this statue was 'now the only memorial left of so illustrious a family'. So the earthly afterlife of Octavius was secured both by the physical statue of him and by the family thereby honoured.

Regarding Servius, therefore, Cicero thinks it 'of consequence, in order that posterity may recollect it, that there should be a record of what the judgment of the Senate was concerning this war'. A statue of Servius will serve as witness to the fact that the war was 'so serious . . . that the death of an ambassador in it gained the honour of an imperishable memorial'. Thus such a statue would be as much a monument to the war in whose service he died as to Servius (or his family) personally. Nevertheless, opines Cicero, the statue would also serve to repair the injury done to Servius personally by ignoring his legitimate excuses (concerning his state of health) for not being appointed to the embassy that had led to his death:

Restore then, O conscript fathers, life to him from whom you have taken it. For the life of the dead consists in the recollection cherished of them by the living. Take ye care that he, whom you without intending it sent to his death, shall from you receive immortality. And if you by your decree erect a statue to him in the rostra, no forgetfulness of posterity will ever obscure the memory of his embassy. For the remainder of the life of Servius Sulpicius will be recommended to the eternal recollection of all men by many and splendid memorials. The praise of all mortals will forever celebrate his wisdom, his firmness, his loyalty, his admirable vigilance and prudence in upholding the interests of the public. Nor will that admirable, and incredible, and almost godlike skill of his in interpreting the laws and explaining the principles of equity be buried in silence.[15]

In this last passage we have a clear statement both of the idea of an earthly afterlife and of the ambitious expectations of an everlasting fame worthy of the term 'immortality'. Ironically enough, it is through Cicero's recorded oratory rather than through the long forgotten physical monuments, as well as through the writings of Servius himself (which have no connection with his fatal embassy), that the earthly afterlife of Servius persists, however tenuously, down to the present day.

II

Apart from the distinction between otherworldly and earthly immortality, there are important distinctions to be observed within the latter category itself. The most basic of these is the distinction between the immortality of family and the immortality of fame. It is this distinction that provides the starting point for the discussion of earthly immortality in Plato's dialogue *Symposium*, where Socrates recounts to his companions what his teacher Diotima had to say about immortality in the course of her teachings on love. Love, says Diotima, 'may be described generally as the love of the everlasting possession of the good'. She explains that what every kind of lover has in view is 'birth in beauty, whether of body or soul'. What are born are either physical children (through bodily love and procreation) or children of the soul (through works executed by various means):

Those who are pregnant in the body only, betake themselves to women and beget children – this is the character of their love; their offspring, as they hope, will preserve their memory and give them the blessedness and immortality which they desire for all future time. But souls which are pregnant – for there certainly are men who are more creative in their souls than in their bodies, creative of that which is proper for the soul to conceive and bring forth: and if you ask me what are these conceptions, I answer, wisdom, and virtue in general – among such souls are all creative poets and artists who are deserving of the name inventor. But the greatest and fairest sort of wisdom by far is that which is concerned with the ordering of states and families, and which is called temperance and justice.[16]

It is obvious which type of immortality Socrates and Diotima regard as superior, for 'Who, when he thinks of Homer and Hesiod and other great poets, would not rather have their children than ordinary human ones? Who would not emulate them in the creation of children such as theirs, which have preserved their memory and given them everlasting glory?'[17] Superior to any of the 'soul-children' produced by artists, poets or statesmen, however, are the 'soul-children' which take the form of works of wisdom created by philosophers.

This hierarchical schema set out by Socrates is based on the idea of begetting, through intercourse with the beautiful, some kind of off-spring which outlasts the begetter. Those who beget physical progeny do so through the insemination of beauty in the form of a sexually attractive woman.[18] Those who beget 'soul-children' do so through another kind of intercourse with the beautiful (albeit one understood through the metaphor of sexual intercourse) – they are 'spiritually preg-nant' and give birth (that is, are creative or productive) when in the presence of beauty, when discoursing with others or when reflecting on such experiences in solitude. In the case of poets, artists, states-men and so on, the resulting works of art, inventions, laws and more are but 'images' of the beautiful. But in the case of the true philoso-pher, the resulting 'children' (works of philosophy) reveal Beauty itself. The distinctions of value Socrates draws between the various kinds of 'soul-children' obviously reflect the priorities of Platonic philosophy, and in particular the doctrine of the soul's ascent through different manifestations of beauty to ideal beauty. What is important for the present discussion, however, is the fact that each of the different kinds of earthly immortality identified by Socrates represents the survival of something that outlasts the earthly life of its begetter – children, works of art, books, laws, virtuous behaviour and so on.[19]

Explicit in Plato's text is the idea of producing progeny, literally or metaphorically, in fulfilment of the desire for earthly immortality. What is implicit is the idea that such immortality also depends upon others – those who co-operate in bringing such progeny to birth and those who recognize and cherish the progeny once born. In common with other idealized accounts of earthly immortality, however, Plato's text makes no mention of the negative and unintentional aspects of such immortality – the failures and vagaries of human memory, the destructive processes of human history, the possibility of being dishonoured rather than honoured by posterity, and so on. Nor does Plato's account make anything of the fact that most forms of earthly immortality will almost always be composite in nature – that is, made up of different kinds of 'progeny'.

By way of further illustration, let us briefly consider the case of the Chinese leader Mao Zedong (1893–1976), whose legacy can be said to constitute a well-established, if complex and ever-changing, earthly afterlife. The business of 'minding' the mortality of a great public figure begins, of course, with the question of what to do with the body. In the great mausoleum in Beijing (modelled on Lenin's in Moscow) where the carefully preserved body of Mao lies on display, an inscription describes the great man as 'forever eternal without corrupting' (*yung ch'ui pu hsiu*). Whether this refers to his legacy as a whole or only to his body, Mao's preserved corpse undoubtedly forms an important component of his earthly afterlife – though it must be said that Mao's corporeal afterlife (like Lenin's too) has been a markedly unexciting one in comparison with the afterlives lived by the corpses of other famous individuals. This is certainly the case with some of the Christian saints, whose bodies or bodily relics were often divided up between different shrines or moved, officially or unofficially, from one site to another (the body of St Mark, for example, was stolen from Orthodox Alexandria and shipped to Catholic Venice). As regards secular figures with particularly busy corporeal afterlives, special mention should be made of the various adventures attributed to the embalmed corpse of Eva Perón (1919–1952).[20] Whether the episodes in question – such as the shunting around to different locations of the embalmed corpse and two skilfully fashioned decoys, the relentless pursuit of the corpse by Eva's fanatical followers, or the obsessed army major's sexual abuse of the corpse – are historically accurate, somewhat exaggerated or purely fictional, all have become components of Eva's earthly afterlife.

As regards Mao's literal progeny, there are (to date) descendants through three generations from each of his four marriages. His earthly afterlife in this respect too is well-established. It is not for the details of his family and personal life that Mao will be mainly remembered, of course, but for his life and work as leader of the Chinese people. His military and political leadership are part of the historical record but also the subject of legend. Given that an earthly afterlife develops a life of its own, the presence of legendary or fictional elements within it raises crucial questions about how we judge the relationship between a subject's earthly life and earthly afterlife. Some of these questions are examined in the next section. Similar questions arise in respect of Mao's intellectual and literary legacy. It is not only the thoughts of Chairman Mao as presented and understood while he was alive that contribute to Mao's intellectual afterlife. The latter is also made up both of new interpretations of his thinking and of new thinking within the broader tradition that is identifiable as Maoist thought. In this respect, a person's earthly afterlife becomes less and less exclusively his or her own.

Finally Mao's earthly afterlife is constructed not only out of the remainders of his private and public life, but out of reminders which are not remainders. Some of these are official, such as state-endorsed images, statues and commemorative events, as well as the above-mentioned mausoleum and the 'cult' associated with it; other reminders are unofficial, and in many cases critical if not hostile, and include satirical images, jokes, anecdotes and critical biographies.

Given the complexity of many earthly afterlives, and not only those of great public figures, drawing distinctions between different types of earthly afterlife can easily become misleading. On the other hand, there are earthly afterlives which do seem focused on one particular kind (or even instance) of remainder or reminder. For example, the 'children' who, for Socrates, define Homer's earthly afterlife are exclusively his poetic works. By contrast, there are some whose earthly afterlife is defined exclusively in corporeal terms – for example, those 'Unknown Soldiers' whose bodies are interred in churches and other shrines around the world. It is possible, in any case, to identify a number of at least theoretically distinct modes, or strands, of earthly immortality such as will assist discussion and analysis of this idea. The five modes I identify here emerge from the examples already given in this chapter, and will be further illustrated in subsequent chapters. All that is needed here, therefore, is a brief character sketch of each.

The first of them, *corporeal immortality*, needs to be confronted immediately, since some people will follow Socrates in considering the corpse the least suitable material for immortality. But his impatience with funeral rituals and indifference to what happens to his body has not been shared by others, who are perhaps the majority. Many people care a great deal about what happens to their body after death, not always in connection with religious belief or ritual, but in a purely worldly sense. It is their own bodies which, however briefly, will play a part in representing them, so to speak, when they are gone. It is almost as if in dying we give birth to a new entity, namely our corpse, and then leave someone else holding the baby, so to speak.

In some parts of the world, as much effort and ingenuity are devoted to preparing the body before burial or cremation as to actually burying or burning it. Nor do the elaborate procedures involved have anything to do with the fate of the deceased in the next world, as they did for example in ancient Egypt. They are carried out either to fulfil the wishes of the deceased or to meet the requirements of the bereaved. The lengths to which embalmers in the United States have gone to beautify a corpse have been entertainingly documented by Jessica Mitford, among others. The purpose of lavishing so much attention on the corpse was first and foremost in order that the body would appear to viewers to be in 'an attitude of healthy repose'.[21] What better way to begin one's earthly afterlife than by at least appearing to be peacefully asleep rather than dead?

But the natural processes of assimilation into the elements are artificially suspended only for the relative few. Most people would agree that if one of the blessings of this planet is life itself, then another is that it allows for the disposal of its dead. Of the dead, Robert Pogue Harrison says this:

> To realize their fate and become truly dead they must first be made to disappear. It is only because their bodies have a place to go that their souls or images or words may attain an afterlife of sorts among the living. We should be infinitely

grateful, therefore, for the hiding and receiving power of this terracqueous [*sic*] globe, which Michael Serres . . . rightly calls 'a tabernacle . . . a receptacle for all decompositions'.[22]

As Harrison also reminds us, the cycle of exchange between dead and living matter has been at work for millions of years, with new life emerging from the matrix formed by the decomposed bodies of living organisms. To this extent it is wrong to think of corpses in the rather negative way in which they do tend to be thought about.

The more obviously positive role of the body in earthly immortality is the sexually reproductive one, and this is the basis of the second mode of immortality, *progenitive immortality*. This is the immortality of family, which is achieved through having children who will have children in their turn. People do see themselves, and just as crucially are seen by others, as 'living on' in their children and their children's children. In Diane Samuels's play *Kindertransport*, one of the characters, Helga, compares children to precious jewels, handed on through the generations as one's legacy: 'We all die one day, but jewels never fade or perish. Through our children we live. That's how we cheat death. Otherwise we're really finished.'[23] This mode of earthly immortality may be accounted the strongest, most tangible and most primitive idea of an earthly afterlife. It is a mode of earthly afterlife which the living can taste in advance. They not only experience the lives of their children and grandchildren before they die, but as children themselves they know what it means to carry the name and memories of their own parents and ancestors. Posterity, in other words, can be experienced from two different directions.

What makes the idea of progenitive continuity an appealing and apparently concrete form of an earthly afterlife is precisely this fact that individuals have direct experience within their own lifetimes of what it means to live on through their descendants. Not only could their own existence be presented as living proof of the success and security of their ancestors' desire for progenitive survival, but they themselves have or will have children and grandchildren who in many cases will resemble them, behave like them and even pursue the same interests and occupations. The satisfaction that human beings derive from the birth not only of their children but of their grandchildren and great-grandchildren is difficult to exaggerate. Much of this satisfaction may have to do with the idea that their own lives and values are being extended or repeated in their living and future descendants. This is well understood by those regimes or tyrants who seek to destroy the earthly afterlife of a particular group or family by systematically exterminating their offspring.

In Diotima's account, it is suggested that the motive for having physical offspring is the hope that these offspring will, by preserving their parents' memory, give their parents the blessedness and immortality which they desire to have in the future. In many cases, of course, having children is not reasoned out in this way, if indeed it is reasoned out at all. Where having children is planned, as often it is not, it will be seen by parents as the natural, normal or 'right' thing to do. Even where having children is reasoned out, the motive (or better, perhaps, the justification) is more likely to be in terms of a duty to keep alive the family name rather than in terms of a desire to keep alive one's own particular name or memory. Having children can indeed be seen as taking a step towards one's own irrelevance and death. If so, being remembered by future generations would be more in the nature of an unintended bonus.

Having progeny as one's earthly afterlife can also be seen as a bonus in a religious context. As the early Christian writer John Chrysostom (349–407) declared,

> At first, the procreation of children was desirable, so that each man might leave a memorial of his life. Since there was not yet any hope of resurrection, but rather death held sway, and those who died thought that they would perish after this life, God gave the comfort of children, so as to leave living images of the departed and to preserve our species . . . But now that the resurrection is at our gates, and we do not speak of death, but advance toward another life better than the present, the desire for posterity is superfluous. If you desire children you can get much better children now, a nobler childbirth and better help in your old age, if you give birth by spiritual labor.[24]

The last sentence echoes Diotima's teaching on the different kinds of offspring that human beings are capable of generating.

The third and fourth modes of earthly immortality, which I call *creative immortality* and *performative immortality*, are two forms of the immortality of fame. The creative mode occurs where the remainders and reminders of a person's life take the form of works of art, ideas, inventions and so on; the performative mode occurs where the remainders and reminders take the form of public achievements in the sphere of, for example, national leadership, military victory and social reform. Here too the authors of such achievements can taste in advance the fame they will enjoy after death, though this is not invariably the case. There are many examples of individuals whose work (or at least its true value or significance) was ignored, or rejected, during their lifetime, only to be rediscovered and celebrated after their death.

The creative and performative modes of earthly immortality are close alternatives, not always differentiated in effect or value. In Campbell's poem, for example, 'mankind' is 'served' equally by 'sword or voice'. In many contexts the kind of fame for which the dead are celebrated is likely to be of one kind rather than another. In the Old Norse Eddic *Hávamál*, for example, it is clearly leadership and military prowess that Odin sings about in the following verses:

Cattle die, and kinsmen die,
And so one dies one's self;
But a noble name will never die,
If good renown one gets.

Cattle die, and kinsmen die,
And so one dies one's self;
One thing I know that never dies,
The fame of a dead man's deeds.[25]

Where certain forms of human activity or creativity are valued above others, the different kinds of fame may even be arranged into a hierarchy. Thus in Plato's account, Socrates regards the immortality represented by the works of the philosopher superior to those of the lawgiver just as the latter are superior to the works of the poet. In Renaissance Europe, however, it was poetry that gained one the highest and most secure forms of earthly immortality, some poets being confident enough to regard poetry as capable of seeing off any other means of securing immortality. This was an idea drawn from Classical sources, and most famously expressed in the ode by the Roman poet Horace in which he claims to have created in his poetry 'a monument more lasting than bronze / and loftier than the royal structure of the pyramids'. *Non omnis moriar*, he boasts – I shall not wholly die.[26] In a similar way Edmund Spenser, in *The Ruines of Time*, contrasts the futility of attempts to attain immortality through either noble deeds or physical monuments with the true immortality conferred by poetry:

> For deeds doe die, how ever noblie donne,
> And thoughts of men do as themselves decay,
> But wise wordes taught in numbers for to runne,
> Recorded by the Muses, live for ay,
> Ne may with storming showers be washt away;
> Ne bitter breathing windes with harmfull blast,
> Nor age, nor envie, shall them ever wast.

> In vaine doo earthly princes then, in vaine,
> Seeke with pyramides, to heaven aspired,
> Or huge colosses, built with costlie paine,
> Or brasen pillours, never to be fired,
> Or shrines, made of the mettall most desired,
> To make their memories for ever live:
> For how can mortall immortalitie give?[27]

Spenser's poem, whatever its contribution to his own posthumous fame or that of the poet Philip Sidney whose work it extols, was explicitly written to 'eternize' the recently deceased Earl of Leicester and other members of the Dudley family.[28]

Poets and others have attached special importance to poetry because it preserves, as a living tradition, the finest human thoughts and thereby the memory both of authors themselves and of those who are the subjects of their poems. But the written word has also been recognized as having a wider importance, in its power to conjure up, vividly and in detail, the otherwise vanished life of the past. For it is not only individuals who can be said to have earthly afterlives, but the otherwise forgotten events and circumstances, as well as peoples, of history. It is this point that Thomas Carlyle makes in his own praise of books above any other physical remains:

> Certainly the Art of Writing is the most miraculous of all things man has devised. Odin's *Runes* were the first form of the work of a Hero; *Books*, written words, are still miraculous *Runes*,

the latest form! In Books lies the *soul* of the whole Past Time; the articulate audible voice of the Past, when the body and material substance of it has altogether vanished like a dream. Mighty fleets and armies, harbours and arsenals, vast cities, high-domed, many-engined – they are precious, great: but what do they become? Agamemnon, the many Agamemnons, Pericleses, and their Greece; all is gone now to some ruined fragments, dumb mournful wrecks and blocks: but the Books of Greece! There Greece, to every thinker, still very literally lives; can be called up again into life. No magic *Rune* is stranger than a Book. All that Mankind has done, thought, gained or been: it is lying as in magic preservation in the pages of Books.[29]

Looking back at the four modes of earthly immortality reviewed in this section, it is worth noting that in respect of each an earthly after-life can, long before death, be anticipated and to some extent shaped by those solicitous of their own and others' post-mortem legacy. Even so, these four modes of earthly immortality could all be described as broadly passive in nature, in the sense that each of them represents some aspect of an earthly legacy unalterable after death, albeit in some cases subject to endless reinterpretation or indeed misinterpretation. But the fifth and final mode of earthly immortality to be identified here, *legal immortality*, is characterized by an active element, in so far as the wishes and interests of now deceased persons continue to be advanced, and developed, through the agency of the law. The wills, trusts and other legal instruments created by such persons during their lifetimes are capable of having a significant impact on the lives of the deceased's heirs, beneficiaries and indeed opponents.[30] By the same token, we also have a context within which the dead might be said to suffer legal harm – for example, where the provisions of a will are not fulfilled, or where the known wishes or interests of the deceased are ignored or sabotaged.

In some cultures, obligations to the dead may be expressed other than through written laws or legal documents. Thus certain rights or responsibilities may be inherited by elder sons, or by sons rather than daughters, on whom the obligation falls to maintain the family name and estate. There are obvious links here with progenitive immortality. Thus it may be considered important, as part of a deceased person's earthly survival, that the children of this person bear the same name, own the same property, maintain the same profession or marry within the same group (endogamous marriage).

Lawyers and philosophers may consider not only who or what can constitute a 'legal person', but whether and in what sense one can remain a 'legal person' after one's death.[31] One author, reviewing the legal rights of descendents under American law, observes that the living cannot be sued for the libel or slander of the dead, and also that 'the right to medical privacy substantially erodes at death'. Nor is posthumous marriage allowable, as it is for example under French law.

> On the other hand, various legal institutions have spent considerable time trying to protect the rights of the dead. As a result, most testamentary distributions, burial requests, and organ donation designations are held to be valid even if they contradict the preferences of the living. Certain destructions of property requested in wills are honored even though they may have a negative impact on the living. Some states even statutorily recognize a posthumous right of publicity, and recent case law suggests there may be a posthumous right to reproductive autonomy.[32]

The same author dismisses the idea that laws protecting the rights of the dead are to be explained simply as ways of regulating the actions of the living, arguing that there is an innate desire to honour the wishes of the dead, even when this conflicts with the interests of the living. The fact that 'rights' language is often used in law suggests something more than merely a self-interested desire on the part of the living for their own wishes to be honoured after death. The consistent use of rights language suggests that judges and legislatures are guided by social and cultural norms informed by ideas about respecting and honouring the dead. This rights language, it is further argued, is best understood in terms of 'Interest Theory', according to which certain categories of persons currently unable to make choices – such as infants, the mentally incapacitated and, as argued here, the dead – are recognized as having rights and interests that need protecting.

> While it is true that only a subset of interests may survive death, and even a smaller subset receive legal protection, death does not necessarily cut off all interests, and consequently, it

does not end all legal rights. Recognition of posthumous legal rights gives the dead significant moral standing within our legal system, as would be expected if lawmakers are driven by a desire to treat the dead with dignity.[33]

III

Each of the five modes of earthly immortality reviewed above can assume either a personal or an anonymous form, though for all of them there is a constant drift towards complete anonymity: as physical bodies decay they obviously become increasingly anonymous; one's progeny, especially after the first generation, will not necessarily remember one or even bear one's name; a work of art or body of ideas can be appreciated just as well without as with the author's name attached, not least where the names of authors are likely to be the only thing known about them; historical events or social movements can be celebrated in ignorance of their originating individuals; and so on. Something approaching an anonymous immortality can be found even in the case of legal immortality, where one might assume the identity of a named individual to be essential. For there are objective entities such as buildings or works of art, or more abstract entities like an idea or a business, which continue to be protected by law long after the name and original interests of their founders have sunk into obscurity.

What divides personal from anonymous forms of earthly immortality, and hence justifies the idea of posthumous personhood, is a surviving personal identity; and this is usually represented by a name. In modern culture, where language, and in particular naming, is generally understood as having a purely instrumental function, it can be difficult to appreciate the significance that names and naming have had in traditional cultures, and may still have deep down within our own culture. In many cultures, ancient and modern, the name of a person, and even of a thing, is widely regarded as consubstantial with the essence or soul of that person or thing. To know the (real) name of something or someone was to know the essence of, and to have power over or access to, that person or thing. Many readers will be familiar with the fairy tale (collected by the brothers Grimm) about a girl who promises her firstborn child to a dwarf named Rumpelstiltskin in return for the gift of spinning gold from straw. When the dwarf comes to collect the child, he tells the girl that the only way to cancel the debt is for her to discover his name – which eventually, to the dwarf's extreme annoyance, she succeeds in doing. In parts of the ancient world, such was the magic of the name that the erasure of one's name from public monuments and documents was tantamount to the erasure of one's identity full stop, and perhaps of one's welfare in the afterlife too. Knowledge of the secret names of gods, spirits and other forces is crucial to the coercion and communication which make up much of magical and religious ritual.[34]

The power of the name is recognized even in modern secular culture, where explicitly magical and mythological thinking has largely been eclipsed. For example, a sense of the power of the name persists in the phenomenon of euphemism. To refer to something or someone unpleasant indirectly or elliptically is to acknowledge that uttering the 'real' name of that thing or person is to make present, or to risk making present, that person or thing. More generally, the name still functions as a kind of shorthand for everything else associated with a person. According to Rolf and Elsa von Eckartsberg, for example, 'the names of the dead are their addresses in our living language through which we can visit their presence and commemorate when alone or in discourse with one another.'[35] In earlier centuries, the importance of remembering the names of one's ancestors was dictated largely by ritual concerns – for example, through intercessory prayers to the saints, and pious actions performed, which were believed to assist the souls of those now in purgatory.[36] Nowadays, at least in secular cultures, people are more likely to connect with their ancestors through the 'hobby' of genealogy, researching their family history with the help of the extensive archives and online databases now available.

The importance of active as well as passive elements in the phenomenon of preserving the name finds one of its classic expressions in the worship of Yahweh in ancient Israel. In Psalm 113, for example, we read that 'Thy name, O Lord, endureth for ever; and thy memorial, O Lord, throughout all generations.' The Hebrew word here rendered as 'memorial' has in other translations been given as 'remembrance', 'renown' or 'fame', and all these words remind us that however creatively powerful the name of a god, it is his worshippers who keep the name alive through a living scriptural and liturgical practice. We can see the same active and passive elements in Laurence Binyon's famous poem 'For the Fallen' (1914) – first published in *The Times* newspaper, 21 September 1914 – the fourth verse of which is engraved

on war memorials and recited as part of the annual Remembrance Day
ceremony at the Cenotaph in London:

> They shall grow not old, as we that are left grow old:
> Age shall not weary them, nor the years condemn.
> At the going down of the sun and in the morning
> We will remember them.

Binyon's poem, not in any explicit sense a religious one, suggests that
those who have sacrificed their lives in war have attained a glory and
immortality comparable to that of the host of stars illuminating the
night sky, stars which will go on shining long after we are dust.

In this poem, as in so many expressions of the idea of earthly
immortality, it is never quite clear in what exactly the idea of the
earthly afterlife of the dead – their posthumous personhood – consists. An earthly afterlife is, undeniably, a social construction, based
on the memories and activities of the living, and on the remainders
and reminders of the deceased. And yet the idea of an earthly afterlife
cannot always or in every respect be kept apart from the idea of an
otherworldly afterlife. There is certainly a tendency, among unbelievers
as well as believers, to speak of earthly immortality in terms borrowed
from the vocabulary of otherworldly immortality. Either these elements can be abstracted from the idea of an earthly afterlife or they
must, after all, be part and parcel of its meaning. In either case, questions arise as to the status of an earthly afterlife. Is it never anything
more than a poetic but potentially misleading name for the way the
living remember and memorialize the dead? Or is it more than simply
the sum of its parts, a mode in which the dead do somehow continue
to exist among us?

One way of testing out the idea of post-mortem personhood in
an earthly afterlife, without presupposing their existence in an otherworldly afterlife, is to consider whether the dead can, in any sense, be
harmed. Alternatively and more positively, one might ask whether the
dead can be benefited in any way. In fact talk of posthumous harm
(or benefit) is a conveniently emblematic way of referring to a whole
array of positive and negative actions (or failures to act) in regard to
the dead. Thus one can talk about wronging, or dishonouring, the dead
as well as about harming them. More positively, one could talk about
duties and obligations towards the dead, the neglect of which might

be examples of wronging or harming them. Among these obligations might be some of the legal ones already touched on in the discussion of the legal mode of earthly immortality. Some people talk about making reparations to the dead for wrongs done them in the past (as distinct from making reparations to their living descendants). The idea of 'posthumous harm', the strongest of all the effects the living might have upon the dead, usefully serves to represent them all.

The first thing worth noting is that those who most vociferously deny the possibility of posthumous harm tend to have special interests in its impossibility, as illustrated in this exchange between two characters in a crime novel by P. D. James:

> 'And now you'll let them blame the murder on Caroline and Amy, both dead and both innocent?'
>
> 'Innocent? Of that, of course. Perhaps you're right and the police will find it convenient to assume they did it, one of them or together in collusion. From Rickards's point of view it's better to have two dead suspects than no arrest. And it can't hurt them now. The dead are beyond harm, the harm they do and the harm that is done to them.'
>
> 'But it's wrong and it's unjust.'
>
> 'Meg, they are dead. Dead. It can't matter. Injustice is a word and they have passed beyond the power of words. They don't exist. And life is unjust. If you feel called to do something about injustice concentrate on justice to the living. . .'[37]

In this conversation the claim that the dead are 'beyond harm' looks very much like an excuse masquerading as a fact. The character making it also proclaims that 'Injustice is [only] a word.' The attitude of the other character (Meg) is probably more representative of the views of the majority, who variously feel, think or behave at least *as if* the dead can be harmed, which is by no means always because they consciously subscribe to some relevant religious beliefs about the dead. One has only to think of the care and respect with which people treat corpses, and even the possessions of the dead; or of the efforts people make to carry out the wishes of the dead or to promote their projects and interests. (That we tend to see these activities as examples of 'not harming' rather than of actively 'helping' the dead suggests an asymmetry in our general attitudes to the dead, the tenor of which is that the dead should be left in peace.) Much of this behaviour can no doubt be explained as a secular relic of behaviour which in the past (as still in some cultures today) is explicitly related to a fear of the (otherworldly) dead. Although this may be so, it is the fact that such behaviour is well-established in a purely or mainly secular context that concerns us here.

'How is it possible to harm someone who no longer exists?' asks Joan C. Callahan, who observes that 'the notion of harming the dead is paradoxical for those of us who ascribe to no theory of [otherworldly] human immortality.'[38] Many people would surely accept that a person's reputation or 'image' can be damaged or, alternatively, restored after their death, or that the desires and intentions they expressed during their lives, and perhaps at the very end of their lives, can be ignored or misrepresented by others. Is this not already to affirm the reality of a deceased person's earthly afterlife?

Let us consider the following hypothetical case. A person who while alive has been seen as leading an uneventful and perhaps even worthless life has in fact secretly been spending long hours of research on the trail of a universal cure for cancer. Suppose that this person, having at last discovered the cure, is diagnosed with a terminal illness which leaves no time to prepare the research findings for publication. This person asks an acquaintance to see through the publication of the research material. Let us now imagine three alternative outcomes to this story. The first and most obvious one is that the acquaintance does what is requested; the research is published, millions are cured of their disease and its discoverer, after whom the cure is named, becomes world famous. A second possible outcome is that the acquaintance claims credit for the discovery and becomes famous (and perhaps also rich). The third possibility is that, before the material has been published, the acquaintance is killed and the research material destroyed in a tragic fire. It can be argued as to whether in the last case the millions of cancer sufferers, born or yet to be born, can be said to have been harmed by the accident. What it seems more difficult to deny is that in the first outcome the researcher's reputation would be transformed overnight, that in the second the researcher would have been harmed in the sense of being wronged, and that in the third the researcher would have been harmed but not actually wronged. In all three cases the idea of an earthly afterlife seems like a useful device for 'placing' these changes in how the deceased person is remembered, celebrated, judged and so on.

To say this, however, is not to attribute to the dead some kind of mysterious status intermediate between that of a living human being and that of an otherworldly person, as some have been inclined to do. Theories of posthumous harm often seem to rest on the idea that the wishes, interests, duties, obligations and other things with which individuals identify themselves when they are alive can somehow continue to exist when these individuals no longer exist, thereby allowing the living to maintain a moral relationship to the dead, and perhaps also vice versa.[39] Callahan's view is that such ideas are pre-theoretic intuitions for which we wrongly seek philosophical justification, and she suggests that

> our pretheoretic intuitions regarding harm and wrong to the dead are not genuine moral convictions at all but are, rather, judgments we are inclined to make simply because we think of the dead as the persons they were antemortem. They are sentiments which are to be accounted for psychologically.[40]

What some of those considering the question of posthumous harm have tended to ignore is the extent to which selfhood or personhood is not an atomistic property but one that depends upon, or is even defined by, the relationship between persons. Human beings are irreducibly social; they cannot but exist as members of an interconnected plurality of persons. When an individual dies, the surrounding plurality is disrupted, but for the same reason this plurality maintains the imprint of the individual's individuality. One might draw an analogy here with a piece from a jigsaw puzzle. Each of the various pieces of a jigsaw derives its particular significance in large part from the several pieces with which it interlocks. When an individual piece is removed, its shape remains, defined by the pieces which surround it, and it can to some extent be 'reconstructed' from the information in these surrounding pieces, but only for as long as these themselves remain in place.

This kind of analysis by no means undermines the idea of an earthly afterlife or the value of thinking of the dead as the absent 'subjects' of such an afterlife, subjects to which various epithets can be applied or withdrawn. Rather it frees the idea from the suspicion, and disadvantage, of being a piece of specious metaphysics possibly at odds with more genuinely metaphysical views about the afterlife of persons. Some philosophers have tried to have it both ways, by suggesting that the dead do have some kind of existence separate both from the world of the living and from any kind of otherworldly existence. Palle Yourgrau, for whom 'the problem of the nonexistence of the dead ... beckons us along the path of metaphysics', proposes that the dead belong to the class of real but non-existent (because no longer actually existing) entities. The dead cease to exist but do not become nothing. The dead (unlike, say, fictional characters) are non-existent entities that nevertheless have being. 'Possible people, like the dead and the unborn, are not a peculiar kind of abstract existent, but rather a perfectly ordinary kind of concrete object like you and me, who merely have the bad luck not to enjoy existence.'[41]

To deny that the dead can be harmed, because they are no longer subjects susceptible to harm, is not to deny that the dead have some kind of earthly afterlife, such as might be represented in terms of reputation, interests, rights, responsibilities and so on (though one might not want to define an afterlife in terms of all of these). The social and psychological benefits of thinking of the dead as still a part of our lives are plain for all to see. A not dissimilar status, though obviously much vaguer, attaches to the next generation or to future generations more generally. But it is also evident that for many people who think this way, though by no means for all of them, the idea of an earthly afterlife of the dead functions merely as the front end, so to speak, of an otherworldly afterlife. For others, who doubt or deny an otherworldly afterlife, an earthly afterlife may function as a (usually temporary) surrogate for an otherworldly afterlife.

The posthumous personhoods represented, or created, by earthly afterlives are in most cases fragile and short-lived. Some of the earthly afterlives of the famous may be well-established, but in many cases their one-dimensional character fails to do their subjects justice. The cessation or fading away of a posthumous personhood could be described as the 'second death' of the earthly individual. Thomas Hardy, lingering in a churchyard, imagines the dead complaining not that they are dead and buried but that they will suffer the 'blank oblivion' of a 'second death' when the living eventually do forget them. Those who have already suffered this 'deeper death' are 'quite forgot': 'They are as men who have existed not; / Theirs is a loss past loss of fitful breath.' Until then,

We here, as yet, each day
Are blest with dear recall; as yet, can say
We hold in some soul loved continuance
Of shape and voice and glance.

Soon enough, however – and unlike the famous few 'whose memory none lets die' – they will join the ranks of the anonymous dead:

But what has been will be –
First memory, then oblivion's swallowing sea;
Like men foregone, shall we merge into those
Whose story no one knows.[42]

On one view of the relationship between the living and the dead, it would make perfect sense for the dead to be anxious that the living had forgotten them, if their welfare in the afterlife depended upon the living making prayers and offerings on their behalf. From another point of view, however, it might seem absurd for the surviving dead, or at least for the long established dead, to worry that they were slipping beyond the range of human memory. The voices of Hardy's 'dead', however, are not the voices of the surviving dead, but rather the voiced anxieties the living have about being forgotten after death.

Despite the kind of pessimism represented in Hardy's poetry, however, the earthly lives of individuals are not necessarily lost or negated by being eventually forgotten. On the contrary, personal afterlives are succeeded by, or give place to, what I shall define as anonymous forms of earthly afterlife, and these might well be said to represent a superior form of immortality. This is the subject of the next chapter.

FOUR

ANONYMOUS IMMORTALITY

But because being here means so much, because everything
here, so fleeting, seems to need us and strangely
concerns us. Us, the most fleeting of all. Once only
for everything, once only. Once and no more. And we too,
only once. Never again. But this
time of being here, albeit only once,
this earthly belonging, can never be undone.
RAINER MARIA RILKE[1]

I

The key to the persistence of posthumous personhood in, or as, an earthly afterlife is memory. More precisely, it is memory reinforced by information and intention. Memories alone will not carry the dead very far posthumously. There must also be something in which memories are grounded and something which keeps memories alive, in addition to which we must be desirous of remembering, commemorating and honouring the dead. By the rather clinical term 'information', I mean not only information about the dead, such as we might find in books, letters, diaries, photographs, digital data and so on, but the other kinds of 'remainders' of the dead discussed in the previous chapter – anything from the bodies and personal possessions of the dead to the works they created or the deeds they performed.

From this it is clear that with the decline of memory and intention on the one hand, and the loss or degradation of information on the other, an earthly afterlife of a personal kind is a precarious reality which will eventually, either suddenly or gradually, come to an end. For the vast majority of the deceased, indeed, posthumous personhood is maintained by a narrowly circumscribed group of family and friends and is relatively short-lived. For the famous few, by contrast, posthumous personhood will be sustained, if not expanded, by a much larger group over a much longer period. For the bereaved, of course, no earthly remainders or reminders can ever compensate for the loss of the unique individuals who have died. Whatever reminders or remainders of the deceased may be cherished by others after their deaths, the deceased have gone forever. This felt insufficiency of any earthly afterlife is poignantly expressed in the second stanza of Edna Millay's 'Dirge without Music'.[2] For Millay there is scant consolation for the disappearance, into indiscriminate dust, of individuals who once flourished as lovers and thinkers: 'A fragment of what you felt, of what you knew, / A formula, a phrase remains, – but the best is lost.' The problem with an earthly afterlife of the personal kind is not just that it comes to an end, like the original life itself, but that its necessarily fragmentary nature serves only to bring home the immensity of the loss it signifies.

It may be, therefore, that posthumous personhood is not the most important thing to be hoped for or cherished in, or as, an earthly afterlife. For an earthly afterlife of a personal kind is not the only kind of earthly afterlife, and its ending or decline does not negate the contributions of those already or soon to be forgotten. What individuals have been or said or done have consequences extending far beyond the limits of their earthly lives and far beyond the extent of their personal earthly afterlives. The personal earthly immortality which the dead 'enjoy', or rather which the living enjoy on their behalf, is succeeded by, or becomes part of, a post-personal afterlife – one that I shall define as an 'anonymous immortality'. The varieties of this anonymous immortality are the subject of this present chapter.

Because it lacks reference to particular characteristics or achievements, it is easy to discount an anonymous afterlife as something weaker, or thinner, than a personal earthly afterlife. But it is also possible to see it as the stronger form of an earthly afterlife precisely because it is no longer dependent on particular memories or specific material items, and hence no longer subject to decay and misrepresentation. Because all forms of earthly immortality tend towards anonymity, anonymous immortality could indeed be regarded as the natural form of earthly immortality. What I shall also be considering here is the idea that it is even the superior form of earthly immortality.

Anonymity, in any context, can come either from a desire to remain unknown, whether through selflessness or secretiveness, or from the accidental loss of identifying characteristics. A donor or benefactor may wish to remain anonymous, but so too may a maker of obscene telephone calls. There are also degrees of anonymity. In the case of complete anonymity, there is no longer anyone to be described even as anonymous. An anonymous composer is at least known to have been a composer, and the nature of the works he or she composed may well tell us something about him or her. By the same token, a person can be rescued from anonymity. An identity can be rediscovered or reconstructed, through archival research, archaeological discovery or DNA analysis. A completely anonymous composer would be an unknown composer, or a lost composer.

Anonymity depends on a lack or loss of identity (or more precisely, on a lack or loss of identifying information), but literally the term denotes the absence of a name. Yet the mere possession of a name is not really a guarantee against what we normally mean by anonymity. If a name cannot be identified or associated with a particular person, or with a particular person's history or achievements, that name scarcely rescues a person from anonymity. Telling persons suffering from amnesia what their name is makes no difference to their sense of their own anonymity. Calling otherwise anonymous assassins by some nickname, such as 'Jack the Ripper' or 'the Jackal', hardly blows their cover, or solves the mystery of their identity, though it might provide a convenient core around which relevant identifying data can be assembled.[3]

The point is that names alone do not a person make – unless, of course, one accepts the magical idea of the name as the revealing or controlling essence of a person.[4] We might picture two tombstones side by side, one whose identifying name and other items of information have worn away and the other with the name and other information still visible. If, on the latter, the remaining information cannot be identified with a particular individual, then the occupant of this second grave will hardly be considered less anonymous than the occupant of the first. Names can promote or hasten a referent's virtual anonymity in other ways too. This can happen, for example, when an inventor's name becomes so closely identified with the invention itself that its original referent is forgotten. Such is the case with the names 'biro' (for a type of pen) and 'hoover' (for a vacuum cleaner), two examples of surnames which have become the names of objects. These, of course, are not perfect examples, or at least not complete examples, of virtual anonymity. If they were, we should not be able to cite them as examples. There is, behind the conflation of name and invention, a vast array of available information about the lives of these two individuals (Biró and Hoover), certainly enough to ensure for them some form of posthumous personhood.[5] But it is conceivable that just as there are some deceased individuals of whom nothing identifiable remains except their name – in a book or on a tombstone, for example – so are there others whose identities have been completely eclipsed by an achievement or invention which may or may not actually bear their name. Such individuals could be said to have exchanged a personal earthly afterlife for an anonymous one. Nor, one imagines, would such an exchange be regarded by most of these individuals as any kind of misfortune, given the likelihood that their names would otherwise have been completely forgotten.

II

As I have emphasized, all forms of earthly survival tend towards anonymity, and it is easy to present anonymous immortality in a negative light, or as a very poor relation of posthumous personhood. But anonymous immortality can also be viewed in a positive light, and even as a form of immortality superior to any form of posthumous personhood. Anonymous immortality is, it can be argued, not only the socially more beneficial form of earthly immortality, but the form more congruent with an individual's own ambitions and ethical ideals. The difference between the two could be regarded as comparable to the difference between leaving one's body for medical research or organ donation,[6] and leaving it in a costly tomb whose main purpose is to perpetuate if not glorify one's own memory.[7] Before looking at what may be regarded as the intrinsic virtues of anonymous immortality, however, I shall review some of the ways in which such immortality arises through the loss or decline of a personal earthly afterlife.

Once again I shall begin with the corpse, that most tangible and poignant symbol of the disjunction between life and death. The corpse is a deceased person's most obvious, and in some cases only, earthly legacy. As the first and most obvious 'remainder' of a recently deceased person, it can function as a potent 'after-image' of the living individual. The presence and appearance of a deceased person's bodily remains constitute the most basic form or phase of an individual's earthly afterlife. In the case of many saints, for example, the persisting corpse plays a crucial role in a person's earthly afterlife – albeit one also linked to the idea of an otherworldly afterlife.[8] But the persistence (in whatever form) of a person's bodily remains only comes into its own, so to speak, in the context of the attendant rituals and customs of disposal and commemoration. Funerary apparatus in the form of tombs, memorials and rituals of commemoration are set against the natural tendency of human remains to slip into complete anonymity. As for the vast majority of the billions of human dead distributed across the planet, these have passed even beyond anonymity, the organic materials that once constituted their bodies now reassimilated into the matrix of nature.

The identity of a human body or set of human remains is maintained, where it is maintained at all, by its known location and by any accompanying monuments and inscriptions. The identity and 'personality' of the smallest fragment of bone contained within the reliquary of a saint may depend, ultimately, upon a single inscription (though in many cases the identification may well be spurious). Reminders of the remainders of the dead take a variety of forms, and in most cases can be preserved or renewed indefinitely (and in theory perpetually). Their meaningful survival as reminders, however, requires a social basis and historical memory which, once lost, can be difficult if not impossible to recover. What is true of bodies is also true of the personal possessions which contribute to the idea of a person's earthly continuance. Such possessions may be more resistant to decay than bodies, but many of them, once divorced from any association with their former owners, easily become anonymous items which on their own have no particular story to tell. (On the other hand, the more nondescript a bodily relic or artefact, the greater the canvas it gives to the imagination.)

Except where efforts are made to halt or delay the natural processes of dissolution, the corpse with all its distinctive features is naturally or artificially reduced to a set of increasingly anonymous remains. Whether a naturally decaying human body ever becomes completely anonymous (assuming it is still identifiable as a body at all) is a moot point, particularly now that techniques of facial and bodily reconstruction and of DNA analysis have become so sophisticated. In many cultures, however, the dissolution of the body is regarded as a good thing, and the process of reduction may be hastened artificially, through cremation or by other means.

The soul may have no further life after the death of the body; however, the body certainly lives on after the soul passes away. Here, we can definitely speak of a *life after death*, because a corpse is active throughout: after death, it remains active in that it elapses, decays, and decomposes. This process of decay is potentially infinite – one cannot definitively say when the process ends because the body's material substances remain identifiable for a long enough time. Even if the vestiges of the corpse can no longer be identified, it doesn't mean the body has disappeared, but simply that its elements – molecules, atoms, etc. – have dispersed throughout the world to such extent that the body has practically become one with the entire world.[9]

One set of human remains may be, or at least may appear to be, indistinguishable from another set of remains, but the fact is that each numerically distinct set of remains is that of a unique human individual. In cases such as the exhumation of mass graves or the recovery of bodies from the site of an air crash, maritime disaster or burnt-out building, immense efforts will usually be made to recover the bodies or remains in question and to establish their identity. Very real distress has been caused to families in cases where it turns out that they have been given the wrong cremated ashes, since to them the ashes of their loved ones are as unique as any embalmed body. One woman in Memphis, Tennessee, who eventually discovered, from an identifying tag within the urn, that the ashes supposedly of her mother were in fact those of someone else, felt she had been deceived: 'I talk to her every morning. I thought I was talking to her every morning . . . All this time it's been somebody else.'[10] In many cases, however, relatives seek to move beyond the illusion of posthumous personhood created by the retention of ashes in an urn. Scattering a loved one's ashes in the sea or river, or at a particular location on land, suggests more of an acceptance of the inevitable anonymity of death, at least at the purely physical level. The letting go of the ashes is a letting go of the person too, at least as an erstwhile fellow inhabitant of the Earth.

Left to themselves, the bodies of the deceased become increasingly anonymous through the natural processes of decay and dissolution. In so far as the body plays a continuing role in the earthly afterlife of the dead, this is usually effected through some kind of *image* of the body rather than through the body itself. Painting and sculpture, and in more recent times of course photography and film, are the chief means of extending the bodily afterlife of the dead. Preserving a body artificially or displaying the bodily remains of particular individuals are practices usually motivated by religious interests (for example, mummification in ancient Egypt, the Christian cult of saints, or beliefs about resurrection). The retention or preservation of bodies does of course render them vulnerable to various kinds of neglect, abuse or indignity, some of which are intended and some unintended. The bodies of the dead have sometimes been exhumed and symbolically humiliated in various ways, even during the lifetime of their immediate descendants. Persons whose bodies are excavated by archaeologists or displayed in museums could be said to be enduring an earthly afterlife which they themselves, during their lifetimes, would have regarded as either grotesque or inimical to their otherworldly well-being. On balance, anonymity might well be considered the better destiny for a corpse.

The second way in which the body, or the bodily, plays a part in an earthly afterlife is through the production of progeny, this being the basis for what in the previous chapter I defined as progenitive immortality. One's body may decay, and even the place of one's disposal be forgotten, but one's name, and one's physical and mental traits, can live on in one's children, one's children's children, and so on. Particularly in secular contexts, perhaps, this progenitive extension of one's personal existence may be affirmed in an individualistic or even selfish sense as a comforting counterweight to the prospect of one's personal annihilation. *I may die*, people may say (or at least think), *but offspring bearing my name and my personal and physical features will live on.* Thus understood, however, such progenitive continuity offers very poor returns, since names and features can change within a generation or two. Memories of deceased family members are more likely to be sustained, or renewed, by document, image and artefact than by the observation of the physical or psychological characteristics of progeny. No matter how many children and grandchildren one has, and no matter how closely some of them may resemble oneself physically or mentally, one's slide into anonymity within a family begins early. An earthly afterlife defined by one's physical or mental traits is most likely to be noticed, and perhaps even cultivated, in the families of persons whose earthly afterlife is already well established in the public record – persons such as monarchs, statesmen, scientists, inventors, artists, film stars and so on. On the other hand, instead of viewing these physical and mental traits as one's own personal legacy to one's progeny, it is surely more realistic to see them as inherited traits belonging to no one individual or family in particular – traits of which one's own life has been yet another ephemeral expression. It is in this context, of course, that writers such as Richard Dawkins emphasize the priority of genus over species and the persistence of genes over the lives of the individuals who are their temporary carriers.[11]

Biology is certainly no respecter of the individual. Bodies decay into the anonymous elements of nature, and the memories of individual progenitors are lost rather than preserved in the tide of succeeding generations. New generations arise in ignorance of all but their most recent predecessors. The struggle against anonymity arguably has greater success in the case of what I have called creative and performative immortality.

Creative survival is relatively secure, since many of the things people write, make or invent tend to be carefully preserved and widely reproduced. Only a truly cataclysmic turn of history would threaten the survival of Shakespeare's plays, Beethoven's music or Picasso's pictures. Like every other form of earthly survival, however, creative survival becomes increasingly impersonal over time, creative achievements gradually eclipsing any detailed knowledge of their creators and in many cases even their creators' names, as we noted earlier. Ironically enough, it is sometimes the enduring fame of one individual that will contribute to the occlusion of another's. Most people have heard of Charles Darwin, but relatively few of the equally important figures of Alexander von Humboldt or Alfred Russel Wallace. Of Humboldt, a recent biographer writes as follows: 'Humboldt's disciples, and their disciples in turn, carried his legacy forward – quietly, subtly and sometimes unintentionally. Environmentalists, ecologists and nature writers today remain firmly rooted in Humboldt's vision – although many have never heard of him. Nevertheless, Humboldt is their founding father.'[12] In every field of human endeavour, perhaps inevitably, those important figures standing in the limelight of fame vastly outnumber those who now dwell in its shadows. There is simply not enough room for them all on the world stage.

Think of all the inventions we take for granted but whose actual inventors have been largely, if not completely, forgotten. How many of us know who invented the electric light bulb, for instance? Indeed, in many cases the names of authors, composers, artists or inventors become little more than devices for identifying their respective creations; as when we talk about a Botticelli painting or a Mozart symphony, for example. Nor does living in the full light of modern history guarantee that one's achievements will be securely pinned to one's name in the public mind, whatever the importance of these achievements. Consider, for example, the turbojet engine. The impact of this invention on modern civilization is almost impossible to exaggerate. But how many of the millions of people who now take for granted the benefits of air travel know the name of, let alone give any thought to, the person who changed the course of human history through this invention? The name is Whittle – Frank Whittle. This individual can surely be thought of as 'living on' the lives of millions of people to a degree few others have done, and yet he does so largely anonymously.[13]

As Oscar Wilde's character Lord Henry observes, the only thing worse than being talked about is not being talked about.[14] But perhaps what is even worse than not being talked about is being talked about inaccurately or for the wrong reasons. It may be only for negative things that one is remembered by later generations, or it may be that what is said about one is simply not true, or indeed the opposite of the truth. For example, although sufficient historical records exist to guarantee the earthly afterlife of the Danish king Canute,[15] who ruled England between 1016 and 1035, this king is remembered by many people today, if he is remembered at all, through the complete misrepresentation of one particular incident in his life, the quite possibly legendary status of which does not negate the basic point about misrepresentation.[16] Tired of the flattery of his courtiers, Canute summoned them all to the beach and there commanded the incoming waves to stop. His purpose was to demonstrate, by the fact that the waves would obviously fail to stop, that he was an ordinary human being with no special powers. More often than not, however, Canute is 'remembered' as a king who arrogantly thought he had the power to command the sea. To add insult to injury, the term 'Canute-like' is sometimes used to refer to a person arrogant enough to think he can hold back the inevitable.

It may well be a distinct advantage, therefore, for writers, artists, inventors, statesmen and so on to become 'relatively anonymous' – that is, to become so closely identified with their works or deeds that almost nothing else, good or bad, is remembered about them. Such relative anonymity certainly fits the case of Homer, whose very historicity (as a single author) is sometimes doubted; but it is also, in effect, the case with many undoubtedly historical figures such as Shakespeare, the use of whose name calls up a body of plays and poetry rather than a historical individual. Creative and performative immortality depend actively on human memory, cultural interests and technical skills of one kind or another, but passively on the survival and accessibility of material entities of some kind, all of which are subject to loss and decay. These material entities are especially vulnerable where they are rare or unique. Even the toughest buildings and monuments are not only subject to the ravages of time, but dependent on changing cultural fashions and the vagaries of human memory. Nor does the mere survival of a building or monument by any means guarantee that its original function – memorial or otherwise – will be maintained. Some monuments may indeed become memorials to the very facts of neglect or forgetfulness. The irony conveyed by a ruined monument to a long forgotten individual who intended to be remembered through such a device is captured in Percy Bysshe Shelley's famous poem 'Ozymandias' – although, arguably, Ozymandias (a Greek name for the Egyptian pharaoh Rameses II) would have had the last laugh in knowing that his monuments, through the medium of Shelley's poetry, have in fact secured his memory as never before.[17] Despite the secondary irony of its giving Ozymandias a new lease of earthly afterlife, Shelley's poem remains a telling satire against the folly of imagining that we can ever insure ourselves against oblivion. A walk through any neglected or overgrown cemetery will yield much the same impression as that brought back from the desert wastes by Shelley's 'traveller from an antique land'.

III

Rather than thinking of anonymous immortality as a weak or failed form of posthumous personhood, however, it is possible to think of it as a mode of immortality equal if not superior in value to the latter. In this section, therefore, I consider some of the more positive interpretations that can be given to the idea of an anonymous earthly afterlife, again starting with the earthly afterlife of the body.

In the case of a corporeal afterlife, what Edna Millay laments as the 'indiscriminate dust' to which all individuals return can also be regarded as a contribution to the fecund matrix from which all new life forms will emerge. For example, advocates of what is known as 'green' or 'natural' burial turn the bodily dissolution wrought by nature into a fact to be celebrated rather than lamented. People take comfort from knowing that their own bodies and the bodies of their loved ones will dissolve to become part of the cycle of nature. Even so, for many people the specific earthly location in which the body of their loved one is laid to rest ceases, for them, to be an anonymous piece of land and takes on a more personal character.

One commentator on burial customs offers a tentative explanation as to why cremation rates, usually quite high in non-Roman Catholic countries, are much lower in Norway and Finland than they are in Denmark or Sweden, and why even the USA, again a mainly Protestant country, has an unexpectedly low cremation rate. The suggestion is that because Norway and Finland were, up to the beginning of the twentieth century, both occupied countries, burial in the national soil came to be regarded as an act of patriotism. In the United States like-wise, inhumation 'is similarly seen as the ultimate form of national belonging (which also helps to explain why Americans are keen to repatriate the remains of soldiers killed abroad, for interment in their native soil)'.[18] In these cases, the relative anonymity of the grave itself is mitigated by the knowledge that, physically, the deceased is united not simply (and rather vaguely) with the natural elements but also with a particular national territory (and people).

In the previous section I pointed out that intentions or expect-ations of securing a personal earthly afterlife through the production of progeny are easily or eventually frustrated. Once one abandons any narrow desire for personal immortality through one's progeny, how-ever, broader conceptions of a progenitive immortality come into view. Thus one might gain great satisfaction, or consolation, from anticipat-ing one's anonymous immortality not only within future generations of one's own family but within a wider constituency. The prospect of a more generic kind of progenitive immortality is part of the idea that the interests of individuals and their families are subordinate to those of the larger human community, and that it is this larger com-munity which should be the ultimate object of our concern for the future. One's individual memory might not be preserved, but some of one's physical and mental qualities will be passed on, or rather some of the things these physical or mental qualities have enabled one to say or do or create may survive to influence or bear fruit in the lives of others. Looking at progenitive immortality from the point of view of those looking back rather than forward, some people take consider-able pride in the fact that they are the direct descendants of this or that well-known historical personage.

In its most extreme or abstract form, an anonymous progenitive immortality would transcend even the more generic forms of communal identity preserved in families, tribes and nations, the ultimate subject of such immortality being neither individuals nor groups of individuals but the gene pool of humanity as a whole. This variety of anonymous progenitive immortality we might call *genetic immortality*. The science of DNA has shown that the ancestry of particular individuals or groups can be traced back not merely over centuries but over millennia. Such knowledge is not always welcomed by those who like to think of themselves, their families or their nations in terms of direct descent or racial purity. Perhaps the most positive result to come from the genetic understanding of humankind is our greater awareness of the unity of humankind, as deriving from whatever we choose to identify as our ultimate origins and the interconnectedness of humanity throughout history. Complex strands of causation, genetic and social, give rise to an endless procession of unique individuals, each of whom will play a larger or smaller part in shaping the lives of future persons and events.

An anonymous progenitive immortality, whether understood in generic or genetic terms, need not imply a devaluation of the unique characteristics of individual human beings. The suggestion by some biological reductionists that individuals are *merely* the means of reproducing a species' genes, understood as the real subjects of life and its evolution, is a purely arbitrary one. We might just as well say that the genes are the means of reproducing the individuals. In any case, why stop at genes or species? Why not say that what really matters is the survival of life as such, even if this means the extinction of this or that species (genus, and so on) in the process. Indeed, why not subordinate life itself to its alleged pre-biological physical components? Elevating the evolution of living matter over its older and more resilient non-organic components is no less sentimental than elevating the existence of individuals over that of their component genes.

Just as our bodies decay and return to the matrix of nature, and our individual physical and mental characteristics continue to manifest themselves as part of the genetic inheritance of future generations long after we are forgotten as historical individuals, so too may the things we have said and done in our lives ripple on as part of our anonymous immortality, quite independently of any surviving objective manifestation of our individual lives, and even when such manifestations have themselves been lost. Although what I defined as the creative and performative forms of posthumous personhood are among the most resilient forms of an earthly afterlife, for the vast majority of people these forms of earthly afterlife do not apply. Yet the lives of ordinary folk lives can become immortal in equally productive albeit quite anonymous ways. We may think here of George Eliot's character Dorothea Brooke, whose anonymous immortality, representative of so many others, is celebrated in the famous last paragraph of the novel *Middlemarch* (1871–2). Dorothea's qualities may not have been 'widely visible' and her full nature may have 'spent itself in channels which had no great name on the earth'.

> But the effect of her being on those around her was incalculably diffusive: for the growing good of the world is partly dependent on unhistoric acts; and that things are not so ill with you and me as they might have been, is half owing to the number who lived faithfully a hidden life, and rest in unvisited tombs.[19]

Taking my cue from George Eliot, I shall define as *diffusive immortality* the kind of anonymous immortality that subsists in the long and potentially endless chain of skills, influences and effects that individuals generate through word or action in the course of their lives. These skills, influences and effects will be variously individual or social, intellectual or emotional, practical or aesthetic. Human culture and civilization depend on these anonymous skills, influences and effects no less than on manifestations of culture more objectively preserved in books, works of art, inventions and so on. Unlike the latter, however, such influences and effects will be largely anonymous, in the sense that they ripple outwards from the life of an individual into the lives of others, and from one generation to the next, with substantial but unpredictable consequences.

A particularly eloquent expression of this diffusive immortality appears in a passage of Thornton Wilder's novella *The Bridge of San Luis Rey* (1927), whose underlying themes are the brevity and uncertainty, but interconnectedness, of individual human lives. One of the characters in this story, Mother Maria, an abbess in charge of an orphanage, is looking back on the lives of the five individuals who plunged to their deaths when the suspension bridge they all happened to be crossing suddenly gave way. She begins by acknowledging the ephemeral nature of the human memory on which any kind of personal earthly immortality depends.

> But even while she was talking, other thoughts were passing in the back of her mind. 'Even now,' she thought, 'almost no one remembers Esteban and Pepita, but myself. Camila alone remembers her Uncle Pio and her son; this woman, her mother. But soon we shall die and all memory of those five will have left the earth, and we ourselves shall be loved for a while and forgotten. But the love will have been enough; all those impulses of love return to the love that made them. Even memory is not necessary for love. There is a land of the living and a land of the dead and the bridge is love, the only survival, the only meaning.[20]

What is true of love – and perhaps of love above all – is also true of other important aspects of human life; it is true of knowledge, of skills, of language, of ideas, of emotions. These are perpetuated, wittingly or unwittingly, through the complex chain of influences within and across the generations.

For Mother Maria, as a Christian, the power of love ultimately has a divine source and meaning. Her words are somewhat reminiscent of those written about the limitless power of love by the philosopher Spinoza, who observes of love

> that as it increases more and more, so also it grows more excellent, because it is bestowed on an object which is infinite, and can therefore always go on increasing, which can happen in the case of no other thing except this alone. And, maybe, this will afterwards give us the material from which we shall prove the immortality of the soul, and how or in what way this is possible.[21]

Nevertheless, Mother Maria's description of the diffusive power of love, working its way through human society long after the individuals who manifested it in one's own generation have been forgotten, is perfectly consistent with a purely secular outlook.

IV

The positive forms of anonymous immortality reviewed in the previous section are all versions, or extensions, of the four basic forms of earthly immortality discussed in the previous chapter – versions, that is, of corporeal, progenitive, creative and performative immortality. In this section I turn to examine two potentially far more ambitious forms of anonymous earthly immortality. These two forms of anonymous earthly immortality, which I shall call *collective immortality* and *cosmic immortality*, differ from the previous forms in being anonymous by definition. Both rest on the idea that, no less after death than during their lifetimes, persons are united with, or are a part of, something greater and more lasting than their own individual lives. Both conceptions of immortality tend to assume a teleological form, the first of them grounded in ideas about a future society as well as a common humanity, and the second in ideas about an evolving Nature or cyclical Universe. From one point of view, these two forms of anonymous immortality can be regarded as the purest forms of such immortality, but from another as arguably the emptiest. Or, to put it another way, perhaps they escape from emptiness only by assuming a metaphysical front.

The collective form of anonymous earthly immortality affirms the value of a social entity that transcends the lives and interests of particular individuals. The entity in question, although it transcends individual personhood, is not for this reason completely impersonal. Thus the entity might be the tribe or the nation, or on a grander scale humanity as such. Or it might be a more abstract humanistic entity, such as human civilization or human evolution. In the modern world, where traditional differences between humankind and other animal species tend to be minimized, the overarching entity could be regarded as the animal kingdom as a whole, or indeed the ecosphere or 'living planet' as a whole.

Bertrand Russell, for one, locates the enduring value of human life within the context of what he calls the 'stream of life':

> To be happy in this world, especially when youth is past, it is necessary to feel oneself not merely an isolated individual whose day will soon be over, but part of the stream of life flowing on from the first germ to the remote and unknown future. As a conscious sentiment, expressed in set terms, this involves

no doubt a hyper-civilised and intellectual outlook upon the world, but as a vague instinctive emotion it is primitive and natural, and it is its absence that is hyper-civilised. A man who is capable of some great and remarkable achievement which sets its stamp upon future ages may gratify this feeling through his work, but for men and women who have no exceptional gifts, the only way to do so is through children.[22]

The last part of this passage recalls the distinction made by Plato's Diotima between the inferior form of earthly immortality guaranteed by the children of one's body and the superior form created through the 'children' of one's mind.

It is only relatively recently in the history of humanity that individuals have been valued independently of their place within a family, tribe or nation. Nor for a social animal does such valuation always sit comfortably with more deep-rooted customs and assumptions. In many cultures still, individual lives and interests are subordinate to family, tribe or nation. The family, tribe or nation is the entity whose identity and continuity must be protected at all costs. It is the function of individual progeny to preserve and carry forward the family, tribe or nation – not of the family, tribe or nation to preserve and to carry forward the individual. Indeed, with the further development of a global culture, and in an era characterized by global crisis, there may even be a return to this more collective view of humanity, people coming to regard humanity as a whole to be the entity whose survival should take precedence over that of smaller groups, families and individuals. To the extent that this shift in consciousness occurs, however, it is still likely to be expressed from within the confines of smaller groups. There might thus be a hierarchy of values which people seek to affirm: by looking after one's family one is helping to preserve the tribe or nation, and by preserving the tribe or nation one is helping to ensure the future of humanity.

The idea of a common humanity is one to which all human beings can relate, as can be seen from the ways in which people talk about the collective future of the human race despite the fact that they, personally, will have no part in it. In almost any kind of society, however, people tend to talk about the future, even the distant future, in the first person plural, as if they themselves will be present to witness, participate in or benefit from some particular event or state of affairs. Go to any crowded place and contemplate the hundreds if not thousands of individuals present there. In a hundred years' time, all or almost all of these people will be dead, and in another hundred years all but a handful of them totally forgotten. And yet many of these individuals will express fears about global warming, environmental pollution or nuclear warfare, or hopes about a cure for cancer, interplanetary travel or pollution-free energy, almost as if they themselves were going to be there to suffer or benefit from these things. What they really mean, of course, is that future generations, and not necessarily even their direct descendants, will be there to suffer or benefit from them.

What needs to be emphasized about some conceptions of collective immortality is that the human society of which such an immortality is predicated is not simply the inevitable result of generation after generation surviving into the future, one to which one contributes simply by having existed, but an intentionally crafted 'entity' whose future character (and perhaps very existence) depends on appropriately directed actions and intentions of successive generations. It is seen not merely as something that comes about but as something that is brought about. One of the clearest expressions of this idea is found in the writings of the youthful Karl Marx, in a passage from a short essay in which he writes that

> the chief guide which must direct us in the choice of a profession is the welfare of mankind and our own perfection. It should not be thought that these two interests could be in conflict, that one would have to destroy the other; on the contrary, man's nature is so constituted that he can attain his own perfection only by working for the perfection, for the good, of his fellow men.
>
> If he works only for himself, he may perhaps become a famous man of learning, a great sage, an excellent poet, but he can never be a perfect, truly great man. History calls those men the greatest who have ennobled themselves by working for the common good; experience acclaims as happiest the man who has made the greatest number of people happy; religion itself teaches us that the ideal being whom all strive to copy sacrificed himself for the sake of mankind, and who would dare to set at nought such judgments?

If we have chosen the position in life in which we can most of all work for mankind, no burdens can bow us down, because they are sacrifices for the benefit of all; then we shall experience no petty, limited, selfish joy, but our happiness will belong to millions, our deeds will live on quietly but perpetually at work, and over our ashes will be shed the hot tears of noble people.[23]

This is not the place to enter into discussion about the rights and wrongs of any particular social system or political programme based on (or at least promoting) the idea of current generations sacrificing their lives (or having their lives sacrificed by others) for the sake of future generations. All that is necessary here is recognition of the fact that such sacrifice has often been rationalized, or idealized, in terms of some form of what I am defining as an anonymous earthly immortality. Self-sacrifice, whether through work or war or by some other means, is often seen as a contribution to a future good in which, although one will not oneself directly participate in it, one's contribution will somehow be acknowledged. The human tendency to think or act communally or globally can of course be harnessed either for good or ill by different kinds of political system or political leader – positively in order to give the people a common purpose in achieving certain goals, negatively in order to control them or deflect attention from their present condition of suffering or servitude.

But the idea of a (present or future) collective humanity as the medium in or through which individuals realize their yearning or instinct for immortality can manifest itself quite independently of any social or political programme. In particular, it can manifest itself as an ethical ideal or more simply as a psychological insight. As such, of course, the idea is easily dismissed as empty rhetoric. But the idea or ideal of identifying with a common or universal humanity, and the actions characteristically associated with such identification, have a clear historical development that prove it to be a cultural achievement of enormous consequence.[24] The idea of a common humanity is an ancient idea, one that lies behind the word 'cosmopolitan', from the Greek κοσμοπολίτης, 'world citizen'. It was the fourth-century BCE Cynic philosopher Diogenes of Sinope who famously described himself as a 'world citizen' when asked where he came from.[25] The idea of world citizenship became especially important among Greek and Roman Stoic philosophers, according to whom the world as a whole could be regarded as a single 'city state'. For Marcus Aurelius, by sharing the common law of reason all human beings can be regarded as fellow citizens of a single state[26] – of 'that higher city of which all other cities are mere households'.[27] This ancient idea of world citizenship was to exercise a powerful influence on later European thinkers.[28]

Nor does a cosmopolitan outlook conflict with other, more local allegiances. The seventeenth-century poet and historian Edmund Bolton, for example, states that historians are 'charged with a fourfold Duty', namely that of writing '1. As a Christian Cosmopolite ... 2. As a Christian Patriot ... 3. As a Christian Subject ... 4. As a Christian Paterfamilias.'[29] Immanuel Kant, in his essay on establishing peace between nations, distinguishes three progressively more inclusive kinds of civil constitution: the *ius civitatis*, 'conforming to the civil law of men in a nation', the *ius gentium*, 'conforming to the law of nations in their relation to one another', and the *ius cosmopoliticum*, 'conforming to the law of world citizenship, so far as men and states are considered as citizens of a universal state of men, in their external mutual relationships'.[30]

Sociometric studies have demonstrated that 'identification with all humanity is more than an absence of ethnocentrism ... and more than the presence of dispositional empathy, moral reasoning, moral identity, and the value of universalism.'[31] Such identification is a crucial element in the recognition of human rights, in the development of egalitarianism and in the behaviour of those who risk their lives to save the lives of the victims of persecution.[32]

For many people it is enough to think that individuals achieve some kind of earthly immortality through what they pass on to others within the ongoing life of humanity, by contributing to future social or political goals within human history, or simply by having been a small element within the total history of the world. This first kind of purely anonymous earthly immortality is well summed up by Benedetto Croce in his short essay on 'Our Dead':

> Those who have died, we who shall one day die, wish only the welfare of those we love; and since that welfare is inseparable from the continuation of our best work, what we would have is that continuation, which is nothing else than a transformation. We are, in reality, nothing but what we do; and that is all of us that we would have immortal. Our specific individuality is an

appearance labelled with a name – it is, in other words, a mere convention; it could persist only as Non-being persists, as a tremor in the void; whereas our affects and our works persist as Being persists, serenely, eternally, in the new reality which they occasion. What is this life of ours but 'a hastening unto death', death of our individuality, that is; and what is achievement save death in our work, which is at once detached from him who does it to become something outside him and beyond?

And is not this glory real glory, real survival – something far superior to the humming of many voices around empty names and vain appearances?[33]

The anonymous immortality described by Croce represents the unvarnished totality of the acts which constitute all that we really are. We are no more and no less than the sum of the actions making up our lives; our individuality is and always has been nothing more than a name and a passing appearance. It puts the collective above the individual.

The idea that a collective form of earthly immortality is a real and worthy goal for finite beings like ourselves, and more than merely a surrogate for the personal immortality that our finite natures deny us, has been developed systematically by the philosopher Mark Johnston, who sets out to show that 'a good person quite literally survives death.'[34] He does so quite differently from the way a person is conceived to survive death through having an immortal soul or by being miraculously resurrected. Since human beings are not substantial selves in the first place, but temporary conjunctions of mental and material factors, there can be no personal afterlife; but we can achieve an anonymous immortality through the survival of our best dispositions within 'the onward rush of humanity' – a phrase (adapted from John Stuart Mill) that recalls Bertrand Russell's image of 'the stream of life'.

For Johnston, belief in any kind of personal immortality is a form of idolatry – an idolatry of the self. A personal afterlife would be just another arena for pursuing the endless satisfaction of our self-centred desires. If we can overcome our selfish interests and desires, however, and cultivate a radical and impersonal altruism that sees the needs and interests of others as no less important than our own, we shall overcome death by surviving in the collective future of humankind. Those with a sufficiently good will have 'a disposition to absorb the legitimate interests of *any* present or future individual personality into one's present practical outlook, so that those interests count as much as one's own'.[35] For Johnston, such persons can be described as having a 'Protean' identity – an identity that embraces not only their own individuality and personality but the minds and bodies of all those whose needs and interests come within the scope of their altruism. Thus (to use a simple example of my own), if I am one of a number of people whose disposition is to save a rainforest threatened with destruction, I will identify with these others while I am alive and after my death live on in their continuing lives, since what constitutes me is not my individual biology and biography but the interests and dispositions I share (or shared) with these others. This becomes a rational as well as a moral attitude once it has been recognized that the individual self is an illusory entity.

If there are no persisting selves worth caring about, then that special self-concern people typically expect and cherish has no justification. 'One's own interests are not worth considering because they are one's own but simply because they are interests, and interests, wherever they arise and are legitimate, are equally worthy of consideration.'[36] Ideally, one's altruism would embrace the lives of all others. As Johnston puts it, truly good people, those who identify sufficiently deeply with the interests of others, 'acquire a new face every time a baby is born and begins to develop into an individual personality'.[37] Thus 'the good after death are conscious, they deliberate, and they act – all of this in and through the multitude that come after.'[38] This, if it makes any sense taken literally, is surely about as strong a statement of earthly immortality as there could be. Taken metaphorically, such a statement represents little more than the sentiments that anyone might express regarding the hope or expectation of an earthly after-life 'lived' through one's children, one's creative work or the beneficial effects one's life may have for future generations. If such statements are to be taken literally, however, one might well be inclined to agree with the verdict given by another philosopher: 'To accept Johnston's theory that identity is relative, that persons are protean, and that we could survive death by coming to identify with future human beings, would require at least as large a dose of wishful thinking as belief in the immortality of the soul or the resurrection of the body.'[39] Johnston is in fact as much a theologian as a philosopher, but one who is looking for a secular reinterpretation of traditional religiosity.

The second of the two most anonymous forms of earthly immortality is *cosmic immortality*. As the name implies, cosmic immortality
works on a scale even grander than that of world history. Attempts to
find a significant place for the ephemeral individual within the ongoing history of humankind seem modest indeed in comparison with
attempts to justify an individual's significance within the history and
constitution of the universe as such. At death, human lives may be lost
as individual lives, but what they uniquely were is never lost within the
total history of the universe, and their unique existences will forever
be a part of any total explanation of the universe. Moreover, once a
particular person has existed it will always be true that this person has
existed, so that – to put it in its most extreme form – even if the universe were entirely to disappear (whatever this might mean), it would
continue to be true that this person had existed. Whether this idea
of nothing and nobody ever being lost is regarded as a trivial point
whisked up into specious profundity, or instead valued as a genuinely
profound insight, is likely to depend on one's metaphysical viewpoint
and in particular on one's theory of time. In its most modest form it
may simply be recognized as an expression of the poignancy of the
fleeting nature of human life, as expressed in the lines from the ninth
of Rilke's *Duino Elegies* quoted at the start of this chapter.

The idea that we should take comfort from, and rejoice in, the
fact or truth that nothing of what each individual has been will ever
be entirely lost within our vast and ever-changing universe I shall
dub the 'stardust philosophy', not least because it is frequently voiced
by philosophically minded physicists and cosmologists. Here is one
enthusiastic expression of it:

> The amazing thing is that every atom in your body came from
> a star that exploded. And, the atoms in your left hand probably
> came from a different star than your right hand. It really is the
> most poetic thing I know about physics: You are all stardust.
> You couldn't be here if stars hadn't exploded, because the ele-
> ments – the carbon, nitrogen, oxygen, iron, all the things that
> matter for evolution – weren't created at the beginning of time.
> They were created in the nuclear furnaces of stars, and the only
> way they could get into your body is if those stars were kind
> enough to explode. So, forget Jesus. The stars died so that you
> could be here today.[40]

The last two sentences betray the anti-religious animus that lies behind this summary of what is a scientifically unexceptionable set of facts. Others have viewed the same set of facts, whether on an earthly or a cosmic scale, in somewhat less exalted terms. Consider, for example, Hamlet's pessimistic thoughts about Caesar's 'indiscriminate dust':

> Imperious Caesar, dead and turn'd to clay,
> Might stop a hole to keep the wind away:
> O, that that earth, which kept the world in awe,
> Should patch a wall to expel the winter flaw! (*Hamlet* v.i)

The sentiment here is close to that of the Book of Ecclesiastes – that all is vanity, that the constitution of the universe is such as to wipe out the greatness of human beings and their achievements as if they had never been. (It is an irony, of course, that the anonymity of Caesar's clay is capable and worthy of Hamlet's comment only because Caesar's historical fame is already securely preserved through other manifestations of his earthly afterlife.)

In other contexts, it is not clear whether the post-personal 'absorption' of the dead within the natural cycle is to be regarded as enrichment or impoverishment. In what is perhaps the best known of Wordsworth's 'Lucy' poems, the dead child is described as somehow one with nature now that she is free of human awareness:

> No motion has she now, no force;
> She neither hears nor sees;
> Roll'd round in earth's diurnal course,
> With rocks, and stones, and trees.[41]

This stanza along with the first stanza of the poem have been subject to very different interpretations, ranging from the pantheistic optimism discerned in much of the poet's other work to the melancholy affirmation of human transience. One critic, whose view falls somewhere between these two extremes, describes the 'calmness of this stanza as the calmness of death', and its tone as that of a 'desperate consolation' deriving from the 'fact that the dead girl is now at last secure beyond question, in inanimate community with the earth's natural fixtures'.[42]

Closer to the melancholy reading of Lucy's fate after death is the one that Philip Larkin envisages for human beings after death. In 'The

Old Fools' (1973), a sharp distinction is drawn between the pregnant oblivion that comes to an end with our birth and the empty and permanent oblivion that follows our death. We break up at death, and the bits that once were us are dissipated forever.

> It's only oblivion, true:
> We had it before, but then it was going to end,
> And was all the time merging with a unique endeavour
> To bring to bloom the million-petalled flower
> Of being here.[43]

Larkin does at least celebrate, in passing, the 'miracle' of our having existed in the first place, but what his poem does not acknowledge is that the disintegrating and unobserved bits that once were us will presumably go on to be parts of the 'million-petalled' flowers that will be (or could be) the existences of other persons. The idea that the universe is, before our individual lifetimes, forever preparing itself for our several unique existences can be seen as the mirror image of the idea that the universe is forever changed by the lives of all those who have ever existed within it. Larkin's observations are nevertheless compatible with a vision of cosmic immortality in which the living and the dead are bound together in an eternal cycle. This more unitary vision is explicit in the poetry of Walt Whitman. In his poem 'Continuities', for example, we find a vision of cosmic immortality which goes beyond merely scientific truths, hinting even at some kind of religious idea:

> Nothing is ever really lost, or can be lost,
> No birth, identity, form – no object of the world.
> Nor life, nor force, nor any visible thing;
> Appearance must not foil, nor shifted sphere confuse
>   thy brain.
> Ample are time and space – ample the fields of Nature.
> The body, sluggish, aged, cold – the embers left from
>   earlier fires,
> The light in the eye grown dim, shall duly flame again;
> The sun now low in the west rises for mornings and for
>   noons continual;
> To frozen clods ever the spring's invisible law returns,
> With grass and flowers and summer fruits and corn.[44]

V

The ideas which form the basis of anonymous earthly immortality – that the death and dissolution of one's body is an integral part of the life cycle of the planet, that one's words and deeds continue to have effects into future generations, that individual lives find purpose within the ongoing march of humanity, and that the fact of our brief existence on Earth and within this universe can never be erased – are commonly affirmed as real consolations in the face of our otherwise personal extinction, and form important components in arguments for the meaning and dignity of our earthly existence.

The more such ideas are elaborated, however, the more difficult it is to differentiate them from ideas about otherworldly immortality. There are two respects in which this is so, one relating to the cultural sources of these ideas and the other to the metaphysical tendency to which any theorizing about the meaning of life and death is subject. Moreover, as emphasized in earlier chapters, there is no essential incompatibility between earthly and otherworldly forms of immortality. There is no contradiction in anticipating (or indeed in investing in) some kind of earthly afterlife, while at the same time believing in, or hoping for, an otherworldly afterlife.

It is hardly surprising that many of the ideas and practices concerning earthly immortality derive from, or depend upon, ideas and practices relating to otherworldly immortality. They do this in a way analogous to that in which the Victorians sought to add gravitas to important secular buildings by designing them in the style of cathedrals. Nor is it surprising that ideas and practices relating to an earthly afterlife tend to flourish in the spaces left by the decline of religious beliefs and practices, where they are presented not as mere surrogates for the latter but as rational alternatives and successors.

Some of these points can be illustrated by reference to the content of secular funeral services. In such services, while there are distinctive elements which affirm a secular as distinct from a religious outlook, some of the ideas and practices are borrowed from religious services. In these funerals, the main emphasis is on 'celebrating' the life of a unique and irreplaceable individual, on the fact that this person will live on in the memories of family and friends, and on the value of his or her contributions to the lives of others. They concentrate, that is, on the more personal forms of what I have called an earthly afterlife.

At the same time there is a reaching out towards something beyond the individual. One passage commonly used as a reading in humanist funerals comes from the writings of the poet and critic Herbert Read, whose favourite symbol was that of the tree of life:

> The death of each of us is in the order of things; it follows life as surely as night follows day. We can take the tree of life as a symbol. The human race is the trunk and branches of this tree, and individual men and women are the leaves which appear one season, flourish for a summer and then die. I too am like a leaf on this tree and one day I shall be torn off by a storm, or I shall simply decay and fall and mingle with the earth at its roots. But, while I live I am conscious of the tree's flowing sap and steadfast strength. Deep down in my consciousness is the consciousness of a collective life, a life of which I am a part and to which I make a minute but unique contribution. When I die and fall, the tree remains nourished to some small degree by my manifestation of life. Millions of leaves have preceded me and millions will follow me; but the tree itself grows and endures.[45]

Read was a romantic with atheist and humanist sympathies. His attitude was, according to one critic, 'essentially Wordsworthian',[46] and yet in Wordsworth's life and thought Read perceived what was to him the fundamental flaw of humanism, caught as it is between a tendency to affirm the infinity of the human mind and a tendency to emphasize humanity's subordination to nature. Read's own work, especially as an art critic, constantly impelled him to look for pattern and meaning in the realm of nature, for absolutes against which to measure human life and its achievements. The passage I have quoted suggests an act of faith of precisely the kind that, as a sceptical rationalist, he rejected. The more pertinent question here, however, is why the passage quoted is deemed so appropriate for humanist funerals. Do people find it consoling or illuminating because of – or despite – what might be called its 'transcendental' drift?

One can of course see why this elegantly written passage impresses, but what, if anything, does it amount to philosophically? Of what, exactly, is the 'tree of life' a symbol here? Surely it is not a symbol simply of nature's cycle of birth and death, or of nature's evolutionary course?

The suggestion is that behind the coming and going of individual lives, there exists something greater to which our human consciousness contributes and of which it is intuitively aware. Yet it is difficult to maintain this kind of language with any seriousness without escaping the pull of some kind of metaphysics – for example, the kinds of ideas associated with figures such as Bergson, Whitehead or Teilhard de Chardin, all of whom have a broadly religious view of the Universe. Traditions of literary rhetoric all too easily allow good observational natural history or biology to shift into something resembling a religiously or metaphysically informed cosmology.

These remarks apply most of all perhaps to the two most anonymous forms of earthly immortality – those I have called collective and cosmic immortality. In the case of collective immortality, a metaphysical and even mystical tendency is clearly present in what is surely a classic source for the idea of a collective immortality for humanity – namely, Hegelian Absolutism. Hegel's system embodies a critique of religion that is itself religious in some respects, so that it is difficult if not actually inappropriate to try to disentangle the religious from the secular elements. This fact is itself an important illustration of the impossibility of framing a vision of anonymous earthly immortality free of religious influence or metaphysical implication. Whether or not Hegel held any distinct view of a personal afterlife remains a matter of dispute among scholars, whose difficulty deciding whether the term *geist* in Hegel's writings should be rendered as 'spirit' or as 'mind' is further testimony to the ambiguity we find in these writings. What is more important, however, is that Hegel clearly regarded the collective immortality guaranteed for humanity in and through the evolving manifestations of the World Spirit as of greater significance than any personal immortality.

In Hegel the ephemeral individual can be regarded as an abstraction from the concrete and ever-present reality of Absolute Mind or Spirit. But while the elements of Hegel's system may thus work against the idea of a personal immortality, what his system equally works against is the idea that individual lives have no meaning or come to nothing. In the historical dialectic between spirit and matter, individuals live on within the onward progress of humankind. As expressions of, or vehicles for, the self-affirming Spirit, individuals can be said to be aware of the eternity of the Spirit they represent while not being themselves eternal or immortal entities. The dark side of this (arguably) optimistic vision, however, is its tendency to encourage others to see individuals as merely means to an end rather than as ends in themselves.

There are echoes of the Hegelian view of collective immortality not only, and most obviously, in Marx and Russell, but in philosophical or theological ideas of the kind already seen in the work of Mark Johnston. The key point, again, is that it is difficult if not impossible to present ideas about an anonymous human immortality without invoking or drawing upon metaphysical if not explicitly religious ideas. Not only this, but such ideas are also liable to follow familiar religious paradigms. In the case of Johnston's vision of our anonymous survival within the ongoing rush of humanity, it is difficult not to see a dependence on (or reversion to) the very kind of religious ideas to which this vision is ostensibly opposed. Johnston presents us with the possibility of a kind of secular redemption – one that takes place before death rather than after it; and yet for the vast majority of human beings the level of selfless altruism or agape required for such redemption is impossibly high. In fact Johnston's idea of redemption through anonymous immortality admits of degrees. Only the relatively few whose wills are perfectly or thoroughly good can be redeemed as full participants in the future of humanity. By contrast, those who are thoroughly self-centred will fail to have any place within the future of humanity, and thus will be lost forever. For these, 'the obliteration of their individual personalities is the obliteration of everything of real importance to them.'[47] What can be reasonably expected by most people, however, is that they will live lives good enough to allow them to see beyond their own deaths to the future flourishing of others.

Now where have we come across this kind of thing before? Most obviously we meet it in those religious eschatologies which separate the dead into the saved and the damned. There are closer parallels still with those systems which recognized different degrees of moral perfection, such as the Manichaean system to which the young St Augustine was so attracted, or the Cathar heresy which spread throughout parts of medieval Europe. Johnston's version of redemption through anonymous immortality could be described as a semi-secular eschatology, combining as it does a Buddhist theory of human selfhood with a demythologized notion of God (or the 'Highest One') as the benign 'self-disclosure of Existence itself', of which we ourselves are individual and temporary expressions. In arguing that it is through the persistence of our beneficent dispositions rather than as separate substantial selves that we survive into humanity's future, Johnston seems to want to eat his cake and and yet have it. Why not rest content with the more modest kind of impersonal anonymous immortality I defined earlier on as diffusive immortality?

The rhetoric of trans-individual survival also applies in the case of the form of anonymous immortality I called cosmic immortality, although arguably – as Pascal's famous thoughts bear witness – it is more of a challenge to find either meaning or consolation in contemplating the immensity of the universe or the relentless nature of the laws of physics.

> When I consider the short duration of my life, swallowed up in the eternity before and after, the little space which I fill and even can see, engulfed in the infinite immensity of spaces of which I am ignorant and which know me not, I am frightened and am astonished at being here rather than there; for there is no reason why here rather than there, why now rather than then. Who has put me here? By whose order and direction have this place and time been allotted to me?[48]

Earlier on, I quoted a passage illustrating the 'stardust philosophy' to which the writing of some physicists and cosmologists is prone. Similar passages have also become resources for readings at secular funerals. One such passage comes from the physicist Brian Cox:

> Our story is the story of the Universe. Every piece of everyone and everything you love, of everything you hate, of everything you hold precious was assembled in the first few minutes of the life of the Universe, and transformed in the hearts of stars, or created in their fiery deaths. When you die, those pieces will be returned to the Universe in the endless cycle of death and rebirth. What a wonderful thing to be part of that Universe. And what a story. What a majestic story![49]

Once again we have a reference to the endless cycle of death and rebirth, but no explanation of why this fact should be comforting to people, and in particular to people whose loved ones have died. While no symbol equivalent to that of the 'tree of life' is deployed in this passage, the universe is described as having, if not being, a 'story' – a 'majestic story'. But no real justification is given for viewing the universe in this way, or for saying that being a part of this universe is such a 'wonderful thing'. These kinds of statements seem vulnerable to the same kinds of criticisms made against people who claim to have discovered religious meaning or a divine presence in the universe: namely, that they are like those who see faces in the clouds which are not really there.[50] They are certainly far removed from Hamlet's or Larkin's gloomy observations about our posthumous future in the universe.

The more important question here, however, is whether those confronting death – whether their own death or that of another – do indeed find comfort or meaning in statements about death being part of the order of nature. It is possible that some people feel that they ought to be deriving consolation from such statements when in fact they do not, or that whatever kind or degree of consolation they do derive does not address their deepest needs. It may well be thought that such statements refer more to the 'problem' than to its 'solution'. One person, contributing to an online forum on the anniversary of a friend's death and identifying herself as an 'atheist and scientist', questions the adequacy of Cox's words in the passage quoted above. She finds some solace in Cox's words – yet, somehow, these words are not enough.

> When I think of my friend, I feel that the matter and energy from which his body was constructed was not him, any more than a story is the paper and ink of the book containing it.
>
> It seems more relevant to me, if we are to address the issue from a scientific viewpoint, to think about the fate of the information content my friend encapsulated in his mind rather than the matter and energy content of his body. His identity lay more in the complex pattern of his consciousness – in his story rather than his paper and ink. Did that pattern of information just cease to be?[51]

These comments remind us, first, of the importance of consolation, whatever one's religious beliefs or lack of them; and, second, that consolation is not always separate from the desire for (or the belief in) some kind of earthly immortality. In this particular case, the bereaved person is indicating that deeper consolation would come from knowing that the information closely associated with the deceased's identity as a conscious individual had been preserved in some way. Of course, some forms of consolation have nothing to do with either earthly or otherworldly immortality. For example, bereaved people often derive consolation from knowing (or believing) that the deceased suffered no pain in dying, or that whatever pain they did suffer is now over.

For some people there can be no consolation without representation, so to speak; that is, only if a deceased person's attributes or achievements remain accessible to future generations can that person truly be the subject of an earthly afterlife capable of consoling and inspiring others. For other people, however, posthumous personhood offers diminishing returns, so that what little survives of a person serves only to remind one of all that has been irrevocably lost. For those who think this way, the paradoxical idea of an anonymous immortality may offer greater consolation when thinking about the legacy of deceased persons.

A more radical alternative, however, is not to look for consolation of any kind, whether in an earthly or an otherworldly afterlife, but rather to accept, and even celebrate, the essentially finite nature of a human life. In the next chapter I consider the position of those for whom 'doing without an afterlife' constitutes the most honest and realistic strategy for managing mortality.

FIVE

DOING WITHOUT AN AFTERLIFE?

... Earth's the right place for love:
I don't know where it's likely to go better.
I'd like to go by climbing a birch tree,
And climb black branches up a snow-white trunk
Toward heaven, till the tree could bear no more,
But dipped its top and set me down again.
ROBERT FROST[1]

I

One of the ways in which people come to terms with mortality – whether their own or that of others – is through the belief, or hope, that in some way the dead live on after death. They may live on literally, either by continuing their existence in an otherworldly afterlife, or by being reborn into another life on Earth. Quite apart from this, however, the dead can also 'live on' as subjects of the kinds of earthly afterlife, personal or anonymous, discussed in the two preceding chapters. Such beliefs, or hopes, not only give consolation to the bereaved, but help people find meaning in their present lives. If the stories of our lives continue after death, or form part of some larger story, then perhaps our lives are not as accidental or as meaningless as they might otherwise appear to be.

But finding meaning and purpose in one's present life does not necessarily depend on the prospect of an afterlife. Relatively few of the people who believe that their lives will end in personal extinction find life either meaningless or tragic. Living one's life without the prospect of an afterlife is for many people more a matter of regret than despair. The various strategies for 'managing mortality' can do much to soften the regret. Thus one can determine to make the most of this life while it lasts, keeping all thoughts of death at bay; or, by familiarizing oneself with death, one can so 'domesticate' it that it loses its power to frighten or disturb. Such strategies may also be deployed by those who do not believe that life ends in personal extinction, but who are nevertheless fearful about, or regretful of, its ending. In so far as death is accepted as an opposing or limiting reality, these attitudes and strategies remain essentially negative ones. Doing without an afterlife is, in this sense, doing without something we should nevertheless prefer not to have to do without. It is like learning to live alone when ideally one would like to be living with others.

But there are other, seemingly more positive ways of 'doing without an afterlife'. It is possible to see life as enjoyable and fulfilling because of, rather than despite, its mortal nature. For those who take this view, the idea of an afterlife is either redundant, or else is a positive hindrance to the authentic living of one's life; anticipating, or trusting in, an afterlife in order to give one's life meaning and purpose can only detract from the full and proper living of it. One can find meaning and purpose in life from within one's own experience of life. The idea that one's present life can only be fulfilled by, or in, some kind of afterlife represents not just an inability to accept the fact of human mortality but a failure to enjoy and value human life on its own terms. These criticisms apply as much to conceptions of an 'earthly' afterlife as they do to conceptions of an 'otherworldly' one. Living one's life with an eye to posterity makes life go no better, to use Robert Frost's phrase, than living it with an eye to heaven.

The intellectual and existential strategies of those who live or seek to live without regard to an afterlife are not necessarily linked with a secular worldview. Doing without an afterlife could mean living one's life on the assumption that there is no afterlife (or at least no afterlife worth waiting for). Or it could mean living one's life on the assumption that the idea of an afterlife makes no sense, or living it with complete indifference to the question of an afterlife. But it could also mean living one's life independently of any concern with an afterlife rather than independently of any belief in one. This means that religious as well as non-religious (or anti-religious) people could live their lives doing without an afterlife.

II

As I have said, there are both negative and positive ways of doing without an afterlife. The difference between them could be represented as the difference between saying 'this life is all we have' and saying 'this life is all we need'. The difference here is a real but not necessarily a

simple one. In the first case, a negative insight can nevertheless call
forth a positive response: this life is all we have, so let us make the most
of it. To say that we should make the most of the one life that we have
sounds both positive and optimistic, and yet it is an attitude typically
informed by regret, and sometimes fear – regret that human life is
finite, and perhaps also fear lest it end sooner than we might expect.
Death is seen as a limiting boundary, an ever-present danger, a harm
to which all must sooner or later succumb. By contrast, to say that the
one life we have is the only kind of life that we need, and even that
its finite and fragile nature are essential to what makes it fulfilling (or
potentially fulfilling), implies that death is an enabling rather than a
limiting boundary, and mortality an essential property of life itself. This
second way of living life appears, or at least aspires, to make all thoughts
of an afterlife redundant. I shall call these two ways of doing without
an afterlife the 'quantitative' and the 'qualitative' ways respectively.

The quantitative approach to living without an afterlife calls forth
an attitude often described under the rubric of *carpe diem* (literally
'seize the day'), a phrase which first appears in an ode by the Latin
writer Horace: '. . . Be wise, strain your wine; and since life is brief, /
prune back your long-term hopes. Even while we speak, envious time
/ flies by: so seize the day, trusting as little as possible to the future.'[2]
Making the most of life while it lasts can mean either pursuing life's
pleasures to the full, or devoting oneself assiduously to more serious
tasks, though these two things are by no means mutually exclusive. It
does not exclusively suggest excess or irresponsibility. If anything, the
vinicultural reference in Horace's poem suggests prudent management
rather than self-indulgent hedonism.[3]

Similar recommendations – to enjoy life's pleasures or to dedicate
oneself to one's work – appear in several biblical texts, where their
import is more secular than religious. 'Let us eat and drink; for tomorrow we shall die' (Isaiah 22:13).[4] 'Then I commended mirth, because a
man hath no better thing under the sun, than to eat, and to drink, and
to be merry' (Ecclesiastes 8:15). 'Whatever your hand finds to do, do it
with all your might, for in the realm of the dead, where you are going,
there is neither working nor planning nor knowledge nor wisdom'
(Ecclesiastes 9:10).

The encouragement to make the most of what life has to offer
before it is too late is also familiar as part of the strategy of the
ardent lover, at least in literature. Thus Andrew Marvell presses his

'coy mistress' not to delay in consummating their love, since with the passage of time

> Thy beauty shall no more be found;
> Nor, in thy marble vault, shall sound
> My echoing song; then worms shall try
> That long-preserved virginity,
> And your quaint honour turn to dust,
> And into ashes all my lust;
> The grave's a fine and private place,
> But none, I think, do there embrace.
>
> Now therefore, while the youthful hue
> Sits on thy skin like morning dew,
> And while thy willing soul transpires
> At every pore with instant fires,
> Now let us sport us while we may,
> And now, like amorous birds of prey,
> Rather at once our time devour
> Than languish in his slow-chapped power.[5]

One can also see, in this and in similar poems, how from an aware-ness of the destructive passage of time a more negative attitude might emerge, one that by dwelling on the fact of mortality tends to inhibit rather than enhance the living of a full life. This attitude, that of *timor mortis* (fear of death),[6] is the melancholy and sometimes morbid cousin of *carpe diem*, which perceives the shadow of death everywhere, and at its worst leads to debilitating states of depression. It is a common trap for those experiencing bereavement, and also for certain kinds of religious temperament, especially in traditions which lay emphasis on sinfulness and death. Although often associated with particular strains of religiosity, however, the attitude of *timor mortis* is just as likely to express itself in purely secular terms.

As a practical adage, the principle of *carpe diem* seems an eminently sensible one, as difficult to argue with as with the recommendation that one should 'strike while the iron is hot' or 'make hay while the sun shines'.[7] One has only to consider what appears to be its oppos-ite number – the habit of procrastination, well described by the poet Edward Young as 'the thief of time'.[8] Why should one ever hesitate to 'seize the moment'? One answer, perhaps, is that *carpe diem* evinces an essentially materialistic view of life, all too easily becoming an excuse for impatience, greed and self-indulgence. In any case, whatever positive motives or consequences may be associated with *carpe diem*, these are not to be confused with the second approach to living without an afterlife – the qualitative approach.

The qualitative approach, which views the present life as providing all that we need to be completely fulfilled, might also be characterized as the 'plenty is plenty' position. The finitude of human life is to be valued and even celebrated as a good in itself, not as something that requires extension, renewal or substitution of any kind. One life is more than enough if we know how to use and enjoy it; and those who do not know how to use and enjoy it will not benefit from having more of the same. Those who take this approach lead their lives neither anticipating an afterlife nor regretting the absence of one. They neither hear, nor indeed listen out for, 'time's winged chariot'. Rather, one might say, they are actually riding the chariot.

The 'plenty is plenty' position, it should be noted, has its negative counterpart in what can be called the 'enough is enough' position. This is the approach taken by people whose indifference to an afterlife expresses world-weariness, or a sense of life's meaninglessness or worthlessness, or in extreme cases self-hatred. Or it is the position of those who share the Wordsworthian lament that 'the world is too much with us'. None of this is to be confused with 'otherworldliness' or with impatience for another life, which if anything are examples of living *with* or *for* an afterlife.

According to the philosopher John Stuart Mill, were it not for the unhappy circumstances of their present lives that make the prospect of a life hereafter so alluring, people could 'easily reconcile themselves' to the idea of annihilation 'and even consider it as a good':

> it is no unnatural part of the idea of a happy life, that life itself be laid down, after the best that it can give has been fully enjoyed through a long lapse of time; when all its pleasures, even those of benevolence, are familiar, and nothing untasted and unknown is left to stimulate curiosity and keep up the desire of prolonged existence. It seems to me not only possible but probable, that in a higher, and, above all, a happier condition of human life, not annihilation but immortality may be the

burdensome idea; and that human nature, though pleased with the present, and by no means impatient to quit it, would find comfort and not sadness in the thought that it is not chained through eternity to a conscious existence which it cannot be assured that it will always wish to preserve.[9]

This passage reminds us that many of the arguments that human beings are better off without the prospect of an afterlife will be identical to the arguments (considered in Chapter Two) that human beings would not find greater happiness or fulfilment in the indefinite prolongation of their earthly lives.

There are two variations on the theme that, in a human life of finite duration, 'plenty is plenty'. These I shall call the 'more is less' and the 'less is more' variations. This first of these puts the quality of life above its mere duration. Thus the normal span of human life can be regarded as more than adequate for one's individual fulfilment – though this does mean, of course, that a life cut short would still tend to be regarded as a tragic loss or a waste of life. As to what would count as a 'normal span', there may well be significant cultural or historical variations on the biblical 'threescore years and ten'.[10] But such variation hardly affects the main point, which is that individuals know at the start of their (adult) lives that they have, as it were, a limited canvas on which to paint their lives. Representing life as a work of art, or alternatively as a story, emphasizes the fact that a life reaches a point where it can be regarded as complete, or as complete as it ever will be. (In the case of a life cut short, one would lament not so much its brevity as the fact that it was incomplete.) Or one might invoke the image of a cup being filled to the brim: to add more liquid would simply be to spoil the whole.[11] What these metaphors suggest is the idea that a human life, to be good and fulfilling, must have some kind of shape or structure.

Whereas the 'more is less' variation on 'plenty is plenty' emphasizes the shape or trajectory of human life, the 'less is more' variation emphasizes the brevity of human life as its principal virtue, turning on its head the idea (associated particularly with *carpe diem*) that brevity is human life's fundamental weakness. The point here is that the brevity, and associated fragility, of human life are what give this life its intensity, beauty and value in the first place, without reference to how long or short each individual life actually turns out to be. It suggests that one's enjoyment of life will only be compromised by nourishing the hope of its indefinite continuation, whether on Earth or in some otherworldly state. Moreover, one's very awareness that this life is unique and unrepeatable is an essential part of one's sense of life's richness and value. Even someone who dies in childhood or in early youth will not necessarily be regarded as having led a life any poorer, or less meaningful, than that of someone who lives into their nineties or beyond. Indeed a life cut short might well be an acceptable price to pay for a life lived intensely or a life lost in the pursuit of some valued project or activity. Towards the end of an intellectually rich and politically eventful life, the English politician Enoch Powell (1912–1998) was asked what his greatest regret was. He replied that he would like to have died in the War.[12] This was not just the expression of the guilt sometimes felt by the survivors of combat. What Powell seems to have meant was that, given the inevitability of death and the disappointments life brings, dying for a good cause in the prime of life would somehow have completed or validated his life. As one commentator observes:

> During the Second World War his own experience of utter certainty chimed with that of his comrades. There was no controversy, no disappointment, only the knowledge that they were all doing the right thing. And not only that, but they were young. And the young have not the fear of death that many of the old possess.[13]

If it is not the length or persistence of a life that gives it its value or meaning, but rather something we do or complete at any point within this life, then perhaps it would make rational sense for a person to be ready for life to end, and even willing to take steps to bring it to an end. This one might wish for the ending of one's life after achieving some particular goal (for example, climbing a mountain, defeating an enemy or seeing one's children grown up). We do sometimes say, by way of consolation, that a person has died doing something he or she loved, or that a person 'would have wanted to go that way'. Strictly speaking, this need not be anything noble or ambitious, so that there could be a certain logic to the slogan we see on the side of the Bercovicz & Co. hearse in Sergio Leone's cinematic epic *Once Upon a Time in America* (1984): 'Why go on living when we can bury you for $49.50?' On the other hand, it might also be argued that the possibility of an even greater achievement coming one's way is sufficient reason never to think one is quitting while one is ahead – there may be another mountain to climb, a greater enemy to be defeated and so on. There might even be a better funeral plan if one were to wait.

It is easy enough to describe particular lives as too brief, or as cut short before their time. But by what standard could a normal human life be regarded as brief or judged to be too brief? In ancient times those bemoaning the alleged brevity of human life may have thought in terms of the cruel or arbitrary decrees of fate; or may have had in mind the contrast with the life of immortal beings such as the gods. The Roman philosopher Seneca the Younger observes that most of mankind (including certain philosophers who should know better) 'complains about nature's meanness, because our allotted span of life is so short, and because this stretch of time that is given to us runs its course so quickly, so rapidly – so much so that, with very few exceptions, life leaves the rest of us in the lurch just when we're getting ready to live'. According to Seneca, however, this belief is a misperception:

> It's not that we have a short time to live, but that we waste much of it. Life is long enough, and it's been given to us in generous measure for accomplishing the greatest things, if the whole of it is well invested. But when life is squandered through soft and careless living, and when it's spent on no worthwhile pursuit, death finally presses and we realize that the life which we didn't notice passing has passed away. So it is: the life we are given isn't short but we make it so; we're not ill provided but we are wasteful of life.[14]

In other words, there is plenty of time for a fulfilling life if one is willing to live it in the right spirit.

What is common to both variations on the theme of 'plenty is plenty' is that any investment in, or hope of, some kind of afterlife, whether earthly or otherworldly, reveals itself as a failure of nerve on the part of finite mortal beings. It is not denied, of course, that deceased human beings become the subjects of an 'earthly afterlife', in the ways described in earlier chapters. The 'plenty is plenty' position is not at odds with developing and cherishing those things that contribute to one's earthly afterlife. On the contrary, it is right that people should derive satisfaction from having children; or that they should hope that whatever is good in their own life will benefit others in the future. But what the prospect of an earthly afterlife should not become is a means either of justifying or of seeking to extend one's present life. Attention to an earthly afterlife only becomes negative where it is symptomatic of a refusal to accept the value or sufficiency of this present life. Within the perspective of the 'plenty is plenty' position, the main value of an earthly afterlife lies in its testimony to a person's unique earthly life having been lived well.

One crucial difference between the quantitative and qualitative approaches to doing without an afterlife concerns their relationship to a religious view of the world. Both approaches are clearly compatible with secular worldviews, and as such are commonly endorsed in secular contexts. But only the quantitative approach is secular by definition, and by the same token subject to critique within various religious contexts. Its nearest equivalent in religious contexts would be the preparatory approach to life: the strategy of making the best of one's life in order to be ready for death when it comes and for what may follow death. Even in religious contexts, however, the strategy of *carpe diem* will often have a secular rather than a religious import. For instance, the post-mortem destiny envisaged for humankind in many cultures of the ancient world was, for all and sundry, of such a bleak character that in effect one's earthly life was all there was, and hence was something to be enjoyed as fully as possible before one entered the gloomy underworld.

The qualitative approach, by contrast, is found in religious and secular contexts alike. It does not entail the non-existence, or indeed the non-importance, of an afterlife. In other words, it is possible to live one's life doing without the afterlife that will nevertheless succeed one's death. There is no paradox here. Consider, as a rough parallel, the difference between those persons who engage in a particular action in order to win admiration or gain social approval – a particular sporting activity, for example – and those who engage in the same action for its own sake (even though they know that they may also win admiration and approval).[15] What doing without an afterlife implies in the case of the qualitative approach is not the denial or rejection of an afterlife, but the rejection of certain ways of relating to this idea. And the same applies to an earthly as to an otherworldy afterlife. Seneca, for example, bemoans the way in which some people spend so much time and energy cultivating a post-mortem legacy that they fail to enjoy their present lives:

So, when you see a man repeatedly taking up the robe of office, or a name well known in public, don't envy him: those trappings are bought at the cost of life. For one year to be dated by their name, they'll waste all their own years. Life deserts some of them amid their first struggles, before the arduous climb up to the peak of their ambition. Some, after they've clambered up through a thousand indignities to arrive at the crowning dignity, are assailed by the wretched thought that all their toil has been for an inscription on an epitaph.[16]

There is no shortage of advice, within secular and religious sources alike, regarding how one should live without an afterlife. In the ancient world, the writings of the Stoics, Epicureans and others provide much practical wisdom on this score. In his *Meditations*, Marcus Aurelius states that 'Perfection of character is this: to live each day as if it were your last, without frenzy, without apathy, without pretence.' If the advice to live each day as if it were one's last could be said to represent the 'quantitative' position, then what might correspondingly represent the 'qualitative' position could be the advice to live each day as if it were one's first, with the kind of freshness and wonder that so many poets have expressed in their work.

Another way of describing this second outlook is in terms of living 'in the present' or 'in the present moment'. The ability to live one's life fully within the present moment is a natural function of the human mind; but it is one that is easily frustrated by the many practical and intellectual demands of human life. For this ability to become habitual requires practice. As such, living in the present moment has been a key feature of some of the world's meditation systems, and perhaps the clearest example of it is to be found in the Buddhist practice of mindfulness. Mindfulness is developed through the insight (*vipassanā*) techniques which constitute one of the two constituents of Buddhist meditation, the other being the concentrative, mind-calming techniques (*samatha*). While *samatha* techniques are used to produce successive stages of mental calm and one-pointed concentration, the analytical *vipassanā* techniques are used to cultivate a non-grasping awareness of what is happening within one and around one in the present moment. These techniques exploit the natural ability of one part of one's mind to 'stand apart' and monitor the rest of what one is feeling and perceiving. In the Buddhist system, mindfulness is exhaustively applied to four different aspects of one's life – bodily condition (one's movements, for example), feelings and sensations, states of mind, and ideas. For example: 'Here, O bhikkhus, a bhikkhu when experiencing a pleasant feeling, understands: "I experience a pleasant feeling"; when experiencing a painful feeling, he understands: "I experience a painful feeling"; when experiencing a neither-pleasant-nor-painful feeling, he understands: "I experience a neither-pleasant-nor-painful feeling."'[17]

Although mindfulness is cultivated through specific kinds of exercise, their cumulative effect is to create an overall habit of mindfulness, with a concomitant falling away of one's anxieties about past or future. One can, nevertheless, also apply mindfulness to one's thoughts (including one's anxieties) about past or future. Indeed the virtue of the *vipassanā* (unlike the *samatha*) techniques is that nothing can ever interrupt them, since whatever intrudes into consciousness becomes potential material for mindfulness. While mindfulness techniques can be tailored to a purely secular outlook, within their original context they serve the Buddhist goal of realizing the 'cool' and enlightened state of *nibbāna*. Meditative techniques broadly similar to mindfulness exist in other traditions, including theistic traditions, though in the latter the focus on the present moment will have a specifically 'religious' purpose: for example, to maintain awareness of the divine presence in everything one does, or to pursue one's daily tasks in conformity with the will of God.[18]

Meditative techniques of living in the present moment tend to promote the view that 'religious ultimate' (however this might be conceived, whether as union with God, *nibbāna* and so on) is an already present reality or a state of being potentially realizable here and now, rather than as some future goal or distant reality. This approach is especially important in the Mahayana traditions of Buddhism. A similar idea in Christian theology is the notion of 'realized eschatology', according to which the 'Kingdom of God' is to be understood not as some indefinitely deferred future event but as a present or at least 'inaugurated' reality: not a state which Christians should hope to attain in the future, but rather a state to which they should be bearing witness to here and now. Those who follow a religion in this way could be said to be living without an afterlife at least to the extent that the afterlife is not conceived as a reality which is ahead of, or other than, one's present life, and hence not as something which overshadows or challenges this life.

It is a feature of some modern, secularizing theology that the lack or loss of faith in the possibility of an otherworldly afterlife leads to a kind of bravado in the face of mortality that does not necessarily reflect a true contentment in the face of mortality. It may indeed smack of disillusion and even a kind of panic. Thus Don Cupitt, in his book *The Fountain*,[19] urges us to abandon the 'old metaphysics of substance' (God, soul, afterlife, and so on) and 'instead be content with our own passing lives'.

> We come to pass, and we pass away. That's it. That's all. We are already in the last world we will ever know, as I believe most people nowadays recognise. We should therefore move on from the kind of outlook that persuades us to spend all our lives preparing for another life beyond this one. We are there already![20]

In explicating his views, Cupitt employs the symbol of 'the fountain', which unlike Russell's essentially historical image of the 'stream of life', represents not merely the onward flow of human history but the contingent flux of existence as such:

> Whether in a city square or in a garden, the Fountain is a focal symbol, sited at a point where many ways meet. As an object it is all foaming transience; but it is surprisingly calm and peaceful to contemplate. It is living water, a symbol of life's ceaseless self-renewal. It is associated with healing and repose. Although it is only a symbol, and there is nothing metaphysical about it, perhaps it may be able to do for us some of the things that God used to do?[21]

Cupitt believes that the fountain, as a symbol of life's ceaseless self-renewal, helps reconcile us to our own complete immersion in time and contingency, and hence to our inevitable mortality. We cannot escape (and should not want to escape) from our utterly transient existence, in which we can get 'so immersed . . . that we get a blissful intuition of the eternal in the very midst of life'.[22] There is no other world to strive for but the one we already inhabit. Cupitt describes this vision of things as a 'mysticism of contingency'.[23] We should ourselves be like fountains; 'we should live by self-giving love . . . by self-outing, pouring ourselves out and passing away all the time.'[24] Cupitt is not interested in how we might 'live on' through what we contribute to the future, but rather in how we can 'live in' the one and only time available to us – the present.

An arguably more profound expression of a religious ideal of living without an afterlife is to be found in the writings of Simone Weil.[25] It is one that brings out a feature of the qualitative position I have not yet specifically addressed, namely the role of death (or of the awareness of death) in enabling rather than threatening what is worthwhile about our lives. In the quantitative approach to living without an afterlife, death is the ever-present (or ever-imagined) opponent of one's joy in living, though paradoxically it may serve to sharpen one's senses just as other dangers tend to do. In the qualitative approach to living without an afterlife, by contrast, death and mortality are what give life its shape and its meaning. Weil's point is that it is death, and not the prospect of an afterlife, that does this. If anything, the prospect (belief, hope, expectation, and so on) of an afterlife serves to rob death of its usefulness. More specifically, a belief in immortality is harmful because it undermines the practical usefulness of death in turning us away from our habitually strong orientation to the future. Where we are strongly oriented to the future we tend to neglect the present, and yet the present is the only place where we can engage with others (and even with God, in the case of religion). In this respect the afterlife, or rather our interest in the afterlife as a future destiny, is as much of a distraction from the present as any earthly future we might imagine or worry about – indeed, it is more of a distraction in so far as it encourages in us an endless deferring of our need to realize, here and now, who we are and what we must do. It is almost as if Weil is substituting for the activating principle of *carpe diem* the activating principle of *carpe mortem*.

Their common emphasis on the here and now suggests that in many cases there may be little difference between the quantitative and the qualitative approaches to living without an afterlife. How, for instance, would one categorize the experience or attitude of an artist absorbed in the completion of a painting? How would one know whether this absorption represented a quantitative or a qualitative view of life? Even so, the worldviews that tend to be associated with each of them suggest potentially important differences between the two approaches. If the quantitative approach were to be characterized as a living *for* the moment, the qualitative approach would be characterized as a living *in* the moment.[26] What living in the moment means in practical terms is giving full and undivided attention to one's present activity or experience. In some cases this will entail looking back to the past or forward to the future. In some cases it may mean keeping death in mind. Only where one's anxieties about past or future actually distract one from being grounded in the present, however, will one fall victim to time, rather than becoming master of it. Mastering time in this way suggests an experiencing of immortality in the present moment reminiscent of William Blake's famous lines:

To see a World in a Grain of Sand
And a Heaven in a Wild Flower,
Hold Infinity in the palm of your hand
And Eternity in an hour.[27]

III

It is now time to look more critically at the attitudes and strategies I have characterized in terms of 'doing without an afterlife'. To begin with, it is worth reiterating what living *with* an afterlife can mean. It can mean, variously, living one's life constantly aware of a future post-mortem judgement (such awareness often causing fear or anxiety); living one's life in such a way as to secure, as one might hope or believe, a happy existence in the next world or in another life; or living one's life in the belief that this life only makes full sense *sub specie aeternitatis*, in the context of a wider-than-earthly existence. In the case of an earthly afterlife, living with an afterlife could mean living one's earthly life with an eye to what people might think of one after one is dead, or with a view to what one might *want* (or not want) people to think of one after death.

In contrast to such conditional and potentially conflicted ways of living one's life, living *without* an afterlife may well seem both a simpler and a healthier strategy, and this is indeed one justification put forward by those professing or aspiring to live in this way. Is it not better to live one's life purely 'on its own terms', without reference to something beyond its boundaries, and even without reference to the past or future within these boundaries? It is of course a central element in the humanist critique of religion that people mortgage their lives to an afterlife that will never come. There are various ethical positions on how this life should be lived on the assumption that it is neither preceded nor followed by any other kind of existence, and strategies such as *carpe diem* will be evaluated accordingly. The same must apply to decisions as to whether this life is worth living at all, including (in the case of those suffering extreme mental or physical pain) whether it is worth going on living rather than deciding to end one's life.

It is not self-evident what the most rational strategy should be for those for whom this life is the only life there is. It is certainly not obvious that those who do take this view apply the strategy of *carpe diem* as consistently or as intensively as they might be expected to do. Most people do not act as if they are under the sentence of death, even when they are diagnosed with a terminal illness. They still let time slip by, watch their spending, concern themselves with life's daily trivialities, worry about future events in which they will have no part, and so on. We might say that the default position for most human beings, including those who know that they are coming to the end of their lives, is to live life as if there were plenty of tomorrows.

Failure to live by one's philosophy of life does not bring that philosophy itself into question. The position of those who claim to be doing without an afterlife will be judged authentic or inauthentic in accordance with the soundness of its underlying assumptions and the nature of the consequences to which it leads. In this respect, the quantitative approach to living without an afterlife is clearly open to criticism on two fronts. In the first place, its presumption concerning the non-existence of an afterlife leaves it open to the charge of dogmatism. It is weakened by even the smallest chance of this presumption being wrong, since its entire rationale depends on it being right: it is a response, or reaction, to the 'fact' that this life is all there is. In the second place, there is a potential utilitarian critique should any of one's quantitative responses to the brevity of life lead to consequences in conflict with the aim of these responses. A simple example would be the suffering brought upon oneself and others through any kind of self-indulgence: 'eat, drink and be merry, and tomorrow you may die prematurely.' Such unforeseen or unintended consequences would also spill over into one's earthly afterlife, this being the sum of how we continue to influence and be remembered by others after we have gone. In short, a hedonistic (or otherwise self-centred) lifestyle might on the one hand compromise one's happiness in the next world (or future incarnation), and on the other hand cause oneself and others unhappiness in this life (and in consequence be part of one's earthly afterlife).

The crucial question here, therefore, is whether a quantitative approach to living without an afterlife could ever achieve its aims without creating collateral damage to others, or indeed even be a coherent strategy. The answer may well be that such an approach could only work coherently if one's strategy were non-hedonistic in its aims, though even those who devote their lives to worthy pursuits or causes may well find that in retrospect, as they near what they must regard as their own personal extinction, all their achievements may seem insubstantial. What one has really accomplished in one's life, or how much of the good one had intended has really been achieved, are questions that most thoughtful people will ask themselves at or towards the end of their lives.

Turning now to the qualitative approach, the first thing to be noted is that this 'plenty is plenty' approach to living one's life is not hampered by any dogmatism concerning the existence or non-existence of an otherworldly afterlife. It is an approach to living without an afterlife that is compatible with either a religious or a secular worldview. In fact, in regard to any kind of afterlife, whether otherworldly or earthly, its watchword might well be: 'Look after this present life, and any next life will look after itself.' Yet this assertion surely exposes a possible flaw in the idea of treating what goes on in any discrete period of time without reference to what might follow it (or for that matter to what might have preceded it). Consider, as a parallel example, the statement: 'Look after childhood, and adulthood will look after itself.' One should certainly keep in mind the case of children so anxious to grow up (or whose parents are so anxious for them to grow up) that they not only miss out on their childhood but possibly ruin their adulthood too. But would leading a life focused mainly on the present (not necessarily the present moment in the narrowest sense) really constitute a fulfilling modus vivendi? Are we not on the one hand forward-looking, future-oriented beings, and on the other hand beings not merely fascinated by the origins and causes of things, but actually rooted in and defined by the past?

It is certainly true that we can be so distracted by what might happen to us in the future, or by what has happened to us in the past, that we neglect both our enjoyment of, and our responsibilities within, the present. Yet is it not possible to make exactly the reverse criticism

– to criticize people for being so absorbed in the present that they neglect their relationship to the past and their responsibility for the future (for example, their duty to understand or learn from the past, or their duty to plan or make provision for the future)? In other words, living with the past and for the future are not merely part of what creates the richness of our lives in the present; they are part of what it means to be a rational, responsible human being in the first place. It can, of course, be argued that the 'plenty is plenty' position does not deny or belittle the past or future orientations of human life, and yet its tendency is to see dwelling on past or future as a betrayal of the richness of what is given in the present. It also underestimates the need people have to find meaning beyond their present lives, or to ground the meaning they do find in their lives in some wider perspective.

A more serious criticism of the qualitative approach, however, is that it tends to make idols both of the finitude of life and of the role of death in bringing life to an end. Let us deal first with the issue of life's finitude. The basis of the qualitative approach is that life should be lived on its own terms, namely as something that has an end as well as a beginning; meaning and fulfilment in human life come from accepting its natural boundaries. A life worth living must have, and must be seen to have, an end. There is, however, nothing about life, and in particular about our experience of life, that makes it essentially or inevitably finite. There is nothing illogical about the idea of a life going on forever. We know that earthly lives do in fact come to an end, and all too soon; but we can at least imagine an earthly life that goes on for centuries, if not forever. Such imagining is undoubtedly important for those who accept the idea of an afterlife, which if it is to be imagined at all can only be imagined in earthly and temporal terms.

For the 'less is more' version of the qualitative approach, what makes life so rich and special is the brevity of life rather than its finitude. And here we have to consider carefully what calling life brief adds to calling it finite. Surely only individual lives can be judged brief or lengthy, not human life as such. Individual lives are judged brief or lengthy by reference to some kind of 'normal' or 'average' lifespan. Moreover, this standard by which we judge a life to be brief or lengthy is itself subject to change. Instead of the biblical three score years and ten, why not four or five or six score years and ten? It would seem arbitrary to place limits on the possible or potential length of a human life – or on the ideal length a life should have if it is to be lived to the full. Human life can only be judged brief in relation to another kind of life that is not brief. Perhaps what is meant by the (relative) brevity of human life is that it is brief in comparison with the lives of other kinds of being we have encountered (elephants, tortoises, oak trees) or imagined (gods, angels, souls in an afterlife). Nature might have appointed things differently, so that human lives could have been exceedingly lengthy in comparison with current human lifespans. Nor is it beyond the bounds of possibility that one day human beings themselves will find genetic or technological ways of substantially extending the human lifespan.

There is, therefore, no logical warrant for thinking of human life as inherently brief. In a way, the 'more is less' version of the qualitative position is making this very point: that we can only be disappointed, or frustrated, if we *think* of human life as inherently brief; better to think of it as something that can be full (or, for some, empty), whatever its length. Where the 'less is more' version of the qualitative position differs from the 'more is less' version is in making the perceived brevity of human life necessary rather than incidental to our fulfilling experience of it. But this 'cult of brevity' may represent little more than a rationalization of the fact that human life is shorter than the lives of other beings, real or imaginary. So, human life being brief or at least perceived as such, we make a virtue of necessity, and affirm the brevity of life to be the 'secret' of a fulfilled or happy life.

The 'less is more' position often seems to be confusing or conflating two quite separate issues: the transience of life's pleasures and the transience of life itself. The fact that the pleasures of life may depend on their transience, and even on our awareness of their transience, does not entail the impossibility or inconceivability of a life in which one were able to enjoy an indefinite if not infinite number of such transient pleasures (and by pleasures one does not only mean pleasures of the sort that would satisfy John Stuart Mill's pig but not Socrates[28]). It is not uncommon to hear people say, perhaps of some journey or holiday rich with intense and novel experiences, that its pleasures would have palled had it gone on longer; but against this we also hear people saying of various events that they wish they had never ended, or had never had to end.[29]

But relatively few people are faced with such exquisite dilemmas. There is, it appears, some degree of elitism in arguments on behalf of the qualitative approach to life, in so far as its model of a life well lived is represented by the healthy and comfortable lives of those with plenty of time and resources for its enjoyment. For millions of people throughout the world, however, life's daily grind offers little opportunity for the kinds of self-improvement or fulfilment envisaged by proponents of the qualitative approach to life. It would take some nerve to say to those who go on struggling for years in order to provide for their families or secure the dignity of their final years that 'more is less', or to say to those whose children or partners have died prematurely that 'less is more'. The ideal of a rich and comfortable life full of opportunities is the preserve of a relative few. One psychologist, Lisl Goodman, observes of the creative individuals she interviewed, such as artists and scientists, that success and fulfilment in their work tended to dispel the fear of death. Generalizing from this, the more complete one feels one's life to be, the less likely one is to fear death. Goodman's findings are echoed in a statement by the poet Ted Rosenthal that she cites several times: 'I don't think people are afraid of death. What they are afraid of is the incompleteness of their life.'[30] There are, however, many people who find their lives unfulfilling precisely through lack of talent or opportunity. Perhaps the cruellest affirmation of the 'more is less' position would come from the likelihood that, for many people, the longer they live, the more they are likely to become aware of the poverty or incompleteness of their lives. It is not surprising if such people are inclined to look for meaning and consolation beyond the boundaries of their present lives, whether in an otherworldly afterlife or an earthly one.

This brings us to arguments about the role of death in the completion or fulfilment of human life. Though sometimes welcomed as a friend, death is in most contexts – and certainly in those where the quantitative approach is uppermost – represented as opponent or enemy. If this life is 'all we have', then one must 'seize the day' while the day is there, resisting to the last anyone or anything that threatens to end it. Positive and life-affirming as this may be, the strategy of *carpe diem* often masks a more pessimistic view, in so far as it lets death set the agenda. As Terry Eagleton puts it,

The frantic jouissance of seizing the day, gathering rosebuds, downing an extra glass, and living like there's no tomorrow is a desperate strategy for outwitting death, one which seeks pointlessly to cheat it rather than make something of it. In its frenzied hedonism, it pays homage to the death it tries to disavow.[31]

The most extreme act of 'homage' to death on the basis of *carpe diem* is that of a rationally contemplated suicide, in so far as one might think that this allows one to set the conditions of one's own death and avoid being 'caught out' by death unawares. The writer Carolyn Heilbrun represents suicide as a case of quitting while one is ahead, thereby avoiding the physical and mental decline of old age. What she fails to address are the negative effects of this act on one's 'earthly afterlife' – that is to say, on the lives of surviving family and friends.[32]

Compared with the perceived role of death in the quantitative approach to life, the view of death as an enabling or advantageous boundary to our lives which is characteristic of the qualitative approach seems both more dignified and more realistic. It is a view sensuously delineated in Wallace Stevens's poem 'Sunday Morning'.[33]

Death is the mother of beauty; hence from her,
Alone, shall come fulfilment to our dreams
And our desires. Although she strews the leaves
Of sure obliteration on our paths,
. . .
She makes the willow shiver in the sun
For maidens who were wont to sit and gaze
Upon the grass, relinquished to their feet.

For Stevens, the beauty and pleasures of this world are necessarily transient, and hence inseparable from death, which we ought therefore to revere. We might yearn for an otherworldly paradise, but this would be nothing more than a pale imitation of the plenitude of earthly existence – silent, changeless, bloodless. A paradise in which ripe fruit never falls from the bough is not for us. This present world is the only paradise we can know. As Stevens says in another poem, 'The imperfect is our paradise.'[34]

Just as the qualitative approach can encourage a 'cult of brevity', so too can it lead to a 'cult of mortality' in which death becomes something we should revere and even celebrate as the key to the meaning of life. It goes without saying that we can learn valuable lessons from death and dying, and that accepting the inevitability of one's own death is one of the most valuable of these lessons. We can learn valuable lessons from all sorts of entities, facts and events in the world, but generally we do not assign absolute value or authority to them. In the case of death, however, there is a striving to attribute some sort of absolute value to the fact or event of death. In many mythologies, the mystery, inevitability and drastic consequences of death are hypostatized into a god. In part, this is an example of the way in which anything powerful and unpredictable tends to be revered. The tendency to absolutize mortality and even revere death occurs as much among those who are not in any explicit sense religious as it does among those who are. As one writer proclaims, without irony, 'When transience is not merely an occasion for mourning, we will have inherited the earth.'[35]

Death is most often over-valued in a purely temporal sense. This is typically expressed in terms of the alleged value death can have in giving us a 'dead-line' against which we can pursue our goals in life. The metaphor of a 'dead-line' originated in descriptions of the practice of setting a line within prisoner-of-war camps which authorized the execution of any prisoner crossing it.[36] It was, it should be noted, a spatial rather than a temporal device, and hence not something one would inevitably cross. The 'dead-line' of death, however, is a temporal constraint and hence something that eventually one is bound to cross. From this fact comes its supposed value in making one enjoy and value all the more whatever time one has left to live. To say that individuals are inevitably better off when facing a deadline than when not is an unwarranted generalization, however – one based on the undeniable fact that in some circumstances some people do indeed benefit from the constraints of a dead-line. But other people, equally undeniably, have flourished precisely through not having such a constraint. Indeed, many of the things done or created by people under the pressure of a dead-line can be judged the poorer as a result. In short, there is no reason whatsoever why people should not lead happy and fulfilled lives without the 'dead-line' of death.

Another way of over-valuing death is a broadly 'romantic' one – often in the more decadent sense of this term.[37] Death may be idealized as something beautiful, as when it is compared to a sleep or rest, for example. There is much in literature, both religious and secular, that reflects this view of death.[38] One can see it also in many forms of art, particularly in certain kinds of funerary monument. Or the alleged beauty of death may be affirmed as part of the beauty of the natural order. Again, as the supposed giver of intensity and meaning to our finite lives, death may be revered as if it were a force or entity in its own right, rather than being seen for what it really is: not any kind of thing at all, but simply a name for the loss or absence of life. The 'less is more' version of the qualitative position is also susceptible to the idealization of a young life cut short by death, often with the implication that death is somehow attracted by the vitality of youth. Here the cult of mortality joins up with the cult of brevity: it is somehow nobler to live a short life packed into a few years than a longer and less intense kind of life. It is a view well-represented by a stanza from the poem 'The Call', by Thomas Osbert Mordaunt (1730–1809):

> Sound, sound the clarion, fill the fife!
> Throughout the sensual world proclaim,
> One crowded hour of glorious life
> Is worth an age without a name.[39]

At its most extreme, the romantic cult of mortality may be expressed in dreams or acts of suicide. Enoch Powell's wish to have been killed in the Second World War may well provide an example here.

IV

In this chapter I have been considering the attitudes and strategies of those for whom a full and authentic life on Earth means 'doing without an afterlife' – that is, living a life whose fulfilment and meaning does not depend on a life beyond this present life, whether this be an earthly or an otherworldly afterlife. But doing without an afterlife does not always mean ignorance of, or indifference to, the *idea* of an afterlife. For one thing, an undercurrent of regret often accompanies the enjoyments and satisfactions of a life lived for its own sake – regret that one's present life and one's own self will one day be extinguished without remainder. Even those who prefer extinction to survival are in their very rejection or dislike of an afterlife living with the idea of an afterlife.

While many people are sceptical of, if not actively hostile to, the idea of an otherworldly afterlife, few deny the reality of what I have defined as an earthly afterlife. While much of the 'content' of our earthly afterlife is beyond our purview or control, we are nevertheless laying down its foundations by the way we are living our lives here and now. People cannot live without some awareness of the nature of the legacy they are bequeathing to the future in the form of their earthly afterlives, however modest this legacy might be. Living without an earthly afterlife is, in this sense, simply not possible. One may profess indifference to one's earthly afterlife, but it is surely a fact of human nature that just as most of us care about what people think of us here and now, so do most of us care about what people might think of us after we are gone.

The idea of living without an otherworldly afterlife raises similar issues, albeit on a grander scale. An otherworldly afterlife is often thought of as something that is, or would be, so far removed from anything experienced in this life that one could only view it as a remote concern with little or no claim upon us in the present. (Something similar might be said about the idea that we have existed in a life or lives before this one.) This is more or less the opposite of how most religious eschatologies represent the afterlife. But if it is we ourselves who continue to exist in an afterlife (and not just some abstract part of us), then this afterlife would have to be regarded as a further stage of the existence we are leading here and now. (By the same token, the life we are leading here and now could only be regarded as an extension of any life or lives we have led before.) We may (for good reasons or bad) be relatively indifferent to a future life in much the same way as we tend to be relatively indifferent to the earthly life we may be leading several years from now.[40] Logically, however, we cannot be completely indifferent to these (eventual or possible) future episodes in our own existence – at least not if we claim to love life, and with it ourselves and others. As future-oriented (but also retrospective) beings we must have some concern about the longer-term (and past) trajectory of our lives – a trajectory that might well embrace what I have called an otherworldly afterlife.

As for those who despite their love of life say they would rather not survive death, what they are saying in effect is that at a certain point they would desire, or be content, to cease existing. But why exactly would anyone who exists ever want to stop existing? (We can leave out of our account here those people who long for death as an escape from some intolerable personal circumstance – extreme pain, debilitating illness or overwhelming debt, for example.) Why would a conscious being who is not in a state of extreme suffering ever want to cease being conscious, either here or hereafter? Even if there were no certainty of a post-mortem afterlife lasting forever, why desire an end to one's life sooner rather than later? It would seem irrational for anyone to eschew a post-mortem existence where this might be expected to be at least as interesting or fulfilling as one's earthly existence has been (or could have been). There is surely a case for arguing that 'more is more' rather than that 'more is less'.

If we were destined for some kind of afterlife, and were certain of it, then as rational beings we could have no option but to acknowledge the fact, even if we did not welcome it, and make the prospect of another life an integral part of how we conducted and evaluated our present lives. Only those who had categorically ruled out the possibility of an afterlife could consistently claim to be living without an afterlife (though never without the *idea* of an afterlife). If it were known there were no afterlife, or if the idea of an afterlife were demonstrably incoherent, then the rational strategy would be to lead our lives purely within the confines of our mortality. The quantitative and qualitative approaches to living without an afterlife both have their merits as rational responses to the assumption that death means personal extinction. But to adopt either of these approaches where there is even the slightest doubt about the possibility of an otherworldly immortality would, at least in terms of what is known as Pascal's Wager, surely be unwise.[41] For time-bound beings like ourselves, living as if there were no afterlife could be as rash a strategy as living as if there were no tomorrow.

SIX

DEATH AND THE END OF THE WORLD

But why bother about the end of the world? It's the end of the world every day, for someone. Time rises and rises, and when it reaches the level of your eyes you drown.
MARGARET ATWOOD, *The Blind Assassin* (2000)

I

P eople do not just die. They die in or from or with a whole world – a world which is (or was) both their own world and a world shared with others; and this world in some sense comes to an end with their death. As the philosopher Wittgenstein put it, 'At death the world does not alter, but comes to an end.'[1] But in what sense or senses exactly does this world come to an end? And what significance might any sense of the ending of the world have for our understanding of ideas about earthly immortality?

In this chapter, I examine three distinct but overlapping senses in which, when talking about the death of persons, we are also talking about the death of a whole world. The first sense covers the experience commonly reported by the bereaved that, for them at least, the world itself has ended with the loss of a loved one. This sense of the end of the world is both a subjective and a figurative one; the world itself does not really come to an end, not even for the bereaved person who is moved to describe it in such dramatic terms. The second sense of the end of the world covers the realization by those confronting their own death that the approaching end of their life means, in effect, the ending of their world. This sense is also a subjective one, but no longer a figurative one. It is literally the case that the world of which one is the subject and centre comes to an end with one's death, while the world as such, the world as a whole, does not. The third and most powerful sense of the 'end of the world', however, refers to the apocalyptic or eschatological possibility of the world itself by some means coming to a complete end for everyone. In this case, the world as a whole objectively and literally ceases to exist. By 'world as a whole' is meant the totality of human life and civilization, rather than the physical planet Earth, although in the more extreme scenarios imaginable the proximate cause of the ending of human civilization may well be the wholesale destruction of the planet itself.

Two points need emphasizing at once. First, and most obviously, all three of these senses of the 'end of the world' – that with the death of a loved one the world has as good as ended, that one's own world ends with one's death, and that the whole world might actually end for everyone – are compatible, intellectually, with a whole range of theories and doctrines about death and post-mortem existence. But second, although all three senses of the 'end of the world' are neutral in regard to any belief about what will or will not happen after death, whatever beliefs one does hold concerning the possibility or impossibility of post-mortem existence are likely to affect both the way one thinks about, and the way one deals practically with, the experiences with which each kind of 'ending of the world' is associated. There is a parallel here with one's beliefs about the nature and role of suffering, for example. While the various experiences of pain and suffering to which all of us are subject are in themselves conceptually neutral, the attitudes we adopt towards them and the ways we actually cope with them will to a large extent be determined by our religious and other beliefs about the world.

II

The feeling that with the loss of a loved one a whole world has come to an end is a common feature of the grieving process. This feeling is by no means always or only a negative one, however. For many people the death of a loved one – never mind the death of one not so loved! – will usher in a complementary feeling: that a whole new world has just begun. These complementary feelings – of one's whole world ending and of a new world beginning – have powerful cognitive and emotional effects on the lives of the bereaved. It is where the feeling is mostly or entirely negative, however, that the impact is the greatest. The loss of someone takes away far more than a particular individual, since that individual has been the centre of a whole world of experiences and relationships. The experience of bereavement, we might say, is more like looking at a jigsaw puzzle from which a particular piece has been removed than like considering this particular piece on its own. Or, to give another analogy, bereavement is like confronting a newly empty chair at the meal table, but confronting it in the same glance which takes in all the other chairs around the table filled with their familiar occupants.

In some cases the grief of bereaved persons will be so severe in its impact that it leads them to desire death for themselves and even to commit, or attempt, suicide. Since their loved one is dead they too might as well be dead. But the sense of the end of the world is for most bereaved people a temporary one, a phase within the complex process of grieving within which people actively or passively come to terms with their loss. For the majority of the bereaved, the simple passage of time will soften the pain of bereavement, though this may be less a matter of healing and more one of learning to live with the loss, rather as one learns to live with some permanent deficit or disability. As Elizabeth Jennings observes in her poem 'Words about Grief', time hides grief rather than heals it, leaving a wound always liable to break open again, with a 'Grief as total as in its first hour.'[2]

Thus what many bereaved people feel, with varying intensity and for longer or shorter periods, is that the world which has literally ended for the deceased has somehow also ended for themselves, or rather – since it all too palpably continues – that the world has been drained of all meaning or purpose, or even reality. Bereaved people often talk about going through the motions of living rather than actually living. Nor is it paradoxical that this feeling of the world having ended requires for its fuel the very continuance of the world; that it is enhanced rather than diminished by the fact that all around them the world and its inhabitants carry on as normal. It may even include the sense, and more rarely the pathological belief, that the world, precisely because it does carry on as normal, is being cruelly indifferent to their loss. For them, the normally functioning world around them presents a striking contrast to the sadness, abandonment and emptiness they feel within themselves.

The sense of the redundancy or worthlessness of the world now that the loved one has gone is not confined to those bereaved through a death. It is a familiar trope in the laments of abandoned lovers, as in the song 'The End of the World', where the singer asks how the sun can go on shining, the birds go on singing or the sea still rush to shore now that the one she loves no longer loves her. Surely they must know it's the end of the world, she complains, wondering how the world can go on as if nothing had happened when it must surely have ended not just for her but for everyone and everything else too.[3] Strictly speaking, such sentiments express not so much the idea that the world has ended as that it should end, or might as well end, now that the loved one has gone. Milder forms of this sense of the 'end of the world' are experienced by those betrayed or disillusioned by someone formerly admired or trusted, or by those who lament the passing of a particular period of history, along with the values it embodied, as the 'end of an era'.

But this first sense of the ending of the world can also be internalized as the feeling that one has died oneself. In Ben Jonson's 'Epitaph on Master Vincent Corbet' (1619), for example, the poet's fulsome praise of the subject concludes thus:

> Much from him, I profess I won,
> And more, and more, I should have done,
> But that I understood him scant,
> Now I conceive him by my want;
> And pray who shall my sorrows read,
> That they for me their tears will shed;
> For truly, since he left to be,
> I feel, I'm rather dead than he!

This feeling on the part of the survivor that it is he rather than the deceased who has really died is, of course, not literally grounded; and yet it is more than merely rhetoric, since it indicates both the depth of the feeling of loss and the strength of the sense that the person who has actually died nevertheless lives on in his good deeds and virtues.

How well or how badly the bereaved cope with their loss, it seems reasonable to suppose, will depend in part on whether they have positive or negative views about death. But we should note at once that positive views about death include not just doctrines of some felicitous post-mortem existence, but also a variety of atheistic and humanistic philosophies in which death as the complete end of our existence is regarded as a good and natural event. By the same token, some religious afterlife doctrines can be regarded as negative, to the extent that they envisage a miserable or painful existence post-mortem. The psychology (and psychopathology) of bereavement is complex and unpredictable, however. How well or badly people cope with bereavement is likely to have as much to do with 'this-worldly' factors, such as the nature of the relationship with the deceased when living, a person's general contentment or discontentment with life, and so forth, as it does with one's beliefs concerning life after death. It is certainly a misconception to suppose that just because someone has a firm faith in a life hereafter they will not feel the grief of bereavement as intensely, or for as long, as one who does not have such a faith. To put it simply, it is the fact that a person has gone, not any belief about where they might or might not have gone, that is the primary source of grief. On the other hand, to say that there is no correlation of any kind between one's behaviour as a bereaved person and one's views about life and death would be to underestimate the known power of ideas and beliefs within a person's life.

Differentiating between the emotional and intellectual aspects of bereavement, therefore, we might say that it should (eventually if not immediately) make all the difference in the world if one believes that deceased individuals continue to exist as conscious subjects of experience in some other world, assuming only (and it would be an assumption) that this mode of existence were not one involving pain or suffering (or at least not one involving greater pain or suffering than experienced in the present world). It is also to be noted that the intellectual comfort the bereaved derive from believing, or perhaps even from knowing (if this were ever possible), that their loved ones continue to exist does not necessarily depend on the idea that they will be reunited with them after their own death, though this belief or hope is certainly affirmed by many. If the prospect of personal reunion were the only motive for hoping or believing that one's loved ones continued to exist, then it might well be judged rather a self-regarding one. In the film *A Chinese Ghost Story* (dir. Ching Siu-tung, 1987), the protagonist helps the earthbound and all too solid ghost of a beautiful girl, with whom he has fallen in love, to escape back into the cycle of human rebirth, knowing that he will never see her again, and certainly never in that particular form, since she will soon be reborn somewhere else as someone else. His last words to her are not anguished or self-regarding, but instead express a noble hortative: 'Be a fine person.'

III

'As our birth brought us the birth of all things,' writes Montaigne, 'so in our death is the death of all things included.'[4] Whereas the bereaved continue to live in a world which some of them may feel has (as good as) ended for them, those facing their own death know that they will cease to exist for this world as surely as it will cease to exist for them. They also know that the world that is about to end for them will continue for others. This second sense of the end of the world is literal despite its being subjective: the real world disappears for, but not with, the dying person whose dying moments (if they are conscious) are indeed their last experience of this world. The 'world as acted in and experienced by oneself' really will end with one's death; indeed, one's death causes its end. But the 'world as acted in and experienced by others' continues of course, even if for some of these others it is a world now noticeably different as a result of one's own disappearance from it. The world goes on as before, lacking only that small unit of activity and consciousness that was oneself. A piece of the jigsaw has been removed.

Only for a solipsist, perhaps, would the ending of the 'world as acted in and experienced by oneself' entail the ending of the world-as-such. The 'otherness' of death can never intrude into the world of the true solipsist. In Henri Barbusse's novel *The Inferno* the narrator reflects on what someone, now dead, had said about his own death:

> 'After my death, life will continue. Every detail in the world will continue to occupy the same place quietly. All the traces of my passing will die little by little, and the void I leave behind will be filled once more.'
>
> He was mistaken in saying so. He carried all the truth with him. Yet we, *we* saw him die. He was dead for us, but not for himself. I feel there is a fearfully difficult truth here which we must get, a formidable contradiction. But I hold on to the two ends of it, groping to find out what formless language will translate it. Something like this: 'Every human being is the whole truth.' I return to what I heard. We do not die since we are alone. It is the others who die. And this sentence, which comes to my lips tremulously, at once baleful and beaming with light, announces that death is a false god.[5]

Unlike the first sense of the ending of the world, moreover, the second sense of its ending – the sense in which the world of one who dies comes to an end – is both literal and permanent. For the bereaved who feel that the world has ended, a new world may eventually open up or their old world revive. For the dying person, however, the experience of this world irrevocably comes to an end, regardless of whether it is succeeded by an existence in another world or by no further experience of any kind.

For the dying, the fact that this world will continue without them is likely to be a source both of regret and of consolation. Those dying or nearing death may say, for example, that they will miss seeing their children or grandchildren grow older, while deriving comfort from the fact that they have had children and grandchildren in the first place, and that these lives will continue. And there will be correspondingly mixed emotions concerning other persons important to them – partners, parents, friends and acquaintances. They will regret having to leave the company of these persons, but be glad that the lives of these persons will continue after their own life has ended. Similar things might be said about their interests, their plans and their projects, assuming that these things have been or will be continued or taken up by others. To die knowing, or even just hoping, that the trees you planted will one day reach maturity, or that the movement you founded will continue to prosper, is likely to be regarded as some kind of 'compensation' for the fact that you yourself will not be there to witness these things yourself. All of this is part of what I have described as the 'earthly afterlife' of the dead.

To describe the outlook of the dying on their imminently disappearing world exclusively in terms of regret and 'compensation', however, is to paint too negative a picture, not least because the attitudes and interests of the dying are commonly of a positive and indeed an altruistic nature. Many people are perfectly ready to die, without actively wishing to die, and despite being fearful of the process of dying. Many face death believing they are fortunate to have lived a full and fruitful life. Or they may see their deaths as part of a natural cycle in which the younger generation benefits from the departure of the older one. Or they may be eager to move on to what they believe, or hope, will be a new life in another world. Nor should we forget that many people willingly give up their lives, not because they want to die but in order to help or save others. Such self-sacrificial dying is widely accepted as one of the noblest acts of which human beings are capable. One of its best known literary expressions is found in Charles Dickens's novel *A Tale of Two Cities* (1859), at the end of which Sydney Carton, heroically taking the place of a friend sentenced to be guillotined, comforts himself with these words: 'It is a far, far better thing that I do, than I have ever done; it is a far, far better rest that I go to than I have ever known.'

Although the 'world as experienced by them' ends with their death, the 'world as changed by them' continues in some measure, forming part of what I have called their earthly afterlife. Because many people dying or facing death see themselves as having continuing interests and even responsibilities in the world they leave behind them, and are seen by those who survive them as having such interests and responsibilities, those dying or facing death are liable to project a 'notional version' of themselves into the world they are leaving behind. These 'notional selves' will be sustained, or not, as the case may be, by those who are left confronting or in charge of their legacy. The convenient fiction of a post-mortem 'notional self' is usually quite independent of any beliefs regarding a person's substantive survival in another world. The deliberate cultivation of such a 'notional self', by oneself before death and by others afterwards, is part and parcel of the phenomenon of an earthly afterlife. As we have seen in earlier chapters, deceased persons persist in a number of ways – through their progeny; through the records and memories of their lives; through the things they have created, said or done; through their wishes being fulfilled and their projects taken up by others; and through all these achievements and personal qualities being remembered and celebrated. They are also seen as physically persisting, through their bodily remains, and through personal possessions and other memorabilia. In more recent times, the earthly afterlives of individuals have been enhanced through technological means – for example, by the freezing of human eggs or sperm for future use, or by the creation of a computer-based 'digital immortality'.

But whatever consolation or encouragement people may derive from the likelihood of their own earthly afterlife, and despite their readiness to die either on their own account or on behalf of others, it is a simple truth that no human beings free of severe physical or mental pain will easily give up their purchase on their life in this world. Even on their deathbeds they may worry about uncompleted tax returns and the like, and not necessarily only out of concern for the unfinished business they might be leaving for others to sort out. The comedian Woody Allen, at the end of a stand-up routine, would take a watch from his pocket, check the time and then say: 'It's an old family heirloom. [pause] My grandfather sold it to me on his deathbed.'[6] People feel and behave as if their life has no end, even when they are rationally aware of its inevitable end, and even when its imminent end is being signalled to them loud and clear. Or, to put it another way, people are too busy living to think about the possibility of no longer living, and sometimes too busy to think about it even when they are dying. Or is it simply that the very boundaries which define one's identity in this life also prevent one from looking beyond this life? If we dig deeper, however, we may find explanations beyond merely the self's inability or unwillingness to contemplate the possibility of its own future non-existence. Perhaps, as an individual self, one is *constitutionally* unable to conceive of, let alone imagine, one's own non-existence. And this might be explained not by a failure of the imagination, or by stubborn optimism in the face of all the evidence, but by some deep-seated intuition of one's own immortality – what William Wordsworth defines as 'an intimation or assurance within us, that some part of our nature is imperishable'.[7] Failure of the imagination would only enter in with a refusal to see one's inherent immortality other than in terms of the indefinite continuation of one's present, earthly existence. One could be right about life continuing indefinitely, but wrong about the way in which it will do so.

'Why aren't they screaming?' asks the poet Philip Larkin about those decrepit 'old fools' for whom the hitherto apparently endless horizon of life is now broken by the looming into view of 'extinction's alp'. One obvious answer is that they too are still too busy living, even when this means, as it does in Larkin's brutal representation of them, that living is now mostly a matter of reviewing a phantasmagoria of retreating memories.

> Perhaps being old is having lighted rooms
> Inside your head, and people in them, acting
> People you know, yet can't quite name ...[8]

In fact, even when memory and other functions are in decline, many old people at the end of their lives continue to live in the present as much as in the past, looking forward to whatever their remaining days have to offer. Life at the foot of extinction's alp need be no different from the life lived before it looms into view.

What is in question is not just an unwillingness or inability to tear oneself away from the world, but the seeming conceptual impossibility of imagining anything other, or anywhere else, than the world we know or have known, and which, even as decrepit and moribund individuals, we still firmly inhabit, whether lucidly or in confusion. The philosopher Bryan Magee, reflecting on what his own approaching exit from the world means for him as a religious sceptic, proposes the following analogy for what might be the closest thing to seeing the world from outside. 'To take a light-hearted comparison, it is a bit like comparing a party surveyed at the door in a valedictory glance by a departing guest with the same party experienced by a wholly engrossed guest in mid-room and mid-hubbub.' While this might also be a description, as he hints, of some kind of 'secular' near-death experience available at the threshold of death, the more important point is that it is impossible to see the world from the outside or to imagine living in any kind of world except in the terms set by the present one:

> The world, like a party, is variegated and indeterminate, but on so unimaginably vaster a scale that it is impossible to convey in language the perception of it as enclosed within experience and yet carrying on separately from oneself. The chief problem in communicating this difficulty lies not in the words 'carrying on' but in the word 'enclosed'. Every possibility I have for apprehending, imagining or inventing, in any way whatsoever, is contingent on the apparatus I have for doing so, and all of it is this-worldly. Even my freest and most imaginative speculations are events in a this-worldly life. I cannot get outside it, or outside its possibilities – except by dying. And as I approach death it is as if I receive tiny, inarticulate glimpses, the barest possible intimations, of the empirical world as a whole. The overriding impression is of its limitedness.[9]

For Magee, as for any reflective person, the looming 'end of the world' inevitably generates thoughts as to whether any kind of conscious experience, however presently unimaginable, might succeed one's death. But instead of seeing this world as an ineliminable obstacle to imagining any kind of a post-mortem world (with the concomitant impossibility of establishing the reality of that world other than by question-begging references to experiences within this one), we could perhaps see this world as a rich source of imagery and analogy for imagining and thinking about that other world. The vicious circle in which Magee is caught up may not be the one he suggests – that of not being able to get outside worldly imaginings – but rather that of not being able to think of a world hereafter in terms of the present world because it has already been decided that any world hereafter would necessarily lie completely outside this world. William Blake, in describing death (or dying) as like going into another room, assumes that this world and the world hereafter are in some way continuous. We might of course want to question this assumption, but so too might we question the assumption made not only by Magee and other sceptics, but by many religious believers, that any future existence would, by definition, be quite other than, and quite separate from, our present existence.[10]

IV

So far I have considered two specifically subjective senses of experiencing the 'end of the world'. Neither entails the end of the world itself; what comes to an end is some individual experience of the world, not the world as such. Not only this, but these first two senses of the world's ending actually depend for their meaning upon the world objectively continuing to exist. The objectively existent world, that is to say, constitutes the necessary precondition for experiencing these two subjective senses of the world ending. But what if the world as a whole should *objectively* cease to exist? What about the death not of individuals but of the human species in its entirety? Two issues come to the surface here: on the one hand, our attitude to our death (and dying) when it is shared with the whole of humanity not as a universal destiny but as a singular historical event (or process); and on the other hand, our attitude to the world (or kind of world) that would be left behind once it were bereft of any human presence and thus of all human subjectivity. The latter issue I address in the following chapter. Here I concentrate on the first issue.

In regard to this first issue, the main question concerning human extinction is how differently we would face death knowing that everybody else alive at the time was facing it simultaneously, and more particularly how we would face it not simply as individuals but as part of some larger community or culture, or even (if this makes any sense) as part of the human species as a whole. Would we face it any differently from the way in which we face our deaths in a world not thus threatened with or certain of destruction, a world we assume will continue not only after we have gone, but long after we have been forgotten? Whether or not there would be any difference, and what such a difference might involve, can be teased out by comparing the answers that people might give to the two following questions. The first and probably more familiar question is this: What would you do, and how might you feel, if you knew you were going to die tomorrow (or within some other brief period of time)? Those asked this question would rightly, or at least reasonably, assume that what is in question is their own individual death and not the death of humanity as a whole. The second question, however, is this: What would you do, and how might you feel, if you knew that you, together with the entire human race, were going to die tomorrow (or within some other brief period of time)?

Faced with this latter possibility, would one's concern be primarily, if not exclusively, the fact that one's own death was imminent, or would it be the demise of humanity as a whole that would take precedence? It is difficult to believe that people would respond to these two questions in exactly the same way. To the extent that the responses were different, moreover, it is likely that the second hypothesis would be considered far worse than the first, and the degree to which one were appalled at the imminent demise of humanity might well be judged a measure of one's own humanity. It is of course possible that some respondents might profess indifference to the fate of humanity once their own fate was sealed. Some might even take a perverse pleasure in the fact that all human beings are going to die. Others might have more humane reasons for finding satisfaction in the imminent end of humanity. Life on Earth might have become intolerable, for example. Certain kinds of religious believer might see a coming cataclysm as a supernatural event bringing human history to its prophesied end. These special cases apart, however, it is likely that the prospect of the total extinction of human life on Earth, ending the usual phenomenon of individual deaths occurring within a self-perpetuating human population, would be considered by anyone facing their own death as a concern of quite a different order from that of their own death. Human beings are social animals, with a concern for others that does not usually come to an end as they approach death. Compared with the deaths of individuals, or with the loss of successive generations, the prospect of the wholesale demise of humanity would be regarded by most people not just as an event beyond the scale of human expectation but as a challenge to, if not negation of, all human values and purposes. Rather as an earthquake threatens to undermine every other form of physical stability we rely upon and take for granted, so could the prospect of the complete extinction of humanity represent a collapse of the framework within which we make sense of our individual and collective lives on Earth. This is a point I shall take up in the next section of this chapter.

Of course we cannot say with any confidence exactly (or even approximately) how this or that individual, or this or that community, would react to the prospect of the annihilation of the entire human race. Where there were no warning of the catastrophe, there could be no reaction to it either. If there were a warning of some kind, then it is likely that people would be too busy trying to forestall (if not deny) the event to give it any systematic consideration. Noah no doubt would have sat down to think about the destruction of the world and its inhabitants only after he and his family were safely aboard the ark. History does offer us some clues, however. For there have been many occasions when it must have seemed to people as if the whole world were coming to an end, but where in fact it was only a part of the world that was destroyed, or ravaged, by some natural or man-made catastrophe. Throughout history peoples and cultures have survived large-scale floods, volcanic eruptions and earthquakes, just as they have survived epidemics and invasions. In many cases there was no time for them to gather their thoughts about such large-scale destruction of their way of life. Did the citizens of Pompeii or Herculaneum, one wonders, have time to consider such questions before they were overwhelmed by the fallout from Vesuvius?

In the obvious absence of any historical indication as to how facing death against the background of the world's total destruction would differ from facing death within the continuing world of the living, we can usefully turn to the imagined worlds of literature, drama and cinema. Within the realm of fiction, there is a large body of narratives, sometimes defined as apocalyptic or post-apocalyptic fiction, which depicts human civilization subjected to, or threatened with, some form of global catastrophe. Strictly speaking, the term 'apocalyptic' (meaning 'revelatory') is a misnomer here. The term originates with those visionary texts, found in several religious traditions, which reveal the existence, or prophesy the coming, of a new order of reality. The emphasis is not so much on the violent or dramatic events that may accompany this discovery as on the significance of what is discovered. Paradigmatic here (and largely responsible for the modern terminology) is the New Testament Apocalypse of John (or Book of Revelation). Even when apocalypse is linked with eschatology, therefore, it is less about the ending or destruction of the world as about what will follow it. In modern secular usage, however, the term tends to be identified mostly if not exclusively with ending and destruction.

Some apocalyptic texts belong within the wider spectrum of 'eschatological' narratives, in relatively few of which is the end of the world also the end of the story. One context where the destruction does seem to be terminal is that of Norse mythology, with its well-known 'twilight of the gods'. In Hindu and Buddhist mythology, by contrast, after the world and all its inhabitants, and indeed all the gods and other beings within the cosmos, have been destroyed at the end of each cosmic cycle, a new world and a new cycle come into being. As a rule, the destruction or dissolution of the world in apocalyptic and mythological texts is linked with creation or regeneration. Classic examples of this are to be found in the flood narratives of ancient Near Eastern mythology, which include the Old Testament Genesis narratives. In purely secular contexts, of course, so-called apocalyptic narratives will tend to focus on the threatened or imminent destruction of the world, and the exclusively earthly response to it – heroic individuals seeking a means of averting or avoiding it, or survivors struggling to maintain or recover some element of civilization. Perhaps a better term for the secular variety of apocalyptic narrative would be 'end of days' narrative.

When we review modern fiction and the cinema, indeed, what is striking is how rarely we find narratives portraying the total destruction of humanity. Most of these narratives envisage a world in which a small group manages to survive, and with it the possibility of rebuilding civilization and thereby continuing the history of the human race. That there should typically be this element of hope, if not triumph, is perhaps inevitable according to the traditional requirements of dramatic narrative. Not even in the darkest tragedy do all the characters die; were they to do so, then we should have a work of nihilism rather than of tragedy, and with it the loss of any purchase on the sympathy or even imagination of the reader or audience. Dramatically speaking, the purpose of introducing into any story a threat of total annihilation is typically to show how the characters in the story avoid succumbing to the threat, however implausibly. Against all the odds, tomorrow does turn out to be another day. To contemplate the absolute end of the world, meaning the irrevocable extinction of human life and culture, seems to allow for no message of hope, no catharsis, no dramatic tension even. Everything simply ends. Dramatizing, or even conceiving of, a complete end of the world and its history faces one obvious problem: where is the narrator situated?[11] (Arguably, fictional narratives in which a group of survivors die, mistakenly believing themselves to be the very last remnant of humanity, would also avoid the charge of nihilism liable to attach to narratives representing the total end of humanity.)

Narratives of 'absolute apocalypse', however, are not entirely lacking. There are stories in which tomorrow, so to speak, will *not* be another day. One twentieth-century novel envisaging a complete 'end of the world' is Nevil Shute's *On the Beach* (1957), of which there have been at least two screen adaptations: a feature film directed by Stanley Kramer in 1959 and a made-for-television version directed by Russell Mulcahy in 2000. In the novel, set in Australia in the weeks following a global nuclear war, the remaining human beings face up, in different ways, to what they gradually realize is not just their own imminent end but the imminent end of the human race as a whole. Whether or not it is any kind of comfort that others are around to share one's experience of this final end of civilization is a moot point. In one scene a couple decide painlessly to end first their child's life and then their own lives rather than succumb to an agonizing death from radiation sickness. For these individuals the ending of the world is experienced with a sad and calm acceptance. By others it is met with defiance and bravado. What is depicted in this novel might be considered practically no different from what has actually happened or what could have happened to groups of people cut off by some disaster within a still populated world. Examples of such groups would include the members of Captain Robert Scott's Antarctic expedition (1911–12), the survivors of the plane which crashed in the Andes in 1972, or the 33 Chilean miners trapped underground for 69 days in 2010. But it is reasonable to argue that for a group of people to die either knowing or believing that they have no successors and that there will be no earthly 'afterlife' either for themselves or for any other human beings would make the last days and hours of that group especially poignant.

In some 'end of days' narratives the plot deals with the plight of an isolated individual struggling in the shadow of what appears or threatens to be the total destruction of human civilization. Uncertainty as to whether such an individual truly is the last person alive or merely someone out of contact with other survivors naturally provides much of the dramatic tension. Dramatically, it is more interesting for the reader or audience if a protagonist who has thought and acted like the last person left alive turns out not to be alone in the world. Where such an individual really is the last person left alive, the narrative is liable to take on something of a mythic or legendary character. One example is Richard Matheson's novel *I Am Legend* (1954), which has been made into a feature film three times. In the original novel, the protagonist is the last true human being left alive, albeit one surrounded by a formerly human population infected by a disease that has turned people into a new race of murderous mutants resembling vampires or zombies (or perhaps a hybrid of the two). The first of the film versions of this story, *The Last Man on Earth* (1964), is faithful to this idea of a solitary figure doomed to be the very last human being. In the second version, *The Omega Man* (1971), the protagonist manages to create a serum against the disease, which he hands to one of a group of uninfected humans just before being struck down by a mutant. In the third version, *I Am Legend* (2007), the protagonist likewise manages to hand over a cure to some uninfected humans whose lives he saves by sacrificing his own. These survivors then journey safely to a colony which promises to form the nucleus of a new human civilization.

Narratives in which an imperilled world is saved, or where there is at least a remnant of survivors capable of rebuilding human civilization, differ in kind from those rarer narratives where the world does indeed end, and end for everyone. In the latter case, whether there is a doomed last individual or a doomed last remnant might well be considered relatively unimportant, given in both cases the imminent finality of an empty world. But one difference would surely be that a last individual is, in a real sense, already living in a world devoid of human society or civilization in any real sense. Narratives featuring a surviving remnant usually suggest the possibility if not inevitability of an eventual recovery for the human race, but with only one individual remaining this possibility is obviously excluded (though perhaps not absolutely if the last individual happens to be a pregnant female). To say that hope for humanity and human civilization continues as long as its last representatives remain alive will also be vacuous if these individuals are, for whatever reason, unable to produce offspring. How long such 'last persons' might survive on their own is a secondary point, even were they to manage to live out a full term of years and die of natural causes. Both a 'last person' and a 'last remnant' would not simply be facing their own deaths, but would be doing so in the full knowledge that human civilization as such, or whatever fragment of human civilization they might be said to embody, would be dying with them. This makes their situation distinct from that of figures like Robinson Crusoe, who assume that the civilization from which they are cut off will continue even if they are never able to return to it (or, perhaps, never want to do so).

The tragedy of a world bereft or soon to be bereft of humankind is a theme well represented in the literature of nineteenth-century Romanticism. In these works we see a shift from the older tradition of apocalyptic narrative, where earthly cataclysm is mitigated if not justified by a religious eschatology, to a newer tradition of science-fictional 'end of world' narratives, where civilization is represented as coming to an end either fortuitously or through human aggression or mismanagement. Thomas Campbell's poem 'The Last Man' (1823) adopts the device of a visionary dream in which the last man on Earth addresses the dying sun that is the cause of Earth's destruction. The destruction is total: 'Earth's cities had no sound nor tread; / And ships were drifting with the dead / To shores where all was dumb!' This poem, despite its immediate scientific basis, retains at its heart a clear religious focus, presenting the last man as a prophetic individual evocative of Adam, the first man. Although his final death is the 'last and bitter cup / Of grief that man shall taste', and although all the works of mankind will be lost, the last man, like all who have died before him, has a destiny beyond the ephemeral Earth:

> This spirit shall return to Him
>   That gave its heavenly spark;
> Yet think not, Sun, it shall be dim
>   When thou thyself art dark![12]

By contrast, Byron's rather similar poem 'Darkness' (1816) presents a world devastated by a dying sun in which there is no glimmer of any religious transcendence. Byron's end of the world is without even a last man to relieve the gloom.

>   The world was void,
> The populous and the powerful – was a lump,
> Seasonless, herbless, treeless, manless, lifeless –
> A lump of death – a chaos of hard clay.

The rivers, lakes, and ocean all stood still,
And nothing stirr'd within their silent depths;
Ships sailorless lay rotting on the sea . . . [13]

A vision of the absolute end of the world unredeemed by any religious hope is also presented in Mary Shelley's novel *The Last Man*
(1826). In this story the world's population is overcome by deadly
plague, until only a handful of survivors are left to wander through a
deserted Europe. Eventually there is literally just one man left alive,
the novel's narrator, Lionel Verney. His musings on the imminent end
of human existence show that hope rises up even in despair:

> But the game is up! We must all die; nor leave survivor nor heir
> to the wide inheritance of earth. We must all die! The species
> of man must perish; his frame of exquisite workmanship; the
> wondrous mechanism of his senses; the noble proportion of his
> godlike limbs; his mind, the throned king of these; must perish.
> Will the earth still keep her place among the planets; will she
> still journey with unmarked regularity round the sun; will the
> seasons change, the trees adorn themselves with leaves, and
> flowers shed their fragrance, in solitude? Will the mountains
> remain unmoved, and streams still keep a downward course
> towards the vast abyss; will the tides rise and fall, and the winds
> fan universal nature; will beasts pasture, birds fly, and fishes
> swim, when man, the lord, possessor, perceiver, and recorder
> of all these things, has passed away, as though he had never
> been? O, what mockery is this! Surely death is not death, and
> humanity is not extinct; but merely passed into other shapes,
> unsubjected to our perceptions. Death is a vast portal, an high
> road to life: let us hasten to pass; let us exist no more in this
> living death, but die that we may live! [14]

Earlier in the novel, when his wife Idris is still alive, Verney talks with
her of 'what might arise on this desert earth, if, two or three being
saved, it were slowly re-peopled'. They also talk of 'what was beyond
the tomb; and, man in his human shape being nearly extinct, we felt
with certainty of faith, that other spirits, other minds, other percep-
tive beings, sightless to us, must people with thought and love this
beauteous and imperishable universe'. [15]

Even where there is no religious hope, the acts and thoughts of 'last men' do not necessarily assume a completely negative or nihilistic character, as is evident in another novel about the end of humankind, Olaf Stapledon's *Last and First Men* (1930). Here there are intimations of an anonymous afterlife for the human race within a far broader perspective than that presented in Shelley's novel. The novel traces the history of eighteen different species of humankind on three different planets across two billion years of history. The last men, now living on Neptune, are destroyed when the sun, having become unstable, swallows up the entire solar system. Before this event, however, it is incumbent upon the last generation to direct their remaining energies into 'designing an artificial human seed, producing it in immense quantities, and projecting it among the stars'.[16] These last men assume an almost mythical status, eschatological counterparts of the culture heroes associated with the origins of human civilization. They project hope rather than despair, epitomizing the glories of the human adventure.

> But there is among us one, moving from place to place and company to company, whose voice all long to hear. He is young, the last born of the Last Men; for he was the latest to be conceived before we learned man's doom, and put an end to all conceiving. Being the latest, he is also the noblest. Not him alone, but all his generation, we salute, and look to for strength; but he, the youngest, is different from the rest. In him the spirit, which is but the flesh awakened into spirituality, has power to withstand the tempest of solar energy longer than the rest of us. It is as though the sun itself were eclipsed by this spirit's brightness. It is as though in him at last, and for a day only, man's promise were fulfilled. For though, like others, he suffers in the flesh, he is above his suffering. And though more than the rest of us he feels the suffering of others, he is above his pity. In his comforting there is a strange sweet raillery which can persuade the sufferer to smile at his own pain. When this youngest brother of ours contemplates with us our dying world and the frustration of all man's striving, he is not, like us, dismayed, but quiet. In the presence of such quietness despair wakens into peace. By his reasonable speech, almost by the mere sound of his voice, our eyes are opened, and our hearts mysteriously filled with exultation.[17]

For many in the modern world, no longer informed by religious expectations or beguiled by mythic or Romantic notions of the end times, one question provoked by end-of-world narratives of all kinds is whether the final disappearance of humankind would represent some kind of failure on humanity's part. An easy response would be to answer in the affirmative if mankind's demise were self-inflicted and in the negative if it were not. This response seems too easy, however. To begin with, how is one to make any clear judgement as to what would count as self-inflicted? For example, would the catastrophic effect of an asteroid impact be attributable to human beings because they had not seen it coming when they might have done, or because they had not taken the measures they could have taken to prevent or mitigate its impact? In 1902 an increasingly pessimistic H. G. Wells, in a lecture entitled 'Discovery of the Future', stated:

> One must admit that it is impossible to show why certain things should not utterly destroy and end the entire human race and story, why night should not presently come down and make all our dreams and efforts vain. It is conceivable, for example, that some great unexpected mass of matter should presently rush upon us out of space, whirl sun and planets aside like dead leaves before the breeze, and collide with and utterly destroy every spark of life upon this earth.

Wells goes on to itemize other possible causes of the end of the 'human race and story': some lethal pestilence, 'some great disease of the atmosphere, some trailing cometary poison, some great emanation of vapour from the interior of the earth'; new animal predators might arise, or 'some drug or a wrecking madness' might overwhelm the human mind. What is in any case certain is that eventually our sun 'must radiate itself toward extinction'.[18] The word 'story' in Wells's lecture suggests, as it did for many late Victorians, the idea of progress in human history. This in turn gives a clue as to what 'our dreams and efforts' might be – presumably Wells has in mind technological advance, social reform and so on. But what exactly would make such efforts 'vain', and is something done in vain equivalent to failure?

In his short story 'The Star' (1897), on which Lars von Trier's feature film *Melancholia* (2011) is loosely based, a 'star' (or more likely a planet) drifts seemingly into a collision course with Earth. The university professor who has calculated the impending disaster defiantly addresses the star (in a manner reminiscent of Shelley's and Campbell's 'last men'): 'He looked at it as one might look into the eyes of a brave enemy. "You may kill me," he said after a silence. "But I can hold you – and all the universe for that matter – in the grip of this little brain. I would not change. Even now."' Later the professor tells his students the bad news.

> The next day at noon, punctual to the minute, he entered his lecture theatre, put his hat on the end of the table as his habit was, and carefully selected a large piece of chalk . . . He came and looked under his grey eyebrows at the rising tiers of young fresh faces, and spoke with his accustomed studied common-ness of phrasing. 'Circumstances have arisen – circumstances beyond my control,' he said and paused, 'which will debar me from completing the course I had designed. It would seem, gentlemen, if I may put the thing clearly and briefly, that – Man has lived in vain.'[19]

In Wells's story, the 'star' does not collide with Earth after all; the world is saved, and lessons drawn. In the film *Melancholia*, however, the expected impact occurs and the film ends with the whole world being destroyed along with all the film's protagonists; no lessons appear to be drawn. An imminent cataclysmic collision with Earth is also the basis for the film *Seeking a Friend for the End of the World* (dir. Lorene Scafaria, 2012), which works within the conventions of light comedy. This film, all of whose characters die along with the rest of the world's population, nevertheless achieves some kind of resolution; the two main protagonists die having recognized and affirmed their mutual love, and their dying young but fulfilled is a circumstance commonly associated with what in the previous chapter I called the 'less is more' philosophy of life. They seem to face death no differently from the way they would face it if the rest of the world were not dying with them.

In *Last Night* (dir. Don McKellar, 1998), another film in which the world actually ends (as a result of an unspecified solar anomaly that has turned night into day), a selection of characters in the city of Toronto prepare themselves for earth's final hour against a backdrop of moderate social breakdown. The father of a family trying to hold on to the familiar routines of life expresses the view that, 'now more than ever, we should be courteous and respect each other's needs. It's a test of our values.' Two other characters, thrown together by chance, end up in a final kiss instead of going through with a plan to shoot each other just before the final catastrophe. (As one of them earlier says: 'I'm not gonna let this world take my life. I am not just gonna pass away.') The director of a gas company meticulously rings everyone on his list of his customers to thank them, wish them well and assure them that everything will be done to maintain a gas supply right up until the end. That this mild character is randomly slaughtered only an hour or so before he would have perished in the final conflagration seems oddly tragic. Not unconvincingly, moreover, the film depicts crowds gathering together in an almost festive mood, as if witnessing the end of the world were not unlike welcoming in the New Year. As one character observes, 'In a way, I feel kind of privileged. I mean, it's the biggest thing that ever happened, and we're gonna be there. I mean, no one was there to witness the beginning, but we're gonna be there at the end.' By contrast, in the film *4:44 Last Day on Earth* (dir. Abel Ferrara, 2012), one character affects complete indifference when his brother reminds him that the world is about to end: 'The world's been ending ever since it started, man. You know, we've been ending ever since we were born. Don't take that shit too seriously.'

Despite what was said earlier, one might want to argue that death is easier to accept on the part of these fictional protagonists (and less tragic for their audience to witness) if it is known that everyone else is to die as well as they. For one thing, there will be no one left to mourn; and to be left behind, as the last person alive, might be considered worse than joining the majority in death. Even so, many people would no doubt share the sentiments of film critic Roger Ebert. 'To me,' he states (in a review of *Seeking a Friend for the End of the World*), 'even worse than this catastrophe would be foreknowledge of it. To die is one thing. How much worse to know that all the life that ever existed on this planet, and all it ever achieved, was to be obliterated?'[20] What is interesting here is the acknowledgement that it is important and comforting for those dying in the ordinary course of the world's history to know that the world (that is, human beings and all their achievements) will be carrying on without them – a point to which we shall return shortly. But it is also interesting, assuming Ebert's comment is at all representative, that some would prefer not to know that the world as a whole was going to end in the near future. There are, of course, smaller-scale examples in the real world where this last sentiment is actually put into practice, as when it is decided, for example, not to tell people that they are terminally ill or dying, or not to tell the dying about the recent death or serious illness of someone close to them. There seem to be two different principles here which can easily come into conflict: one is that we should die, and indeed want to die, in full relationship with the world as it is; the other is that we should not be told bad news or anything else that might cause additional suffering. But if the paramount aim were to minimize suffering and increase happiness, why not also tell dying persons pleasing things that are not true?

V

Returning to the question about the end of the world, why is it important for those contemplating their death, or actually facing death, to assume that the world will be going on without them? The question seems more pointed if cast in negative terms: why should the prospect of one's own death, and one's actual experience of dying, be made worse by the knowledge that human civilization and with it the whole of humanity will also cease to exist? The existential angst caused by such knowledge (however gained) would presumably be of a completely different order from the kind of anxiety caused by the contemplation of specific events likely or certain to follow one's death. For example, a dedicated businessman might die knowing that his company will almost certainly go bust after his death, or an artist might die fearing that her disaffected daughter will destroy all her paintings. Would not such eventualities shrink to insignificance if one also knew that the world as a whole was going to go bust or be destroyed? People do not easily abandon either their grip on their own physical existence or their moral and empathetic interests in the lives of others; and these interests are conjugated not just in the past and present tenses, but in the future and future conditional tenses too. These post-mortem interests, moreover, are not confined to the lives and well-being of family, friends and acquaintances. They extend into the wider human and indeed non-human population of the planet.

A further clue as to why, even when they are leaving it, people do not cease caring about the world and its inhabitants is surely to be found in the efforts they have made (especially in their later years) to do something that will outlast them, whether it is having children, engaging in creative work or pursuing other activities likely to ensure their earthly afterlife. In other words, wittingly as well as unwittingly people bequeath to the future some kind of personal legacy, one that they may themselves anticipate in their own lifetime. But the prospect of an earthly afterlife, even where it is not self-centred, and the natural empathy one has with one's fellow human beings, may not tell the whole story when it comes to explaining why it is important, for those dying or facing death, that the rest of the world should go on existing. If anything, both these forms of human behaviour in the face of death seem to beg the larger question. Here is the place, therefore, to examine the analysis given of this larger question by the philosopher Samuel Scheffler.

Scheffler's analysis of the question, in his book *Death and the Afterlife* (2013), could be described as a systematic answer to a question made famous by Groucho Marx, among others, but originally asked by the Irish politician Sir Boyle Roche: 'Why should we put ourselves out of our way to do anything for posterity, for what has posterity ever done for us?'[21] Scheffler's answer to this question would be that posterity – that is, the continuing existence of humanity – is in fact precisely what gives our present lives the meaning and the values that we find in them. We care about the future of humanity both as a good in itself and as a condition for most of the other things that we value. Indeed, according to Scheffler, we care more about the future of humanity as such – which means people we shall never know and who may not even yet exist – than we do about those closest to us, or even about our own future existence in some otherworldly afterlife (if such is our hope or belief). According to Scheffler, we tend both to exaggerate our own capacity for egoism and to underestimate the extent to which we are concerned to promote the greater good of humanity, not only beyond our own personal interests, but beyond our concerns for the well-being of our own circle of friends, family or tribe.

> the survival of people after our deaths matters greatly to us, both in its own right and because it is a condition of many other things that now matter to us continuing to do so. In some very significant respects, we actually care more about the survival of others after our deaths than we do about the existence of a personal afterlife, and the imminent disappearance of the human race would have a more corrosive effect on our ability to lead what I have called 'value-laden lives' than

does the actual prospect of our own deaths. These facts teach us something about the limits of our egoism and about the limits of our individualism.[22]

Scheffler reasons out this apparently counterintuitive conclusion by imagining our likely reactions in two scenarios – one that he calls the doomsday scenario and another he calls the infertility scenario. In the first, one learns that thirty years after one's own death everyone else will die; in the second, we live in the last period of human history, when the earth's entire population has become sterile.[23] Scheffler suggests that 'it is safe to say that most of us would respond to the doomsday scenario with what I will generically call, with bland understatement, profound dismay.'[24] It is the second scenario that clinches Scheffler's main argument, since our likely reactions here would appear to demonstrate that it is not simply the future of our immediate loved ones that we care about – loved ones who in this scenario would not die prematurely (as many of them would in the first scenario). It might of course be argued that our profound dismay is indeed about our loved ones rather than about humanity at large, albeit in a deferred sense: because we care about our loved ones, we also care about our loved ones' loved ones, and so on. It would, however, become increasingly artificial to differentiate between the larger and the more specific groups here; and it could be said that it is the ultimate relatedness of all human beings that is precisely what fuels our dismay.

Scheffler calls the ongoing existence of humanity we all take for granted the 'collective afterlife', distinguishing this from what he somewhat misleadingly describes as the personal afterlife, the continuation of one's individual existence in another world. This term, or rather this pair of terms, is misleading at least to the extent that it underestimates the fact that this 'personal afterlife' would itself be a collective afterlife. Scheffler does acknowledge this, since he identifies as one of the motives for belief in a personal afterlife the desire to be reunited with one's loved ones, and another as the need to see the injustices of the present world righted. But why only one's loved ones, might one ask? Why would reunion with a larger humanity not also be a motive, given that the loss of a larger humanity is what would undermine our present lives if we knew that the world was going to end? In any case, Scheffler makes it clear that he rejects both the existence and the plausibility of a personal afterlife and hence, one suspects, is not inclined to pursue the logic of the idea further. We can fairly say that he would be content to explain belief in a personal afterlife exclusively in terms of the fear of extinction, the desire for reunion with loved ones and the craving for the resolution of worldly injustices.

Scheffler's main contention, however, is difficult to deny: that, irrespective of our belief or disbelief in substantive survival, we do in fact care about the persistence of the collective afterlife. We care about it both for its own sake and because our confidence in its continuation underpins many of the other things we care about.

> Humanity itself as an ongoing, historical project provides the implicit frame of reference for most of our judgements about what matters. Remove that frame of reference, and our sense of importance – however individualistic it may be in its overt content – is destabilized and begins to erode. We need humanity to have a future if many of our own individual purposes are to matter to us now. Indeed, I believe that something stronger is true: we need humanity to have a future for the very idea that things *matter* to retain a secure place in our conceptual repertoire.[25]

Given either the doomsday or the global infertility scenario, not only would our longer-term interests, projects and responsibilities lose their momentum; even our more immediate appetites, interests and relationships are likely to wither in the shadow of humanity's imminent demise. Why would we even play diversionary games, he asks, when there no longer remains anything serious from which to be diverted?

A key element in Scheffler's argument is that our relationship with the collective afterlife is or can be an active and creative one. We can, for example, use devices such as wills and bequests 'to extend the reach of our own agency beyond death in an effort to help sustain the people and things that matter to us'.[26] Moreover, the fact that the social network to which one belongs will be disrupted by one's death can even be regarded as a positive element of the collective future.

> In a certain sense, it personalizes one's relation to that future. Rather than looming simply as a blank eternity of non-existence, the future can be conceptualized with reference to an ongoing social world in which one retains a social identity. One can imagine oneself into that world simply by imagining

the resumption of one's premortem relationships with people who will themselves continue to exist and to remember and care for one. One needn't fear, as many people apparently do, that one will simply be forgotten as soon as one is gone.[27]

Using a simile reminiscent of Magee's comparison of life in this world to a party, Scheffler suggests that the 'world of the future becomes, as it were, more like a party one had to leave early and less like a gathering of strangers'.[28] This extension of what I earlier called a 'notional self' into a future from which we shall be substantively absent gives us licence to imagine a social identity for 'ourselves' in the world of the future. What Scheffler is describing here is the consolation one may derive from the prospect of one's earthly afterlife – a survival that others, and not ourselves, will actually enjoy (or not enjoy, as the case may be). And just as Scheffler's collective afterlife is the context within which a person's earthly afterlife is sustained (or suppressed) in the future, so does the certainty that there will be such an afterlife provide the motive force for many of the interests and projects pursued by those currently alive. To value something is to want it to continue, and it is through our values that we acquire a stake in the future.

> When we value something . . . we project ourselves into the future and invest ourselves in that future. Our emotions and our future courses of action both hang in the balance; they both depend on the fate of what we value . . . If we valued nothing, then the prospect of post-mortem asteroids or global infertility would lack the power to disturb us in the way that they do . . . [I]n valuing, we lay claim to the future – we arrogate to ourselves the authority to make judgements about how the future should unfold.[29]

Scheffler's analysis is open to a number of challenges and also leaves important questions hanging. That many of our actions and values are based on the assumption that the world will continue indefinitely into the future, even the far future, seems incontrovertible. Scheffler is probably also correct in his optimistic assessment of the balance of egoism and altruism in most human beings. It might nevertheless be the case that, for most people most of the time, the future prospects of humanity at large, as distinct from the welfare of their more immediate circle of family and friends, figure very little in the way they think about the future. Such things as our collective failure in dealing with the problem of climate change, or our readiness to make far-reaching individual or local decisions without consulting a wider human constituency, are difficult to square with rational and far-sighted altruism. The projection of our notional selves into the future could be interpreted less as an engagement with the future and more as a refusal to accept that the future, like the past, is a 'foreign country' of which we ourselves shall never be citizens.

Scheffler's analysis is limited to the argument that the values by which human beings actually live depend upon the rarely examined assumption that humanity will continue into the indefinite future, and to the speculation that, if the end of humanity were ever known or believed to be imminent, the future-oriented lives of those who tacitly affirm these values would rapidly stall. What his analysis does not claim to do, however, is provide any answer to questions about the meaning of life or about the significance of human extinction. It cannot solve the problem of the meaning of life by establishing that human beings, as a matter of fact, find meaning by living in the shadow of the collective afterlife of humanity. Even if this collective afterlife 'can vindicate our worldly concerns and help to stave off nihilism', still our lives have no 'larger cosmic purpose or significance'.[30] All one can do, therefore, is to hope, or assume, that human life will continue to flourish for millennia to come. Scheffler assumes, however, that sooner or later the end of humanity will indeed come, and that will be that. Whether the human race survives for another million years, or another hundred million years, or for some unimaginably longer period of time, its eventual demise must one day be confronted by some particular generation or generations of human beings. There will one day be a generation (or perhaps a few generations) for whom the knowledge and prospect of humanity's end will be no longer a future possible but an imminent historical reality. To these unfortunates Scheffler's book (which we can imagine surviving in some form) will have nothing to say, or nothing to say that will be anything more than descriptive social anthropology. It will offer no consolation for, or explanation of, what for them will have been a simple accident of birth. They will be like people who turn up at the railway station having just missed the last train or arrive at a concert hall after the last tickets have been sold.

On Scheffler's hypothesis, moreover, it can surely make no difference whether the inevitable final chapter of the book of human history
comes sooner or later. If one generation does not face it, then another
will, and the event will be as meaningless if it comes later as it would
have been had it come earlier. We cannot say that the more human
beings that have existed, the more meaningful human existence will
have been. Surely the only way in which such meaning can be found
for humanity at large, and not just for that lucky majority for whom
there was still a human future to give the past, present and future history of the world its meaning, would lie within precisely the kind of
broader metaphysical or cosmological worldview that Scheffler's view
of the matter excludes.

Scheffler's terms of reference do not allow him to think that the
end of human civilization could have any significance beyond being
the final twist of the human evolutionary tale. His view of human life
in the universe might even be described as parochial. He does not consider, for example, the possibility that human civilization might spread
to other habitable planets or become part of a larger community of
intelligent beings in the universe. Alternatively, human beings might
conceivably discover (in accordance with many religious cosmologies)
that human life on Earth is but one manifestation of life in the universe, and that the universe is rich with many other kinds of beings,
including other rationally intelligent beings, occupying ontological
niches, so to say, other than that of our familiar Earth. If humankind
were indeed part of a wider community of intelligent beings in the
physical universe, there already exists a collective afterlife of a broader
kind that will persist even when some particular collective afterlife
comes to an end.

Within a theory of what Scheffler calls a personal afterlife, moreover, the prospect of the complete destruction of this world and its
human inhabitants, disastrous as it would be, would not necessarily
be a cause of despair and meaninglessness. Scheffler himself, however,
can only view such an afterlife in negative terms. Thus, for him, one
potential danger of belief in a personal afterlife is that it 'may reconcile
people too readily to the disappearance of life on earth, and make it
seem less urgent to prevent this from happening'.[31] Scheffler's assumption here is the familiar one of imagining that the personal afterlife
would have no continuities with this world, and its subjects no continuing relationship with those on Earth. In any case, a belief that

the disappearance of life on Earth has no meaning either positive or negative will fare no better in preventing this event from happening, assuming (as do both of his two apocalyptic scenarios) that they are beyond human control. Projecting our human values onto a collective afterlife that is destined, sooner or later, to come to an end amounts to little more than a kicking further down the road, for as long as there is anybody to do the kicking, of the unopened can labelled 'meaning of life'. Quite possibly Scheffler would endorse a view of the meaning of life in line with the bleakly reductionist idea of purpose in the universe suggested by the cosmologist Paul Davies:

> If there is a purpose to the universe, and it achieves that purpose, then the universe must end, for its continued existence would be gratuitous and pointless. Conversely, if the universe endures forever, it is hard to imagine that there is any ultimate purpose to the universe at all. So cosmic death may be the price that has to be paid for cosmic success. Perhaps the most that we can hope for is that the purpose of the universe becomes known to our descendants before the end of the last three minutes.[32]

But questions about the meaning and value of life can be extended beyond human relationships to the entire animate and inanimate world. We need to be here to formulate such questions, of course, but some of them will relate to times and situations when we will (or may) not be here. In Nevil Shute's *On the Beach*, one character says to another: 'It's – it's the end of the world. I've never had to imagine anything like that before.' To this the other laughingly replies: 'It's not the end of the world at all . . . It's only the end of us. The world will go on just the same, only we shan't be in it. I dare say it will get along all right without us.'[33] This is rather a thoughtless, if not actually a cynical, remark to make about a world upon which human beings have just unleashed radiation deadly to most forms of life. What attitudes we should have to what might happen in or to the world after human beings no longer inhabit it, and whether we have responsibilities towards it to be exercised in advance of our absence from it, are questions I take up in the next chapter.

SEVEN

WHAT OF THE WORLD WITHOUT US?

Not one would mind, neither bird nor tree,
If mankind perished utterly;

And Spring herself, when she woke at dawn,
Would scarcely know that we were gone.
SARA TEASDALE, 'There Will Come Soft Rains' (1920)

I

In this book I have been exploring the idea that human beings, even after they are forgotten as individuals, can be said to have attained some kind of earthly immortality simply by having left their mark upon the world. Thoughtful persons cannot live in this world without being aware, sometimes quite vividly, of the impress of the lives of previous generations upon almost every detail of their own. Everything we do, say, see or hear bears the imprint of the known and unknown dead who have gone before us, and indeed made our lives what they are.[1] The world itself, with its future generations, constitutes our collective memory and hence our collective afterlife – a memory stored in books, images, languages, inventions, laws, customs, buildings and the landscape itself. But does the world only have meaning in relation to the human beings who are able to recognize it as a world, their world? What of the world without us? What value, if any, can the world, in all its animate and inanimate complexity, be said to have in its own right, independently of our human habitation of it? Does it make sense to be concerned about the world's own longevity or immortality? What gives point to these questions is the spectre of human extinction – the possibility (or probability, or certainty) that sooner or later all human life will disappear from this Earth.[2]

The likelihood that the world and its non-human inhabitants will outlast the entire human race surely compels us to ask where human mortality and human extinction leave everything else. This may sound like asking what a room looks like when there is no one in it or whether a falling tree in a forest makes a sound when there is no one there to hear it. In fact, and to stick with these two examples, the room and its contents, and the tree and its surrounding forest, are obstinately there despite the lack of human observers. The point is exactly this: that although we will not be there ourselves (as observers or users of it), the world itself will persist, and in particular will bear traces of our former activities within it. In this respect, the world's 'immortality' could be considered part of our own (collective) immortality. A question arising from this is whether, while we are still here, we have responsibilities towards the world that will one day persist without us. These responsibilities relate both to the earth's natural species and also to the aesthetic and utilitarian artefacts we leave behind us. How much do we or should we care about the persistence of natural species and of human artefacts independently of our own use and appreciation of them? As I have said, what brings this question dramatically into focus is the possible, or inevitable, future extinction of the human race.

In this chapter, I first review the diverse possible circumstances in which human extinction could occur, and the bearing these circumstances might have on the theme of earthly immortality. Following this, I explore three contexts within which questions about earthly immortality might arise: the realm of nature; the realm of human culture; and what might be called the astronomical realm – the context within which we consider the Earth not in isolation but as an entity which forms part of a solar system in one of the billions of galaxies scattered across the universe.[3]

II

It would sound odd to say of a deceased individual that this person is, or has become, extinct.[4] This is because we generally reserve the language of extinction for the loss of an entire species.[5] Moreover, the language of extinction does not sit easily with the way deceased individuals are seen as 'living on' in some way – through their children, their work, their friendships and so on. Again, whereas the death of a single person, however sad or traumatic for immediate friends and family, is accepted as an inevitable and even benign part of the natural order, the extinction of the entire human species would be regarded as a catastrophic eventuality. In the case of most species of animal, what will concern us will be the conservation of the species itself rather than the preservation of its individual members. While some may 'mourn' the deaths of individuals from particular species of non-human animal – species such as dogs, horses or elephants, for example – it is generally the species itself that is valued, which is why the culling of some of its individual members is often an acceptable strategy for preserving that species. This in any case fits in with the survival strategy of species themselves, whose reproductive and rearing behaviour subordinates the interests of its individual members to those of the species as a whole. What matters most is keeping the species as a whole alive. In this respect, the interests of human conservationists and the collective instincts of the species itself are in accord.

In human society too, the needs and survival of the group will tend to take precedence over those of its individual members. Nevertheless, individual human beings treat one another quite differently from the ways in which the individuals of most other species treat one another. In any civilized society, each human life is regarded as having intrinsic value, and great care is taken to avoid the death of each of its individual members. Even where, in justification of some perceived or imagined greater good, the lives of individuals are placed in jeopardy, or are deliberately sacrificed, such deaths will be regretted. Inevitably, however, the deaths of individual humans are judged differently, according to whether they are peaceful or painful, timely or untimely, accidental or deliberate, criminal or legal, and so on.

On an evolutionary timescale, of course, species themselves come and go, just as do individuals within a given species. In this respect humans are no different from any other species, and may well go the way of dodos or dinosaurs. Moreover, the animal-like features of human behaviour or the human-like features of animal behaviour,[6] and the fact that we share a very high percentage of our genetic make-up with other species, have encouraged the view that human beings are 'just another' mammalian species, a view which in some quarters fosters an attitude of human self-denigration. It is pointed out that much human behaviour is worse than that found in most other animal species, which leads some people to express the view that the planet would be much better off without us. The argument that there is nothing special about human beings, and that they might well be regarded as inferior to other species, tends to be a self-refuting one. No other animal species can reflect on its own nature in this way, or contemplate its own likely demise, or despise its own status or behaviour. And the fact that human beings are genetically very close to other species might just as well be cited to show the irrelevance of genetics when it comes to understanding the unique nature of human beings within the animal kingdom (or, alternatively, to show that even the slightest genetic difference between species can make all the difference). The claim that human beings are not essentially different from other animals is easily refuted by reference to the rich cultural legacy of humankind. No other animals, however smart, possess the ability to reflect and act on the basis of rational thought within a temporal perspective or a cultural tradition based on the imaginative creation of alternative worlds.[7] For this reason humans are also in the unique position of being capable of either raising or reducing the chances of their own extinction and that of other species.

The survival of humanity is threatened with a number of hypothetical future events or processes, all of which have been discussed by scientists and dramatized in film and fiction. These eventualities could be gradual or sudden, natural or anthropogenic, and terrestrial or extra-terrestrial in origin. Moreover, human extinction could occur either as a singular event, or as part of the wider degradation or destruction of the world's ecosystems. Thus the literal ending of the world discussed in the previous chapter might come about through extreme climate change, pandemic disease, loss of resources, global nuclear warfare or asteroid impact, or even as the intended or unintended consequence of visitation by extraterrestrial beings. Human beings might suffer wholesale extinction instantly; within a few days, weeks or months; in the course of a single generation; or over some much longer period of time. Human populations might dwindle away gradually, at different rates in different places around the world. For as long as at least some areas of the planet were habitable, there could be groups of humans struggling to survive and preserve a modicum of civilization. Even where the eventual destruction of the entire ecosystem seemed inevitable, human beings might consider escape or rescue a possibility. Science-fiction narratives and forward-looking scientists have imagined human beings, or at least a representative sample of them, setting out for new homes elsewhere in the galaxy. Alternatively, if the existence of intelligent beings elsewhere in the universe were taken seriously, human beings might broadcast the equivalent of mayday signals in the hope of advice or rescue.

On the cataclysmic hypothesis, however, humanity's struggle to survive would eventually come to an end with the complete extinction of humankind. Whether human beings would have time to reflect upon their likely or possible extinction would of course depend on the rapidity with which the event occurred. The possibility, or as some would insist the inevitability, of human extinction is one that we can contemplate here and now while the human species, despite all its difficulties, appears still to be thriving. Perhaps the worst kind of confrontation with human extinction would be one where we had advance knowledge of an unavoidable global disaster – a deadly virus with no known antidote, for example, or a giant asteroid on a collision course with Earth.

But subtler forms of human extinction are also possible, or at least imaginable, where extinction is more a process than an event, and where either the gradual nature of the process or our own complicity within it would mean that we remained largely unaware of its significance for us. We might, for instance, perfect ourselves into extinction through an excess of technological interventions within our biological and psychological make-up, transforming ourselves – as some hope and others fear – into what is in effect a new species. In Chapter Two, I suggested that a future, transhumanist version of humankind, devoid of many features of the older humanity, could in effect spell the extinction of the latter. The ultimate transhumanist dream is the development – through genetic manipulation and cybernetic enhancement – of physically immortal human beings. Some would regard this not as the apotheosis of humanity but rather as tantamount to humanity's extinction, on the grounds that it is mortality itself that is the key to our nature. No less disastrously, perhaps, human beings might disappear through interbreeding with another humanoid race such as might be encountered in a future space-faring age. Early *Homo sapiens*, itself once threatened with extinction, was at one stage interbreeding with *Homo neanderthalensis*, a now extinct species (or sub-species, *Homo sapiens neanderthalensis*) whose DNA remains a minute part of the genetic make-up of many modern humans.[8]

But would the biological extinction of a species (or genus) necessarily be equivalent to its complete annihilation? The dinosaurs 'live on' genetically in later species, geologically in the numerous fossils discovered around the world, and culturally in the perennial human interest generated by these creatures. Neanderthal man might be extinct in the obvious sense, but his assimilation or interbreeding with *Homo sapiens* could also be regarded, more positively, as a form of long-term survival. Human beings contemplating the possibility, likelihood or certainty of extinction might take steps to preserve some of their DNA, along with that of other species, in a form and location accessible to any intelligent beings who might sooner or later turn up on Earth. By the same token, spaceships containing DNA material and the memorabilia of human culture could be launched from a doomed or dying planet Earth in the hope that intelligent beings elsewhere might benefit from this material in some way, or might by acknowledging our existence at least keep our name alive.

Even without taking such deliberate steps to preserve memorabilia of human culture (and even DNA samples) for other rationally intelligent beings to discover, an extinct humanity will have left its mark on Earth and in the solar system, come what may. This 'mark' would consist in the accumulated changes made by human cultures to the geology, geography, topography, atmosphere and biology of the planet, and centuries of physical artefacts great and small, as well as the electromagnetic emissions (radio waves, and so on) of recent centuries. How long these traces of humanity would last, once humanity itself had disappeared, has been the subject of some speculation.[9] Superficially, at least, humanity's more obvious traces would disappear relatively quickly, nature rapidly reclaiming all the spaces hitherto occupied by human culture.[10] But, as the geologist Jan Zalasiewicz concludes,

whatever we as a species do from now, we have already left a record that is now indelible, even while the scale of this fossilization event is still in question, and within our power to determine. Humankind has, through its various activities, done enough to preserve its relics into the far future. The environmental changes that we have set in train will, without a shadow of a doubt, be translated into the solid rock of the Earth. The Urban Stratum is now, in substantial part, effectively eternal. More: our actions now will literally be raising mountain belts higher, or lowering them, or setting off volcanoes (or stifling them), or triggering new biological diversity (or suppressing it) for many million years to come. The knock-on effects of our geochemical experiments are unpredictable in detail, but will be substantial and likely surprising. We have left our mark. However we are interpreted in some distant future, there will be little doubt that we will be associated with – and responsible for – some of the most extraordinary geology of this, or any other, planet.[11]

Whether there ever will be anyone to 'interpret' us in the far distant future, and to what extent humanity would have been proud of what it had left behind, are rather different questions of course. One important point that Zalasiewicz makes is that the more definite the marks we leave for future explorers to discover, the more damage we shall be doing to ourselves. 'The deeper the footprint that we leave, the greater will be the immediate calamity that awaits our children.'[12]

Geologists and others have recently proposed that a new epoch in the Earth's history began when human beings started to make irreversible changes to the Earth's climate and geography. This new epoch has been named the Anthropocene Age.[13] It is ironic that an epoch so named could also be defined as the one in which human beings were for the first time capable of bringing about their own extinction. The ultimate irony would be if the nearest humanity came to achieving any kind of collective immortality would be through leaving permanent traces of its self-destruction.

A question worth asking here is whether the disappearance of humanity, under some circumstances or even under any circumstances, would necessarily be regarded (*ex ante* of course) as a negative eventuality? It is interesting that long-existent but eventually extinct creatures, such as dinosaurs, are popularly regarded as having, by becoming extinct, somehow failed where they might have succeeded, so to speak – succeeded, presumably, by surviving indefinitely. Their extinction is a sign of failure and a mark against them, which is why it is a popular insult to describe as 'dinosaurs' those who do not or cannot change with the times.[14] When individuals die, we do not regard their lives as having been a failure, or as having been 'lived in vain', simply because these lives have ended. This is true even if we hold the view defended by some philosophers that it is always better to be alive than dead, or the view that death is bad because it harms the person who has died by depriving them of a good – that of being alive (or of the goods associated with being alive). Individual lives might, of course, be variously judged as cut short, incomplete, wasted or unfulfilled, but none of these judgements amount to saying that a life has been lived 'in vain' or has been a 'failure' simply by virtue of its having come to an end.

The question here is whether we might want to say the same kind of thing about the entire human species. In the previous chapter, I discussed the suggestion by H. G. Wells that all the 'dreams and efforts' of humanity would have been in vain if some cataclysmic event were to bring to an end 'the human race and story'. One might sympathize more with this view in the case of humanity bringing about its own destruction than in the case of such destruction being caused by factors beyond human control or foresight. But the real question here is whether the destruction of humanity, however caused, could be said to amount to a 'failure' of some kind, or to the whole history of humanity having been lived 'in vain'. If humankind were to be destroyed before its science has achieved the ambition of creating an unlimited supply of clean energy or of discovering a comprehensive cure for cancer, it would by no means follow that all human dreams and efforts had been in vain. Nor would it follow that these particular ambitions had been in vain. What counted, it could be said, were the dreams and the efforts themselves. Wells, however, seems to be referring to something more general than simply the failure of humankind to have achieved this or that particular goal.

It could be argued that whether our individual lives are to be accounted failures or not will depend upon the integrity and enjoyment with which we live our lives while we have lives to live, and not upon living for a certain period of time (if not indefinitely) or even upon particular achievements. So too might it be argued that whether or not any given human community or society has lived in vain must depend upon its qualities at this or that point in history, not upon how long it lasts or upon when or how it comes to an end. Would one really judge the Aztec, Roman or Ottoman empires to have been failures simply because they came to an end?[15] Would it not be better to judge these civilizations, in so far as they can be judged at all, by their legacy to later civilizations? Better still, would one not judge them by the lives and achievements of the individuals who made up these civilizations? And, like the Last Man at the very end of Olaf Stapledon's future history of mankind, might one not say something similar about human civilization as a whole?

> Great are the stars, and man is of no account to them. But man is a fair spirit, whom a star conceived and a star kills. He is

greater than those bright blind companies. For though in them there is incalculable potentiality, in him there is achievement, small, but actual. Too soon, seemingly, he comes to his end. But when he is done he will not be nothing, not as though he had never been; for he is eternally a beauty in the eternal form of things.[16]

III

It is misleading to think about human extinction in isolation from the state of the entire planetary ecosystem. Human beings are not alone in this world. They live within, and as part of, a complex ecology ranging from the tiniest microbes to the largest mammals. Human extinction might come about as part of a larger extinction of life on this Earth, or merely as the loss of a single species. In either case, human extinction would not be without dramatic consequences for the planet as a whole. Until relatively recently, most people would undoubtedly have said that the destiny of the human race as a whole is something beyond human control or prediction. They will generally have assumed that the history of the human race would stretch indefinitely into the future, just as it could be seen stretching back millennia into the past. Even for those who believe or believed in an end of history brought about by some kind of divine judgement, indeed especially for them, the idea that the human race might come prematurely to an end is or was unthinkable. Nowadays, however, our knowledge of evolutionary history has made us fully aware of the possibility of human extinction. What should be our attitude to this possibility, not least in view of the fact that the chances of a self-inflicted human extinction are now much higher than at any other time in human history? Individual human beings do not go through life explicitly desiring or promoting something as abstract as the perpetuation of the human race as a whole; but they could be said to be doing so implicitly, in the course of wishing to perpetuate their own families and to protect their own tribal and national identities.

This brings us to a second question. What responsibility, in the light of their own possible extinction, do human beings have for the non-human occupants of this planet and indeed for the planetary environment as a whole? For as long as there are humans around to enjoy and benefit from the presence of fauna and flora, questions about their intrinsic value are easily ignored. Attitudes to the natural world, and especially to the 'higher animals' within it, are variously justified in utilitarian, aesthetic or moral terms. First and foremost, plants and animals supply us with nourishment and with a wealth of other practical benefits, including transport, clothing material, fuel and medicine. Both animal and plant species tend to be referred to as 'natural resources'. Apart from this, we find our lives enriched by the presence of the fauna and flora in our environment.[17] At the same time we also experience strong moral obligations towards the natural world, over and above its practical uses and aesthetic appeal. The familiar idea that human beings are 'stewards' of the natural environment suggests something more than either sentimentality or mere self-interest. It is not just a question of behaving humanely towards sentient beings, nor of having some kind of empathy, especially with the higher animals. There is also a sense that the natural world has an intrinsic value and that it is a human obligation to conserve it for its own sake as well as for our own benefit and enjoyment.

Supposing that this is indeed so, for there is no space to argue it here, an important question arises. Does the obligation to be stewards of the natural environment also oblige us to consider what we should do in advance of the likely event of human beings one day ceasing to exist, not least given our past interventions in the natural environment? One obvious response to this question is to say that taking measures to protect the post-human environment is an activity no different (except in scale) from, say, including in one's will the provision of a sum of money to be spent on one's pet dog after one has died. If we have no trouble understanding this lesser activity, then we should have no difficulty understanding the greater one. Of course our planet will, in some form, 'survive' our own departure from it. But is it enough simply to say that the planet will get on perfectly happily without us, as the character from Nevil Shute's *On the Beach* airily suggests?[18] Much damage has already been done, and human beings could conceivably put in place measures to mitigate this damage which would continue to be effective long after we had disappeared.

Other justifications can be given for human beings doing what they can for the natural environment despite their own likely disappearance from it. It might be thought that such actions would improve, however marginally, the chances of future intelligent beings arising within Earth's ecosystem. Another, arguably more realistic, prospect is that an ecosystem left in the best possible condition could prove that much more useful or welcoming to some other race of intelligent beings such as might happen upon our world. A last remnant of human beings leaving the natural environment in as good a state as possible for the future flourishing of life is on the same continuum as dying persons making arrangements for the future care of their human and non-human dependants. In short, actions directed at maintaining or safe-guarding the natural environment for a future time when there will or might be no human beings left within it require no additional arguments other than those which explain or justify the kinds of humane concerns most human beings already demonstrate. Taking measures designed to benefit the natural environment after we have gone – such as dealing with nuclear waste or atmospheric pollution – would in itself constitute an example of what I have defined as our anonymous earthly immortality.

Some will want to argue that it is impossible to view the world, let alone to value it, independently of our own particular evolutionary position and species interests within it. Even our aesthetic appreciation of the world, in all its animate and inanimate variety, must be subject to the particularities of human biology. It might be concluded, therefore, that the idea of valuing a world bereft of humankind is a meaningless one. But although a purely disinterested view of our world or of anything within it might well be impossible, human beings are nevertheless capable of abstract and speculative modes of thought which allow them to think outside biological and cultural constraints. If this were not so, it is difficult to see how human beings could have come up with the theory of evolution, for example, or how we could ever say that this or any other theory was either true or false. In any case, a non-human as distinct from a human view of the world is not what is in question. Either it makes sense to ask whether human beings can have views about, or attitudes towards, the fate or status of this planet independently of their dependence upon it, or it does not. If it does, then it is hardly a criticism to say that these views and attitudes must express a specifically human viewpoint.

IV

Would the kinds of concern relating to the well-being of the post-human natural environment also arise in relation to the preservation of humankind's own artefacts? By 'artefact' here I mean any utilitarian or aesthetic object, or secondary representation of such an object, of which the following are some of the more obvious examples: books, paintings, buildings, vehicles, tools, furniture, photographs, digital data. Many of these artefacts would of course survive the sudden or gradual demise of humanity, and some of them would survive the more catastrophic event of all life on Earth being extinguished. With forethought, no doubt, it would be possible to extend the longevity of some human artefacts by centuries if not millennia. The question here is whether there would be any interest in doing so, let alone anything approaching a moral obligation in this regard.

The obvious response here is to say that unlike sentient creatures and the inanimate natural environment on which they depend, human artefacts have absolutely no value or meaning in a world devoid of those who alone are able to appreciate or make use of them. Sentient creatures have an intrinsic value and, in relation to them, their inanimate environment (soil, water, atmosphere and so on) has an instrumental value. Thus making sure that all nuclear materials were safely buried so that the well-being of surviving wildlife would not be jeopardized by radiation is an example of the kind of rational and humane behaviour a last generation of human beings might display. By contrast, taking steps to preserve, let us say, the paintings in London's National Gallery against the kinds of degradation that would soon attend them if special measures were not taken would seem to be a meaningless activity, since with the disappearance of any human observer these paintings have a status no different from that of random bits of coloured materials. Why not, instead, leave open the doors and windows of the gallery to admit any creatures who might find something useful there to eat or nest in?

Before simply concluding that members of an imminently extinct humanity would have little or no interest in the fate of its cultural artefacts, and no reason to be interested in them, we should pause to reflect that this conclusion presupposes a view of art, and of cultural artefacts more generally, that is peculiarly modern. According to this view, art has purely social origins and functions; even the aesthetic criteria by which art is valued are dependent on social context. Without this social context, works of art have no meaning. In past eras and other cultures, however, the power and value of art (or of what we now call art) was not purely aesthetic or even anthropocentric. Many 'works of art' and other artefacts had an otherworldly purpose, being considered communications with, or representations (if not embodiments) of, supernatural beings or principles, and as such did not require the presence of an 'appreciative' public to justify them. A disappearing humanity who thought like this might well take steps to protect their artefacts and 'artworks' in a world where there would be no human beings left. We might call this view a magical or a primitive one, but it is one that also persists in modern cultures. Even the immense monetary value we place upon works of art, like the value we place on gold, seems to have, in our terms, a non-rational basis. People have been ready to risk or sacrifice their lives to rescue or safeguard works of art and other cultural items. Such actions are likely to be justified in terms of saving the cultural heritage of a whole society, but what still needs explaining is why such items are worth dying for. Would any of the last persons alive on Earth risk their lives to retrieve a painting, say Botticelli's *Primavera*, from a burning building? Probably they would not do so, but they are hardly likely to be indifferent to it. They would see its destruction as the tragic disappearance of something uniquely human.

Cultural artefacts, along with our imprint upon the natural environment, might well survive to form part of humanity's 'terrestrial afterlife'. In a world in which there were no longer any human beings present to respond to them, of course, such artefacts could hardly be the vehicles of the kinds of earthly immortality, anonymous or otherwise, that they have provided for their creators within the course of human history. And yet there might eventually be a new, albeit non-human, response to these artefacts. We can speculate that there might eventually be a response from a visiting or colonizing extraterrestrial race, one capable of recognizing such artefacts for what they were. Alternatively, there might eventually be a response from another intelligent species such as might eventually evolve in our wake. This latter possibility, of course, assumes that our planet would remain capable of supporting life for as long as it took for a new intelligent species to emerge. What both alternatives assume, moreover, is that at least some human artefacts are themselves capable of surviving through the immense periods of time likely to pass before the possibilities in question could ever be realized.

As Alan Weisman tells us, artefacts made of non-corrosive metals such as gold, platinum or copper – the so-called 'noble metals' – are likely to last forever. Bronze, an alloy of copper, is particularly durable.

That new, 97.6 percent zinc penny will leach away if tossed in the ocean, dooming Abe Lincoln's visage to be filtered by shellfish within a century or so. The Statue of Liberty, however, which sculptor Frédéric Auguste Bartholdi hammered from copper sheeting not much thicker, would oxidize with dignity at the bottom of New York Harbor should glaciers ever return to our warming world and knock her off her pedestal. In the end, Liberty's sea green patina will thicken until she turns to stone, but the sculptor's aesthetic intention will still be preserved for the fish to ponder. By then, Africa's white-backed vultures may also have vanished, except in Mark Rossi's bronze homage to them, in whatever is left of Philadelphia.[19]

Let us suppose, however, that the threat of human extinction (assuming it to be both a gradual and a predictable occurrence) is contemporary with a period in human history when it is taken for granted, or at least regarded as highly probable, that there are other intelligent beings capable of visiting Earth. In these circumstances, it might make perfect sense to do what one could to preserve, for the instruction or even benefit of such potential visitors, at least a sample of humanity's cherished achievements. This would be an extension, on a much larger scale, of the 'time capsules' that have already been left for future generations of human beings to discover.[20] In the case of such historical time capsules, it is assumed that there will be a surviving human culture to provide continuity between those who buried the capsule and those who recover it. In any case, a deserted or even a devastated planet would function as a kind of time capsule by default for any extraterrestrial visitors, rather as an archaeological site does for earthly investigators. One legacy likely to persist for thousands of years, giving eloquent testimony to our skills in the use of the Earth's resources, is the mass of irreducible nuclear and plastic waste that now blights the planet.

The first time capsule of modern times was the 'Century Safe' collection of artefacts deposited by Mrs Charles Diehm in Philadelphia in 1879, but what is probably still the most ambitious one was the 'Crypt of Civilization' organized by Thornwell Jacobs (1877–1956). Inaugurated in 1936, its contents constitute an encyclopaedic inventory of life and customs up to the year 1940. In this same year the crypt was sealed, the plan being it should be reopened in 8113.[21] The term 'time capsule' itself appears to have been coined by the Westinghouse Electrical and Manufacturing Company in the course of planning a promotional event for the 1939 New York World's Fair. In 1938 a 2-metre (7-ft) cylinder, containing microfilm records together with a selection of commonly used items and materials, was buried on the site of the New York World's Fair, with the intention that this 'cross-section of our time' would be opened 5,000 years later. The Vice-President of Westinghouse expressed the hope 'that this pioneer effort will encourage others to deposit even more adequate records of our day in many places, and at such intervals as will provide "futurians" with a complete running history of their past, our future'.[22]

In preparing his crypt, Thornwell Jacobs had in mind not only the future inhabitants of Earth, but the possibility of visitors arriving from another world. With the advent of space exploration, the idea of the time capsule took off, quite literally, in a new direction. The selection and presentation of data specifically designed for discovery by non-human intelligence obviously requires something more than just selecting representative material for some future earthly generation. The Voyager 1 and Voyager 2 space probes, launched by NASA in 1977 and now well beyond the furthest edge of our solar system, each carried

> a gold-plated copper disc . . . containing sounds of Earth, greetings in 55 languages spoken by 87 percent of the world's population, 115 analog-encoded photographs and 90 minutes of music ranging from the bell-pure tones of Pygmy girls singing in a forest in Zaire to Beethoven's Cavatina and Chuck Berry's 'Johnny B. Goode'. To facilitate playback, the aluminum case enclosing each record carries a ceramic phono cartridge plus a diagram showing how to use it . . . The record's case also sports a pulsar map, showing Earth's location at the epoch of launch, and a patch of uranium-238 from whose half-life the time elapsed since launch may be inferred.[23]

The information etched into the grooves of the Voyager record is expected to last at least one billion years.[24]

According to Gregory Matloff, the Voyager 1 and 2 probes, and the Pioneer 10 and 11 probes which went into space before them, are likely to be the longest-lived artefacts of humanity:

Long after the Egyptian Pyramids and Great Wall of China have crumbled to dust, the Stonehenge megaliths have been reclaimed by the English countryside, and the Eiffel Tower and Lady Liberty have fallen, the Pioneer 10 and 11 and Voyager 1 and 2 will cruise the trackless void of the galaxy. Forever silent after the exhaustion of their radionuclide batteries, pitted by occasional impacts of interstellar dust grains, these craft and their successors will be recognisable artifacts billions of years in our future.[25]

Given the extreme unlikelihood that these craft will ever be intercepted by another intelligent race, we might well ask what the real purpose is of their message plaques. Matloff suggests that they represent attempts symbolically to communicate with the cosmos as a whole, somewhat as how the designers of medieval cathedrals sought to connect with the Creator. Perhaps they are, rather, an attempt to communicate with ourselves, as a way of epitomizing the best of human aspirations and accomplishments. Or perhaps it is simply that their creators are seeking 'to immortalize themselves through a form of cosmic graffiti'.[26]

A number of scientists have expressed doubts about making deliberate efforts to broadcast our existence to intelligent species elsewhere. Such activities could, in theory, hasten the extinction of humankind, rather than promote its development.[27] We might nevertheless want to contemplate the possibility of an 'afterlife' for humanity beyond its eventual extinction, however caused, just as individuals facing death contemplate their own earthly afterlives. If we can manage to contemplate something as enormous as the possibility of humanity's complete extinction, it should not be difficult to imagine the possibility that there are in the universe other intelligent beings for whom our own former existence will not necessarily be insignificant. If so, whatever artefacts or information are left from our civilization might prove invaluable to another rationally intelligent species, either materially or intellectually – even if only as a warning from history.

Time capsules are unlikely to add much more to a future knowledge of Earth's past than any accidentally surviving material would do. Quite apart from the possibility that their locations would over time be forgotten, destroyed or rendered inaccessible, the main problem with time capsules is their extremely limited or highly selective content. Any serious attempt to preserve the past for the benefit of rational beings in the future – whether these be a remnant of our present humanity, intelligent beings from elsewhere in the universe or a new race that might eventually evolve upon the Earth – would have to be on a much larger and more systematic scale. The records of humanity's scientific and cultural legacy have been increasing exponentially since the beginning of the medieval period, so that if we are talking about preserving a substantial proportion or even merely a representative sample of this legacy, let alone the whole of it, we are talking about a very large operation indeed.

Ironically enough, the more recent the historical period the more vulnerable are the cultural records and artefacts of human culture to the natural processes of decay. Much of our knowledge of the ancient world comes from linguistic and other signs and symbols inscribed on highly durable materials such as stone, bone, ceramic or metal. Even the papyrus and vellum manuscripts in our libraries and museums are relatively robust compared with the fragile media of recent centuries: paper, film, tape and digital storage devices, some of which depend upon complex electronic equipment whose own long-term survival is in doubt.

One idea would be to transcribe cultural information on durable media such as titanium or magnesium alloy plates, and store them on the Moon or Mars, or in a secure Earth orbit – perhaps with the idea that only a race advanced enough to reach such locations could be trusted to make proper use of such data. Solutions beyond this lie in the realm of scientific speculation or science fiction. For example, in Arthur C. Clarke's Space Odyssey novels, the advanced space beings who make contact with Earth are described as having, in their ceaseless experimenting, 'learned to store knowledge in the structure of space itself, and to preserve their thoughts for eternity in frozen lattices of light. They could become creatures of radiation, free at last from the tyranny of matter.'[28] For the time being, however, we are stuck with material means of preserving information, which means that the information thus preserved is forever at the mercy of time and change. What is more, all our eggs are in one basket – that of planet Earth. Should our planet be destroyed, then the cultural legacy which is our collective afterlife would be destroyed too.

V

In any case, imagining that humanity could hide its existence in a universe containing, and possibly teeming with, other intelligent species would be to bury one's head in the cosmic sand. It would be equivalent to the attempts being made to resist the unstoppable process of globalization, the process by which our world is becoming increasingly interconnected at the economic, political and cultural levels. It is not inconceivable that, in and through the process of globalization, this world will one day come to regard itself, existentially and not just theoretically, as a single community. Ideas about globalization may appear somewhat parochial when set against the idea that humanity could be but one species among others within a broader class of intelligent beings, but they might well function as a propaedeutic for the larger vision. Not every extraterrestrial race would necessarily be confined to a particular planet, and it is beyond telling to what extent and in what ways such races would or would not be indifferent to the existence – and in some cases plight – of beings similar to themselves. Within this extraterrestrial context, the stakes are raised enormously so far as the issue of collective human immortality is concerned. It is reasonable to suppose that thinking about the nature and destiny of humankind, and about its biological and cultural future, will increasingly be conducted not merely within a global perspective but also within, let us say, a galactic one. Such thinking might well be driven by the work of Steven J. Dick, a prominent theorist on the theme of extraterrestrial intelligence, who has identified what he calls the Intelligence Principle as 'the central principle of cultural evolution'. This Principle states that

> *the maintenance, improvement and perpetuation of knowledge and*
> *intelligence is the central driving force of cultural evolution, and*
> *that to the extent intelligence can be improved, it will be improved*
> ...The Intelligence Principle implies that, given the opportunity to increase intelligence (and thereby knowledge), whether through biotechnology, genetic engineering or AI, any society would do so, or fail to do so at its own peril.[29]

Culture has many driving forces, but for Dick none is as fundamental, or as powerful, as intelligence itself. In his view, cultural evolution over thousands or millions of years will very likely result in a post-biological universe populated by artificial intelligence, with sweeping implications for strategies in the search for extraterrestrial intelligence (SETI) and for our worldview. Like many theorists in this and related areas, Dick espouses a transhumanist view of the human future. But an acceptance of something like the Intelligence Principle is perfectly compatible with other visions of the future of humanity, visions in which humans remain firmly biological and keep advanced technology in check.

With knowledge, or at least information,[30] established as the lingua franca of a fully globalized human community psychologically prepared for evidence of the existence of (and even for contact with) intelligent beings elsewhere in the galaxy, the way is also open for information, knowledge and even wisdom to be recognized as common media between one such race of intelligent beings and another. And in this light, the question of human immortality and the possibility of human extinction both take on new aspects. For one thing, the chances of the human race attaining some kind of collective immortality would be much enhanced if our own existence, and the achievements of our own civilization, were to be recognized and in some measure preserved by others. For another, if there were other races in the universe, and especially if the possibility existed of meaningful communication between them, then it could be argued that the extinction of any one of them (for example, the human race) would not be as absolute or as tragic an eventuality as it might be considered if it were the only race. This is a possibility voiced by Stapledon's 'last man' as he contemplates the demise of the human species:

> Yet though we are not at all dismayed by our own extinction, we cannot but wonder whether or not in the far future some other spirit will fulfil the cosmic ideal, or whether we ourselves are the modest crown of existence. Unfortunately, though we can explore the past wherever there are intelligible minds, we cannot enter into the future. And so in vain we ask, will ever any spirit awake to gather all spirits into itself, to elicit from the stars their full flower of beauty, to know all things together, and admire all things justly.[31]

These considerations are all highly speculative of course. Given the parlous state of our own planet, and the apparent total absence to date of any of our hypothetical galactic neighbours, we must be wary of any unduly optimistic view concerning the abundance or security of intelligent life in the universe. The physicist Enrico Fermi, during a lunchtime conversation on the likelihood of extraterrestrials, famously came out with the question: 'Where are they?'[32] The 'Fermi Paradox', as it came to be known, contrasts the immense age and size of the universe, and the likely abundance of habitable planets within it, with the conspicuous absence, within our ever-widening astronomical purview, of any actual signs of extraterrestrial intelligent life.[33] A paradox, unlike a contradiction, has a solution. Not only must there be a rational answer to the Fermi Paradox, but we probably know enough to be able to hypothesize the complete range of its possible answers.[34] At one extreme there is the possibility that we are, after all, the first example – and will perhaps turn out to have been the only example – of intelligent life in the universe.[35] This is in conflict with what it would seem reasonable to assume on the basis of the so-called 'principle of mediocrity': namely, that life-bearing planets like our own must be fairly typical of planets throughout the universe. The principle of mediocrity, whether in science or in daily life, boils down to this: that we should, by default, regard ourselves as typical observers of typical observables. Its cosmological equivalent, sometimes referred to as the 'Copernican principle', is that 'we do not occupy a privileged place in the universe'.[36]

At the other extreme is the possibility that the universe is teeming with intelligent races who (since we have yet to observe them) are somehow deliberately concealing their existence from us – or, alternatively, with beings whose existence we are unable, or not yet able, to register or recognize. In between come various possibilities, such as that the myriad intelligent races in the universe are so far apart as to be, given the laws of physics, forever inaccessible to one another; or that we, in particular, are in an isolated sector of the galaxy, unaware of, and unnoticed by, other civilizations; or, most depressingly of all, that intelligent species, once they have reached their technological phase, are liable to destroy themselves.

This last possibility brings us back to the question of human extinction in particular. Proponents of the so-called 'Doomsday Argument' claim that human extinction is, on statistical grounds, likely to be much closer than we might think (or want to think). Given the exponential rise in population, the jeopardies our species now faces, and the assumption that no species can last forever, the argument is that we are probably nearer the end than the beginning of the total lifespan of humanity.

> One might at first expect the human race to survive, no doubt in evolutionarily much modified form, for millions or even billions of years, perhaps just on Earth but, more plausibly, in huge colonies scattered through the galaxy and maybe even through many galaxies. Contemplating the entire history of the race – future as well as past history – I should in that case see myself as *a very unusually early* human. I might well be among the first 0.00001 per cent to live their lives. But what if the race is instead about to die out? I am then a fairly typical human. Recent population growth has been so rapid that, of all human lives lived so far, anything up to about 30 per cent – figures quoted in this area vary according to, for example, how far back in evolutionary history we see humans and not just apes – are lives which are being lived at this very moment. Now, *whenever lacking evidence to the contrary one should prefer to think of one's own position as fairly typical rather than highly untypical.* To promote the reasonable aim of making it *quite ordinary* that I exist where I do in human history, let me therefore assume that the human race will rapidly die out.[37]

The mechanics and variations of this argument have been much debated, and there are of course serious questions about the assumptions on which it is based. But it should give pause for thought to those who assume that the rise and rise of human beings is only likely to be followed by their further rise. The Doomsday Argument has a decidedly fatalistic ring to it, and other scientists have, on no worse scientific grounds, taken a very different approach, the guiding principle of which is that the future of the universe will be what we decide to make of it. The more extreme or adventurous versions of this approach exemplify the transhumanist philosophy discussed in Chapter Two. The future of the universe as envisaged by the physicist Freeman Dyson, for example, is one in which 'life is free to evolve into whatever material embodiment best suits its purposes'. Dyson describes his own idea of the universe as

> very different from the universe which Steven Weinberg had in mind when he said, 'The more the universe seems

comprehensible, the more it also seems pointless.' I have found a universe growing without limit in richness and complexity, a universe of life surviving forever and making itself known to its neighbors across unimaginable gulfs of space and time. Is Weinberg's universe or mine closer to the truth? One day, before long, we shall know.[38]

Whatever the answer is, or turns out to be, the mere possibility that we are not alone in the universe could be sufficient to change our attitude to the human race and the planet it inhabits, and in particular to our potential extinction, if or when this threatens. Some kind of afterlife for humanity as a whole might well follow our extinction, and this if nothing else should justify conserving both our planetary eco-system and the achievements of human culture as our post-extinction legacy. It would also be consistent with what is finest in humanity if our conservation efforts were to be regarded not simply as a way of securing some kind of symbolic immortality for ourselves within a cosmos inhabited by other intelligent species, but rather as a means of leaving behind us information and resources for the benefit of other intelligent species. On the other hand, these other species might for all we know be totally indifferent to the fact and history of our own existence. In either case, we would not be there to witness it.

One final thought worth pondering here is one expressed by the philosopher Roland Puccetti. It is a thought reminding us of a point made several times throughout this book – namely, that an earthly afterlife is never enjoyed by its actual subjects, but only vicariously by those these subjects leave behind. For these subjects themselves, however, an earthly afterlife can be experienced by anticipation, as a present consolation for a future from which they are by definition excluded. This would apply to our species as a whole and not only to its individual members. Writing about the possible existence of intelligent extraterrestrials in our universe, Puccetti suggests that having good grounds for believing in the possibility, however remote, of the existence elsewhere in our universe of beings somewhat like us physically and socially, and sharing some of our values, would have a beneficial moral effect on the human community.

The search for knowledge, the desire for truth, the willingness to subordinate individual interest to social aims for the common benefit: these are all values without which no community of intelligent organisms could achieve a technological civilisation. If we are convinced such societies exist, though too distant for us to confirm our belief, we may have confidence some of our values may outlast our civilisation. Not that this would make them permanent: life itself is a transitory phenomenon in the history of the cosmos. But at least it could lay to rest the provincial humanist dogma that if we abandon belief on the Divine we have nothing to fall back on but Man's values. What we have to fall back on are the values . . . of a potentially universal community of persons from which we are detached by the accidental dispersion of matter in the cosmos. That is pallid comfort, yet comfort of a kind.[39]

EIGHT

THIS WORLD IS NOT ENOUGH

To subsist in lasting Monuments, to live in their productions, to exist in their names, and praedicament of *Chimera's*, was large satisfaction unto old expectations, and made one part of their *Elyziums*. But all this is nothing in the Metaphysicks of true belief. To live indeed is to be again our selves, which being not only an hope but an evidence in noble beleevers; 'Tis all one to lye in St *Innocents* Church-yard, as in the Sands of *Aegypt:* Ready to be any thing, in the extasie of being ever, and as content with six foot as the *Moles* of Adrianus.

THOMAS BROWNE, *Hydriotaphia* (1658)[1]

I

This book has sought to show how various are the means, both accidental and intentional, whereby we invest our own and others' lives in some kind, or degree, of earthly immortality. It will also have shown how limited is the return on most of these investments. The fragility of human memory and the corrosive passage of time mean that the remembered dead all too soon become the anonymous dead. Only a select minority of named individuals from each passing generation remain recognized subjects of an earthly afterlife, and even then by no means indefinitely. The afterlives of individuals are subsumed into the lives of families, the afterlives of families into the lives of nations, and the afterlives of nations into the history of the human species as a whole. If or when the human species itself ceases to exist, its only afterlife will be on the one hand its legacy within the planet's biological evolution and, on the other, whatever traces remain of its terrestrial impact and cultural monuments. Whether any non-human (or post-human) intelligence would ever be present to acknowledge this posthumous legacy of humankind is, of course, quite another question.

It is easy enough to mock the vanity or futility of memorializing the dead, as Thomas Browne and many others do, or to censure the human desire to stay alive for as long as possible. Those concerned to perpetuate their own memories through a post-mortem legacy of some kind may well be open to the charge of vanity or narcissism, if not to that of refusing to accept their own mortality. But there is nothing unworthy in wanting to leave behind some testament to one's own presence on the Earth, especially where it makes a positive contribution to the lives of coming generations. Still less would one seek to criticize others for cherishing the legacy of deceased persons whom they have admired or from whose lives they have benefited in some way. In particular, it would surely be inhuman for the bereaved not to want to cherish the memory of their deceased loved ones, though there are undoubtedly both healthier and unhealthier ways of doing this. Just as it is natural to want human lives to persist for as long as possible, in the full knowledge that even the longest life must eventually come to an end, so is it also natural to want to preserve for as long as possible the memories and legacies of those who have already died. Inevitably memories will fade, legacies fall into neglect and graves cease to be visited. Yet it would be a mistake to say that the ideas and practices I have described under the rubrics of 'posthumous personhood' or 'anonymous immortality' are worthless aspirations, achievements or consequences of earthly lives. On the contrary, the continuity of human civilization vitally depends upon them and indeed is largely constituted by them. What one writer says of the 'human will to immortality' embraces earthly as well as otherworldly forms of immortality – namely, that it is 'the foundation of human achievement; it is the well-spring of religion, the muse of philosophy, the architect of our cities and the impulse behind the arts. It is embedded in our very nature, and its result is what we know as civilization.'[2]

As for the natural human desire to go on living for as long as possible, there is no good reason to resist the medical advances and improved social conditions that enable people to live healthier and hence longer lives. None of this approaches the kind of challenge to the natural order to which the transhumanists aspire. Although modern times have witnessed lifespans more or less double the biblical 'three score years and ten', these still fall centuries short of the lifespans attributed to the Old Testament patriarchs.[3] According to the *Guinness Book of Records*, the person with the longest fully authenticated lifespan is the Frenchwoman Jeanne Louise Calment. She was born on 21 February 1875 and died on 4 August 1997: only 122 years and 164 days in all. The fact that 'life expectancy has gone spectacularly upwards in advanced countries during the last hundred years . . . does not mean that the very old are any older than they used to be. It is simply that a much higher proportion of people actually reach old age.'[4] We may either empathize with, or else dismiss as an almost childish petulance, Miguel de Unamuno's passionate declaration that 'I neither want to die nor do I want to want to die; I want to live for ever and ever and ever.'[5] It is nevertheless a fact that most people do not want to die, even if this does not necessarily mean that they would want to live forever. Why should one expect human lives to be exempt from the laws governing all other living creatures?

As George Santayana wryly observed, 'The fact of having been born is a bad augury for immortality.'[6] But while earthly immortality in any strict or literal sense may be unattainable, the ambition to keep alive, for a longer or shorter period, the memory and achievements of the dead in an earthly afterlife is neither unworthy nor unrealizable. The motives for this ambition become clearer when we consider the ideas and practices associated with an earthly afterlife in relation to those associated with an otherworldly afterlife. Examining the relationship between earthly and otherworldly immortality is the main subject of this concluding chapter.

II

Earlier chapters have shown how close can be the connections between earthly and otherworldly immortality, in some cases so close as to confuse the distinction itself. But the ideas and practices associated with an earthly afterlife are not typically in competition with those which relate to an otherworldly afterlife. In many cases ideas about these two kinds of destiny proceed along separate lines, each with their own logic. People may believe their loved ones to be in the next world while also working to maintain their legacy in this world. In theory, of course, an individual whose earthly life is regarded as insignificant or even held in contempt may be numbered among the saints in heaven, while someone whose life is admired and celebrated on Earth may occupy the darkest and loneliest corner of hell. In other cases, not only is there no competition between the two kinds of afterlife, but there may be close connections between them. For example, in many cultures the fate of the soul in the next world is closely bound up with the rituals of bodily disposal in this world. It is a classic trope of traditional ghost stories, for example, that those whose bodies have not been given proper burial may continue to trouble the living. In polemical contexts, however, earthly and otherworldly immortalities do, inevitably, come into conflict. Thus Thomas Browne – as we saw in the passage heading this chapter – uses the Christian confidence in resurrection as a stick with which to beat the monumental afterlives of the dead in ancient paganism. In the context of secular humanism, by contrast, the tangible phenomena associated with a person's earthly afterlife are sometimes set against the intangibilities if not implausibilities of survival in another world.

In most cultures throughout history, including European culture up until the period of the Enlightenment, a balance is maintained between the memorialization of the dead in this world and a concern with their status or destiny in the next. That many people, when thinking about the 'future' of the dead, give equal attention to earthly legacy and otherworldly survival (reward or punishment) could hardly be summed up more concisely than in the epitaph for a friend composed by Robert Burns. Having extolled the merits of his friend, Burns hedges his bet with these concluding lines: 'If there's another world, he lives in bliss; / If there is none, he made the best of this.'[7] Whatever hopes it evokes of a life to come, an epitaph, whether lapidary or literary, also constitutes one of the most basic and universal tokens of a person's earthly afterlife. The epitaphic urge is present even in the simplest inscriptions of name and date, which for many deceased persons soon becomes the only surviving record of their lives.

Human beings are equally skilled in the arts of forgetting and of remembering the dead. As time-bound beings, moreover, it is natural for human beings to look both forward and backwards. The experience of bereavement itself involves both 'holding on' and 'moving on', and managing the transition from one to the other. Funerary rituals and customs, whether religious or secular, are as much about distancing (and even protecting) oneself from the dead as they are about maintaining a connection with them. But our longing for the dead is not necessarily unhealthy or backward-looking. Such longing may indeed betray an inability to accept loss, a failure to detach one's own identity from that of a departed loved one. But it may equally well express a healthy desire for continuing communion with a loved one or a belief that the dead remain real, albeit invisible, members of the human community.

Continuing concern and affection for the dead is not extinguished by the simple fact of their death. Much depends on when and how the dead have died, of course. In the chilling but moving Scottish ballad 'The Wife of Usher's Well', the grieving mother of three sons who have died 'over the seas' demands, understandably if unreasonably but in any case with magical insistence, that they 'come hame to me / In earthly flesh and blood'. They do come home, and are welcomed back with food and a bed for the night; but since they are no longer really flesh and blood, at cockcrow they reluctantly depart again, fearing that if 'we be miss'd out o' our place, / A sair pain we maun bide.'[8] They, as well as their grieving mother, are reluctant that they must go.[9]

An acceptance of death does not mean the ending of all relationship with the dead. In many cultures, ritual as well as narrative helps the living to maintain a balance between their connection with and their distance from the dead. A striking example of such a ritual still takes place in Madagascar. This is the Famadihana ritual, when every few years the living exhume the dessicated bodies of their dead, dance with them and talk to them a while, and then reclothe and reinter them.[10] In fact many forms of otherworldly immortality depend crucially upon the existence of a person's earthly afterlife, and especially upon a person's corporeal remains. The bodily remains of persons act as reminders of their former earthly lives and, in many contexts, as a tangible means of connection with their survival in an afterworld. In ancient Egypt, the careful physical preservation and ritual protection of the body was a condition of a person's safety in the afterworld.[11] In Christian tradition, the integrity of bodily remains continues to be part of the logic of the belief in the doctrine of resurrection.

But the priorities and demands of earthly and otherworldly afterlives are not always compatible. Some of the tensions that can arise are well illustrated in a document issued in 2016 by the Vatican's Congregation for the Doctrine of the Faith regarding the disposal of human ashes following cremation.[12] This document emphasizes that the Church, while clearly preferring the traditional custom of inhumation, is not actually opposed to cremation; but it does insist on certain conditions for the conservation of cremated remains. Although cremation does not contradict ideas about the immortality of the soul or resurrection of the body, the practice of inhumation shows a greater esteem towards the deceased and is less likely to lead to the abuse of human remains. Ideally, cremated remains should be buried in a cemetery or other location within the jurisdiction of the Church; they should not be scattered, conserved in domestic residences or divided among different family members.

> The reservation of the ashes of the departed in a sacred place ensures that they are not excluded from the prayers and remembrance of their family or the Christian community. It prevents the faithful departed from being forgotten, or their remains from being shown a lack of respect, which eventuality is possible, most especially once the immediately subsequent generation has too passed away. Also it prevents any unfitting or superstitious practices.

Cremated remains will often be treated with the same degree of respect in secular contexts too. But the various practices of which the Vatican document disapproves are proscribed for specifically doctrinal reasons:

> In order that every appearance of pantheism, naturalism or nihilism be avoided, it is not permitted to scatter the ashes of the faithful departed in the air, on land, at sea or in some other way, nor may they be preserved in mementos, pieces of jewelry or other objects. These courses of action cannot be legitimized by an appeal to the sanitary, social, or economic motives that may have occasioned the choice of cremation.

In many secular contexts, the practice of scattering (rather than burying) cremated ashes at a location significant in some way to the deceased is among the more conservative of the practices associated with cremation.[13] As the Vatican document intimates, more 'creative' alternatives have become popular in recent times. For instance, one modern alternative to scattering the ashes on land or in water is to dispose of them pyrotechnically.[14] Again, human ashes can be turned into personal mementos of the deceased in the form of glass or diamond pendants, rings and the like.[15] Another recently advertised possibility is for ashes to be made into the glaze of a drinking mug.[16] Such permanent memorialization is considered more valuable than the memory of the single event of scattering the ashes in the air, on land or at sea. Those who recoil from such practices might stop to think that many longstanding 'traditional' customs could be criticized as no less barbarous – interring bodies under the floors of churches and other buildings, burying different parts of a body in different locations (fractional burial), displaying the disintegrated bodily parts of saints in religious buildings, keeping a human skull on one's desk as a memento mori, and so on. Nor are some of the more bizarre practices of modern times so very different from customs once practised or still practised in some cultures.[17] Consuming the ashes of a loved one might be regarded as a grotesque if not pathological practice in the modern world, but in some cultures (admittedly not many) this has been a standard mortuary practice.[18] A key difference of course is that such acts are not the deviant practices of single individuals but customs embedded in a wider system of beliefs and symbols.

When we move from the afterlife of the body and of material things to the afterlife of the mind, we find a similar range of conflicts and harmonies between the demands of earthly and otherworldly immortality. The often ambivalent relationship between the aspirations associated with earthly and otherworldly afterlives finds classic expression in Milton's pastoral elegy 'Lycidas'. This poem identifies the desire for worldly fame as, paradoxically, a noble weakness:[19] 'Fame is the spur that the clear spirit doth raise / (That last infirmity of Noble mind) / To scorn delights, and live laborious dayes . . .' But the quest for worldly fame and its prizes is subject to the cruelties of time and fate; it can be cut short at any time:

> But the fair Guerdon when we hope to find,
> And think to burst out into sudden blaze,
> Comes the blind Fury with th' abhorred shears,
> And slits the thin spun life . . .

Nevertheless worldly fame, at least when its aspirants are poets and writers, can be transposed into heavenly fame, a fame that redounds to one's otherworldly as well as one's earthly immortality:

> Fame is no plant that grows on mortal soil,
> Nor in the glistering foil
> Set off to th' world, nor in broad rumour lies,
> But lives and spreds aloft by those pure eyes,
> And perfet witnes of all-judging Jove;
> As he pronounces lastly on each deed,
> Of so much fame in Heav'n expect thy meed.[20]

Milton's poem is in part a working-through of his own concern for an immortality motived by the highest ideals, since he aspired to be ranked among those scholars who 'love learning for itself, not for lucre, or any other end than the service of God and truth, and perhaps that lasting fame and perpetuity of praise which God and good men have consented shall be the reward of those whose published labours advance the good of mankind'.[21]

If in many contexts there is harmony, or at least no conflict, between ideas and practices relating to an earthly afterlife and those relating to an otherworldly one, in other contexts the importance of earthly immortality will be emphasized precisely because an otherworldly immortality is either excluded or denied. In such cases earthly immortality may either be regarded as an important surrogate for the unattainable form of immortality, or else promoted as a form of immortality equal to if not superior to the latter. In the Gilgamesh epic the eponymous hero learns the hard way that immortality in the form of an endless life is unattainable (despite his being two-thirds divine). He must accept his mortality; but as a mortal being he realizes that another kind of immortality is open to him and by implication to all mortal beings who yearn for immortality. This is the immortality of fame, achieved in his case by heroic acts, great feats of building and, above all (and ironically), by the story of his epic but fruitless quest for eternal life. No small part of Gilgamesh's earthly immortality has been achieved by his supposedly recording his fruitless quest on the 'tablets of stone' that enabled our rediscovery of the story in modern times.

Conspicuous by its absence in the Gilgamesh epic is any reference to what I have already identified as the most powerful and probably most ancient form in which people conceive of an earthly immortality: namely, immortality through progeny. In Plato's *Symposium* this is presented as the standard form of earthly immortality, so to say, even though the immortality of fame, and the immortality of literary creation, are regarded by Plato as far superior means of 'living on'. What needs emphasizing about the progenitive form of earthly immortality, however, is that for many religious people it is neither secondary to, nor a substitute for, an otherworldly immortality. For one thing, the survival of the family line is necessary to the maintenance of rituals which ensure the welfare of one's deceased ancestors, whose company one will soon enough be joining. For another, it may be believed that the souls of the dead are reincarnated among the living. Moreover, some cultures place greater value on the destiny of the community than on that of the individual, or rather they identify an individual's destiny with the destiny of the community. What tends to be abolished here is not merely the sharp division between an individual afterlife and a collective one, but also any clear distinction between religious and secular concepts of the afterlife. The family, tribe or human race itself becomes the supreme and sacrosanct entity. Even for the secularist who denies religious hope, survival through progeny constitutes more than simply the best surrogate for an unattainable otherworldly immortality. It is a self-renewing form of this-worldly immortality with its own tangibly and perpetually realized this-worldly 'eschatology'. As the most tangible and egalitarian form of earthly immortality, progenitive immortality remains the most important secular consolation for the lack of an otherworldly immortality.

There has undoubtedly been a greater emphasis on the various forms of earthly immortality in recent decades, as both popular and intellectual belief has increasingly moved away from ideas about an otherworldly afterlife. With the rise of individualism on the one hand, and the decline of belief in the doctrines and authority of the Church on the other, attitudes to death in the modern West now differ sharply both from what they once were in earlier times and from what they still are in many other parts of the world. For many people, death is no longer even a taboo subject. Death has become just a blank – a non-negotiable destiny drained of all eschatological colour. 'Where once people took comfort in the idea of an afterlife that gave death meaning (death as "expiration"), in the wake of urbanization, industrialization, twentieth-century wars, and an over-reaching medical technology, death is "termination".'[22] While some people do all they can to avoid thinking about death and afterlife, and others allow it to overshadow everything else in their lives, the vast majority acknowledge the reality and inevitability of death without giving it too much thought. Such accommodation, although clearly preferable to either denial or obsession, remains an essentially negative attitude. Death is seen as the ultimate constraint among the many lesser constraints of life, rather than as something that might illuminate the meaning of life or help define one's identity and purpose in the world. The truth of human mortality is something to be managed rather than something to be contemplated. People live their lives 'Allowing for death as a mere calculation, / A depreciation, entered in,' as Peter Porter puts it.[23]

What lies beyond death is at best a complete unknown and at worst a total annihilation. Either way, the prevailing scepticism leads people, when confronted with the experience of death and bereavement, to seek meaning and consolation in the varieties of earthly immortality. We see this reflected very clearly in the changing nature of funeral services and mortuary practices. Traditionally these were rituals designed to assist the passage of the deceased from this life into the next, and hence were forward rather than backward looking. But nowadays many funeral services, religious as well as explicitly secular ones, tend to be retrospective and celebratory, looking back on the life of an individual whose possible continuing or future existence, if entertained at all, is left nebulous and uncelebrated. In consequence, there is a greater emphasis on an individual's earthly legacy, howsoever modest this might be.

The dead no longer have the status even of ghosts; they are more like dramatized constructs whose continuing identity depends now upon the fragile memories and memorializing activities of the living. Verbal forms have shifted accordingly, as when people might say, for example of some particular action done on behalf of the deceased, that 'Uncle Arthur would have wanted this' or 'Aunt Alice would have liked that'. Traditionally, although only select categories of the dead – such as ghosts or saints – continued to have any kind of earthly presence or agency, most of the dead were regarded as continuing subjects who, although in another world, might still be aware of, and even able to benefit from, the actions of the living. And just as the living looked after the dead, tending their graves, offering prayers on their behalf, and so on (as well as by managing their earthly legacies), so were the dead understood to look after the living. The dead and the living were locked into a relationship of mutual concern and responsibility. Nowadays, in the eyes of many people, the dead no longer exist anywhere, either to care or be cared for. Or rather the dead can only be cared for as memories, in relation to their earthly afterlives, which are in any case reducible to aspects of our own lives.

III

The disjunction between an earthly and an otherworldly afterlife is not an absolute one in the minds of many people. But although most forms of earthly immortality make perfect sense without reference to any idea of otherworldly immortality, it is difficult not to see the former as a consolation, substitute or even surrogate for the latter.[24] This is true above all of the use made of the term 'immortality' itself, a word borrowed from the vocabulary of mythology and religion to characterize something which in itself has nothing to do with the supernatural. Even those who are not merely sceptical about otherworldly immortality, but who explicitly reject the idea, may find it difficult, when discoursing about earthly afterlives, to avoid language and customs more familiar from religious traditions. In itself, perhaps, this reflects nothing more than changing priorities in the long cultural history of 'managing mortality'. This language and these customs are no more a sign that what we are all really yearning for is an otherworldly immortality than the language of 'horsepower' applied to the internal combustion engine is a sign that we all want to ride horses through the streets. But there are nevertheless indications in the way people engage with the idea of earthly immortality, both for themselves and for others, that what they may also be yearning for, or at least regretting the absence of, is another kind of immortality, an immortality beyond earthly conditions. Perhaps some of us really would prefer to be galloping across the landscape on horseback than riding through busy streets in cars.

Before considering the possibility that the attention paid to earthly immortality reveals deep-seated longings or even convictions regarding an otherworldly immortality, we need to examine the more familiar argument that it is otherworldly rather than earthly immortality that is the real surrogate here. The idea that religion, and in particular the belief in a life after death that is integral to most if not all religions, is a projection or compensation for earthly ills and dissatisfactions has a long and complex pedigree and is even part of the vocabulary of religion itself. It was the Greek thinker Euhemeros who suggested that the gods were otherworldly versions of earthly kings and heroes, while some centuries earlier Xenophanes had argued that if horses, oxen or lions had hands which enabled them to draw as humans do, each kind of animal would represent their gods as having the same form as themselves. Xenophanes' argument was not in itself an argument against the truth of religion; it was more a statement that the divergent concepts or images of the gods peculiar to each nation reflect the differing points of view of the members of each nation. Xenophanes, like his near contemporary Gautama Buddha, seems to have been a religious critic of religion rather than a critic of religion per se. The views of figures like Euhemeros and Xenophanes nevertheless anticipate the more sophisticated secular criticism of religion of later times, according to which religion is the creature of psychological anxiety and social oppression.

Although any particular conception of an earthly afterlife can be independent of, or in harness with, any particular set of religious beliefs and practices, ideas about an earthly afterlife are sometimes presented in a way that conveys, or implies, a challenge to the alleged emptiness of the concepts of otherworldly survival associated with religion. Whereas those I have called 'confident believers' may well consider that much of the attention devoted to the earthly afterlives of deceased persons is compensatory for the lack of belief in their otherworldly afterlife, 'confident sceptics' will tend to regard the idea of an otherworldly afterlife as substituting for more practical, earthly ways of cherishing and celebrating the memory of departed loved ones. For secularists or materialists, belief in or hope for an otherworldly afterlife represents not just an intellectual failure but an expression of hubris, a pursuit of earthly vanity by other means. (This point of view – arguably the default position of the 'confident sceptic' – is even one with which some 'confident believers' can identify, or at least sympathize, in so far as they seek to distance their own views about an otherworldly afterlife from other religious views which they consider false, childish or even immoral.)

Within the broad tradition of religious scepticism, it is not difficult to argue that conceptions of an otherworldly afterlife are projections of our desire to avoid annihilation by living on after death in some blissful celestial environment. Such environments are likely to be represented as idealized versions of the pastoral, horticultural or urban environments of Earth. By the same token, the afterlife experiences we envisage for those who have done evil, and about which some people may be fearful on their own behalf, will be exaggerated versions of the worst kinds of terrestrial experiences we have imagined if not actually witnessed. Counter-arguments to the effect that these concepts of afterlife are supported by empirical evidence, in the form of the experiences of mystics, yogins, shamans and others who have reported visiting higher worlds, obviously meet with a variant of the original sceptical argument: namely, that these experiences are themselves cultural artefacts projecting the familiar desires for salvation or immortality. For Paul Badham, commenting on 'the archetypal imagery of a paradisal heaven of flowery gardens, suffused in warm light and radiant with peace and joy' that informs near-death experiences across different cultures, it is 'overwhelmingly likely that reports from past near-death experiences are what have shaped our traditions and provided the content of our religious imagery concerning the future life.'[25]

This cycle of argumentation can of course go round and round. Even without the universal features of near-death experiences to which Badham and others advert, however, the fact that representations of celestial (and infernal) worlds are couched in earthly terms cannot in itself be a knock-down argument supporting the 'projection' thesis. If post-mortem survival means that humans continue existing, as them-selves, in another world, then a person's post-mortem existence must conform to certain 'rules' of embodiment and identity for this existence to be continuous in any meaningful sense with this person's present existence – in which case a spatially organized world with some kind of topography is precisely what one would expect in an afterworld.[26] If, on the other hand, the accounts of supernal worlds given by mys-tics and others are attempts to represent otherwise ineffable realities in familiar terrestrial terms, then reductionist arguments based simply on the *language* of these accounts amount to nothing more decisive than shooting the messenger.

Thus the fact that descriptions of otherworldly afterlives are inevit-ably couched in earthly terms does not in itself support the argument that these otherworldly afterlives never represent anything other than projections and idealizations of our present, earthly lives. In any case, earthly afterlives themselves are no less explicable as forms of pro-jection and idealization – the preservation of the name, image and activities of deceased persons within a world they no longer inhabit as living subjects, in many cases through the idealization of their lives and personal qualities. A question here is why such idealization (or, more rarely, denigration) of the dead is so compelling an activity for the living. One answer is that the cultivation of a person's earthly immor-tality, unlike the projections and idealizations supposedly represented in otherworldly immortalities, depends upon tangible commemorative and celebratory phenomena one can believe in and to a large extent control – funerals, tombs, portraits, statues, biographies, anniversaries and so on. An earthly afterlife can indeed be initiated by or for a person while that person is still alive. But a contrary possibility is that the idea of an earthly afterlife derives much of its energy and appeal from the belief in or hope for a person's otherworldly immortality – in other words, that the cultivation of one's own or another's earthly immortality is in fact the disguised or sublimated pursuit of an otherworldly immortality. It is to this theme that I now turn.

IV

It is no part of my purpose in this book to assess evidence for or against the possibility of an otherworldly survival for human beings. Whatever I have said about otherworldly immortality, and about its relationship to earthly immortality, does not depend upon taking a view upon this matter. It is nevertheless worth speculating about the significance that the reality of an otherworldly destiny for humankind might have on our understanding of the ideas and practices associated with earthly immortality. Indeed, might not the importance attached to cultivating earthly afterlives for ourselves and others be easier to explain if these afterlives were seen as intimations of an otherworldly afterlife? By the same token, would not some elements in the cultivation of earthly afterlives be exposed as harmful or negative in some sense? Most important of all, were the truth of post-mortem survival ever to be established, might not some of the activities and artefacts associated with the earthly afterlives of persons (memorial services, mementos, and so on) be shown to bring the living and the dead together in some way?

Let us consider an analogy here. Before the discovery of microbial life consequent upon the invention of the microscope (and, much later, the development of germ theory), human lives were obviously being affected, and indeed often terminated, by the existence of such life forms, just as they are today.[27] Following the discovery of microscopic life, human beings were able not only to control and indeed harness the activities of microorganisms, but to explain certain natural and in particular physiological phenomena long observed but not yet understood.[28] For example, it was not understood how grapes produced wine, although humans clearly became very skilled at exploiting the process. Similarly it was not understood why food spoiled, though clearly the conditions under which it did spoil were well known, as were various methods of mitigating the problem.

Let us now pursue the analogy between the discovery of microbial life and the discovery of human individuals surviving in an otherworldly afterlife, supposing that the human survival of death were not just a fact, but a demonstrable fact, and had indeed been demonstrated. What I wish to pursue here is not so much the obvious analogy between a world teeming with microbial life and a universe teeming with discarnate intelligences, but rather an analogy between the kinds of consequence that might follow from these two discoveries. Discoveries are not the same as inventions, even though new inventions often depend on new discoveries. Inventions introduce something new into the world's mix; discoveries reveal what is already there. If the reality of human survival were to be proven, such a discovery would very likely reveal not only some new facts but some hitherto unknown (or unproven) connections between old ones. Definitive proof of the personal survival of death might, for instance, throw new light on the long history of belief in ghosts. The more sceptical (and often quite elaborate) theories about ghostly phenomena might give way to what would now be considered more parsimonious explanations based on the idea of post-mortem human agency. Moreover, there might be greater insight into how and why some of the many rituals and customs connected with the disposal of the dead had developed. Equally important, however, is the possibility that people might now be able to evaluate the propriety of various rituals and customs, just as modern medical science has facilitated the discrimination between effective and ineffective remedies within the realm of so-called folk or traditional medicine. Suppose, for example, that it was discovered that cremating or burying a body immediately after a person's death, or at the other extreme not bothering to dispose of it at all, were somehow detrimental to the newly deceased person's experience in the next world. Or suppose that traditions about the recently dead being wounded by the grief of the bereaved turned out to be more than mere superstition.

If the discovery of post-mortem survival led to the recognition of connections between the earthly and the otherworldly in one area of life, then there is no reason to suppose that there would not also be connections in other areas too. Consider the kinds of activity associated with what I have defined as creative immortality, regarded by many as the worthiest manifestation of earthly immortality. Persons now deceased who have composed music, painted pictures or written poetry, fiction or works of history have through such activities secured for themselves some kind of earthly afterlife. On the hypothesis of post-mortem survival, one might speculate that the living, by engaging with such works, are not simply keeping alive the earthly memory of their authors, but also opening up the possibility of communing with the surviving minds of these authors themselves.

For example, one might reasonably suppose that the life of a surviving Johann Sebastian Bach (whose post-mortem persona we can call 'Bach') might still be taken up with music, and that, whatever this might mean in detail, these continuing musical interests would somehow be continuous with his musical career on Earth. Supposing we further speculate that 'Bach' is (or for a time was) both aware of, and affected by, the posthumous performance and appreciation of his music on Earth, and even that he is (or for a time was) somehow able to inspire musicians and performers on Earth. (It is perhaps worth remembering here that originally 'inspiration' referred literally rather than metaphorically to this kind of connection between earthly and otherworldly intelligence.[29])

In a similar way, it might be suggested that Rembrandt, for example, not only 'lives on' in his paintings in the sense that they serve to keep alive the memory of his life and the genius of his work, but in the sense that those who admire his paintings, or his person through his paintings, could somehow be influenced or inspired by the now otherworldly 'Rembrandt'. Something similar could also apply to other forms of creativity, artistic or otherwise. The point of these hypothetical examples is not to suggest that we are only able to understand or appreciate the life and work of deceased persons because they must somehow be spectrally present to us, but that on the hypothesis of post-mortem survival it could make sense to think of creative work as one kind of medium among others through which communication with, or influence from, the deceased might be realized or facilitated.

Moreover, if on the hypothesis of post-mortem survival it were not absurd to think that we could be in communion with the mind of J. S. Bach when performing or listening to his music, with Rembrandt's when contemplating his paintings, or with Wordsworth's when reading his poetry, so might it not be absurd to think that one could be in communion with, say, one's deceased grandfather when looking at photographs of him, reading his diary or talking to one's children about him; or with deceased loved ones when attending their funeral or memorial service, when visiting their graves, when offering prayers on their behalf, or simply when keeping them in mind. The essential point is that if an otherworldly immortality were indeed part of human destiny, then the various phenomena I have described as constituting our earthly immortality could, without ceasing to be valid in purely earthly terms, also be vehicles conveying intimations of an otherworldly immortality. To this extent earthly immortalities could function not merely as consolations or substitutes for an otherworldly immortality considered doubtful or impossible, or at least assumed to be inaccessible to the living, but as a means through which the persisting lives of the dead might intersect with the lives of the living.

If these kinds of connection between earthly and otherworldly afterlives really did exist, then it is not unlikely that some of the activities undertaken by the living in constructing or maintaining the earthly afterlives of the dead could also be seen as activities oriented towards their otherworldly immortality. A possible example here is, again, provided by the composition and inscription of epitaphs. For William Wordsworth, epitaphs are not merely evidence of the socially developed desire to remember others and be oneself remembered after death. They are also evidence of what is at the root of this desire – evidence, namely, of the intimation we have of our own immortality. As Wordsworth puts it,

> without the consciousness of a principle of immortality in the human soul, Man could never have had awakened in him the desire to live in the remembrance of his fellows: mere love, or the yearning of kind towards kind, could not have produced it . . . Add to the principle of love which exists in the inferior animals, the faculty of reason which exists in Man alone; will the conjunction of these account for the desire? Doubtless it is a necessary consequence of this conjunction; yet not, I think, as a direct result, but only to be come at through an intermediate thought, viz. that of an intimation or assurance within us, that some part of our nature is imperishable.[30]

Epitaphs are typically presented as sentiments voiced by the dead themselves, or voiced by the living on behalf of the dead.[31] It is, of course, only the living who create and read these epitaphs, which traditionally constitute the simplest medium through which the living maintain a publically visible trace of their dead. According to Wordsworth, however, what epitaphs more importantly reveal are the intimations of the otherworldly immortality to which both their readers and their subjects are heir.

Each of the forms of earthly afterlife identified in earlier chapters might well be reinterpreted in terms of what they tell us about aspirations, if not beliefs, relating to an otherworldly afterlife too. For instance, it is difficult to explain the care with which the bodies of the dead are treated even in secular contexts without invoking notions of either religious or superstitious respect. The possessions of the dead also have a mystique which, if taken seriously, points to some kind of continuing power or presence of the deceased which in purely secular terms is no longer possible. Again, many forms of earthly afterlife depend upon the 'magic' of the name as constituting or revealing the essence of a person. Last but not least, the appeal of progenitive immortality depends on family, tribe or humanity itself being seen as an almost transcendental entity that is more than the sum of its parts.

Justifications of earthly immortality, especially in its more 'anonymous' forms, are liable to metaphysical pretensions which do not sit comfortably with their secular character. Here, for example, is an affirmation of what, in Chapter Four, I called the 'stardust philosophy':

> 'You are dust, and to dust you will return.' Yes! Anything else is just being greedy. *We are stardust*, to be exact, and we're going right back to where we came from, to make room for other people to enjoy the remarkable wonder of living and loving . . . I see this now not as pessimism but as a beautiful realism. The universe, and life on this planet in particular, *is* the transcendent reality. It is bigger than any one of us or group of us. It is outside of our control and we don't deserve more than the one life we get.[32]

The secular author of this passage is cheeky enough to quote a biblical passage as his proof text, and yet his idea of the universe as a 'transcendent' reality is metaphysically empty. Indeed this example of secular religiosity might well be dismissed as an example of a secular, scientific view being coloured rather than compromised by religious rhetoric. The same cannot be said of the radical fusion of scientific and religious views found in the work of the cosmologist Frank Tipler, who introduces his explanation of his Omega Point theory as follows:

I shall describe the physical mechanism of the universal resurrection. I shall show exactly how physics will permit the resurrection to eternal life of everyone who has lived, is living, and will live. I shall show exactly why this power to resurrect which modern physics allows will actually exist in the far future, and why it will in fact be used. If any reader has lost a loved one, or is afraid of death, modern physics says: 'Be comforted, you and they shall live again.'[33]

The observation that affirmations of an earthly afterlife sometimes appear to be affirmations of an otherworldly afterlife in disguise must not be confused with the quite separate point – touched upon in an earlier chapter – that ideas and practices associated with an earthly afterlife may derive historically from those associated with an otherworldly afterlife. We have already mentioned how certain customs and practices originally associated with the idea of an otherworldly afterlife may over time come to be associated with the idea of an earthly afterlife. The same is true in the history of language too. For example, much of the language about the dead which originally derived from and made sense in terms of otherworldly afterlife is now, quite legitimately though usually metaphorically, additionally or alternatively employed in references to an earthly afterlife (or the lack of one). The slang description of death as the 'big sleep' derives from, but does not now refer to, the theological idea about the dead sleeping; references to a deceased person as being 'here in spirit' or 'now at rest' no longer refer only to the literal presence of discarnate souls or to some kind of substantive existence in an afterworld; and more colourful expressions, such as those about swearing on someone's grave or about turning in one's grave, have their origins in rituals and superstitions predicated on beliefs that the dead survive in another world. The argument that because references to an earthly afterlife are couched in the language and imagery traditionally associated with an otherworldly afterlife they must therefore be disguised references to the latter is fallacious, and in any case it can easily be turned on its head to produce the opposite argument – namely, that ideas about an otherworldly afterlife are cryptic or superstitious versions of ideas about an earthly afterlife. This is precisely what Bertrand Russell does in his interpretation of progenitive survival. That parenthood is psychologically capable of providing life's greatest happiness is, says

Russell, demonstrated throughout history and taken for granted in almost all literature:

> Hecuba cares more for her children than for Priam; MacDuff cares more for his children than for his wife. In the Old Testament both men and women are passionately concerned to leave descendants; in China and Japan this attitude has persisted down to our own day. It will be said that this desire is due to ancestor worship. I think, however, that the contrary is the truth, namely that ancestor worship is a reflection of the interest people take in the persistence of their family.[34]

In this case, what would one make of the importance attached, in the Hindu tradition, to having a son? The traditional answer, at least, is that without a son to perform the necessary funerary and post-funerary rites one's happiness in the next world would be in jeopardy.

Apologists for an earthly *as opposed to* an otherworldly afterlife consider the former idea superior to the latter, as though the former is comparable to guests gracefully retiring and the latter to guests outstaying their welcome. Given the poor returns on any investment in an earthly afterlife, however, the best forms of otherworldly afterlife must, in an ideal universe, surely trump the best forms of an earthly afterlife. It is difficult to see why one would rationally prefer, either for oneself or for others, anything less than an otherworldly afterlife – assuming that the latter were available, so to speak, and assuming also of course that it would not entail eternal misery or suffering. Clearly many people do not believe in any kind of otherworldly survival and therefore are liable to attach great importance to an earthly afterlife, at least as a consolation for the otherwise total loss of an individual and perhaps also as a surrogate for the otherworldly survival assumed to be impossible.

Those who affirm the possibility or reality of some form of otherworldly afterlife will not deny the reality or decry the value of an earthly afterlife, but they will tend to see the latter as more meaningful when it is linked in some way with the former. Those who deny the possibility or reality of an otherworldly afterlife may well exaggerate the importance of an earthly afterlife or, more stoically, may dismiss most forms of it as little more than icing on the cake of oblivion. Moreover, as was made clear in Chapter Five, there are some people for whom oblivion is by no means the worst destiny.

V

In this book I have considered ways in which human beings confront mortality – their own, that of others, that of humanity as a whole and even that of the world itself. In particular, however, I have examined three rather different ways of managing mortality through various constructions of an earthly immortality. The first of these has, so far in human history, been little more than a dream or fantasy – the fantasy of overcoming mortality by not dying in the first place. Given the laws of biology, the only way of realizing the dream of 'living on' indefinitely in this world would be by changing ourselves into something superhuman, if not into something non-human or even anti-human. Thus human beings might eventually turn themselves into androids or cyborgs – that is, into beings whose given biology is enhanced by and combined with cybernetic elements. It is difficult to believe, however, that even the most sophisticated human android or cyborg could last forever, even if all we mean by 'forever' is the rest of human (or post-human) history, wherever in the universe this history might take place. This is to say nothing of the doubts one might have regarding the identity of such human cyborgs, and nothing about whether such an existence would prove ethically acceptable or socially or psychologically satisfying (if indeed these terms continued to have meaning).

The second means of managing the desire for earthly immortality is to find immortality not in some extension of our brief lifespan but in the richness of our present life, a richness which if anything is enhanced rather than threatened by life's brevity. This kind of immediate or realized sense of immortality may be cultivated through a particular way of living, or it could be dependent on mystical or ecstatic experiences revelatory of some transcendental reality. The trouble with this idea is that an earthly immortality based on an attitude or technique of living in the present moment, without clinging to past or future, must come to an end with a person's extinction. What would it mean at the end of such a life to talk about attaining immortality? How would the ending of life for such a person differ from the ending of life for one who had lived in quite a different way? One obvious answer is that the two individuals in question might at least die differently. One might even say of someone who had died that he or she experienced an immortal life right up to the end.

As for an earthly immortality based on transcendental experiences of some kind, this would not be easy to differentiate from an otherworldly immortality – and might indeed represent the most profound form of otherworldly immortality. The subjects of such experiences could be thought of as having glimpsed or tasted, even during their mortal lives, a quality of life they will know more fully after death. In the Buddhist tradition, which arguably represents the most sustained and serious attempt to deal head on with the tragic impermanence of human life, the mindfulness techniques designed to overcome the suffering caused by desire and impermanence only make sense in relation to the attainment of nirvana, which is a positive and a permanent mode of being.[35]

The third means of managing mortality through the medium of an earthly immortality, and the one with which I have been chiefly concerned in this book, is to anticipate for oneself or for one's loved ones an earthly immortality based on life's legacy, a legacy one can to some extent determine before one's death but which eventually depends on the memories and activities of others who will be its 'custodians'. Earthly immortality through some persisting legacy may take two forms, which I have defined as 'posthumous personhood' and 'anonymous immortality'.

These two types of earthly immortality might well appear, rather negatively, to represent two phases in the inevitable decline of one's effect on and remembrance by others (whether those now living or those yet to be born). This is the theme addressed in Thomas Hardy's poem 'The To-be-forgotten', cited in Chapter Three, in which Hardy imagines the churchyard dead dreading the inevitable time when, forgotten by the living, they will suffer the 'blank oblivion' of a 'second death' when the living eventually come to forget them.

More positively, however, posthumous personhood and anonymous immortality can be viewed as two stages in a process whereby an earthly afterlife is cut loose from being about the remembrance and celebration of a particular individual whose substantial personhood is no longer present in any case. It is possible, in other words, to see one's anonymous immortality not only as the best that can be hoped for in the way of earthly immortality, but as the purest form of the latter. For in this way one survives in and for others, without reference to one's own personhood, which is no longer 'present' to earthly experience.

It is not easy to say how and why it is that the idealizations, substitutions and consolations of an earthly immortality have such a powerful effect both upon the living who imagine their own future earthly after-lives and upon those who live on as the witnesses and custodians of the afterlives of others. To write these effects off as mere sentimentality will not do, since it is the power or depth of the sentiments that we need to understand. It is not difficult to see them as springing in part from an instinct, if not belief, that deceased persons are more than the sum of their now completed lives, or to believe that our fascination with earthly immortalities derives much of its force from their role as vehicles for, or intimations of, otherworldly immortalities.

REFERENCES

PREFACE

1 Peter Moore, *Where are the Dead? Exploring the Idea of an Embodied Afterlife* (New York and London, 2017).

INTRODUCTION

1 Edward Young (1683–1765), *The Complaint: or, Night-thoughts* (London, 1742); Night Seventh, 507–10.
2 See, for example, Yvonne Sherwood, *A Biblical Text and its Afterlives: The Survival of Jonah in Western Culture* (Cambridge, 2000).
3 For a book based on the most literal understanding of what a literary afterlife is, see Bernard A. Drew, *Literary Afterlife: The Posthumous Continuations of 325 Authors' Fictional Characters* (Jefferson, NC, 2009). What is it, asks Drew, about certain literary characters that impel new authors to make them live on long after their original authors have died?
4 Edward Shils, *Tradition* (London, 1981), pp. 24 and 15.
5 Ibid., p. 167.
6 Auguste Comte, *Catéchisme positiviste* (Paris, 1852); *The Catechism of Positive Religion*, trans. Richard Congreve (London, 1858), pp. 76–7.
7 Karl Marx, *The Eighteenth Brumaire of Louis Bonaparte* (New York, 1963), p. 15. Compare this with Voltaire's description of history as 'nothing but a pack of tricks we play upon the dead' (in a letter to Pierre Robert Le Cornier de Cideville, 9 February 1757). See *Complete Works of Voltaire* (Banbury, 1971), vol. CI, p. 448.
8 See *The Poems of Alice Meynell* (New York, 1923), p. 44.
9 In some conceptions of post-mortem existence, individual selfhood is abolished or transcended. In these cases, arguably, the term 'afterlife', with its implication of personal continuance, should not be used.
10 If 'earthbound' ghosts or 'haunting' apparitions were forms of the surviving dead, however, they might well be regarded as in some sense the subjects of their own earthly afterlives. Alternatively they might be regarded as 'supernatural' cases of what I defined in Chapter Two as 'staying on'. Vivid examples of how the surviving dead might share their

earthly afterlives with the living are given in Richard Lloyd Parry, *Ghosts of the Tsunami: Death and Life in Japan's Disaster Zone* (London, 2017).

11 See David R. Unruh, 'Death and Personal History: Strategies of Identity Preservation', *Social Problems*, XXX (1983), pp. 340–51.

12 John Ellis McTaggart, 'The Relation of Time and Eternity', *Mind*, XVIII (1909), pp. 343–62 (p. 343).

13 For more on this, see Eleanore Stump and Norman Kretzmann, 'Eternity', *Journal of Philosophy*, LXXVIII (1981), pp. 429–58.

14 Christopher Cherry, 'Can My Survival Be Subrogated?', *Philosophy*, LIX (1984), pp. 443–56; here pp. 450, 448.

15 The OED gives three meanings for this word: (1) a person's later years of life; (2) a post-mortem existence; (3) a renewed use or influence. One of the examples given to illustrate the third meaning describes a particular disused railway line as having an 'afterlife' as a long-distance footpath.

16 R. S. Thomas, 'The Country Clergy', in *Collected Poems, 1945–1990* (London, 1993), p. 82.

17 The Greek gods, for example, had to drink ambrosia to maintain their existence.

18 For example, the Hindu and Norse mythologies both envisage a time when the universe, including most of the gods, will be destroyed – although this destruction is followed by a new creation.

19 Consider also the words of Hannah Arendt, *The Human Condition* (Chicago, IL, 1958), p. 18: 'Immortality means endurance in time, deathless life on this earth and in this world as it was given, according to Greek understanding, to nature and the Olympian gods. Against this background of nature's ever-recurring life and the gods' deathless and ageless lives stood mortal men, the only mortals in an immortal but not eternal universe, confronted with the immortal lives of their gods but not under the rule of an eternal God.' Compare with this Thomas Browne's statement: 'The created World is but a small *Parenthesis* in Eternity' (*Urn-Burial*, 1658).

20 Andrew Bennett, 'On Posterity', *Yale Journal of Criticism*, XII (1999), pp. 131–44 (p. 131). Elsewhere Bennett quotes William Hazlitt ('On the Living Poets', 1818) on how the greatest poets can afford to wait for lasting fame: 'If their works have the seeds of immortality in them, they will live; if they have not they care little about them as theirs.' *Romantic Poets and the Culture of Posterity* (Cambridge, 1999), p. 4.

21 T. C. Finlayson, *Biological Religion* (Manchester, 1885), pp. 67–8. The work under criticism was Henry Drummond's *Natural Law in the Spirit World* (New York, 1884).

22 There is, of course, a subtle difference between being 'immune to' and 'immune from' something. The former implies an intrinsic immunity, the latter an immunity dependent upon some external factor (for example, the law, military power, God) – an immunity that could, therefore, be withdrawn.

23 As Denis Diderot observes (Letter 4 to Falconet, 4 February 1766), 'posterity properly begins only from the moment we cease to exist; but it speaks to us for a long time before that' (*La postérité ne commence proprement qu'au moment où nous cessons d'être; mais elle nous parle longtemps*

auparavant). See *Mémoires, correspondance et ouvrages inédits de Diderot*, vol. III (Paris, 1830), p. 218. For an analysis of the hopes invested in posterity by Diderot and his contemporaries, see Carl. L. Becker, *The Heavenly City of the Eighteenth-century Philosophers* (New Haven, CT, and London, 1932), Lecture IV: 'The Uses of Posterity'.

24 See J. V. Luce, 'Immortality in Plato's Symposium: A Reply', *Classical Review*, II (1952), pp. 137–41.

25 Rolf von Eckartsberg and Elsa von Eckartsberg, 'Social and Electronic Immortality', *Janus Head*, XII (2011), pp. 9–21 (p. 9).

26 See D. G. Charlton, *Secular Religions in France, 1815–1879* (Oxford, 1963), esp. chs 3–4.

27 Auguste Comte, *System of Positive Polity, or Treatise on Sociology, Instituting the Religion of Humanity* (1851–4); trans. Richard Congreve (London, 1877), vol. IV, p. 90.

28 Charles Hartshorne, 'Time, Death, and Eternal Life', *Journal of Religion*, XXXII (1952), pp. 97–107.

29 See, for example, Robert J. Lifton, *The Broken Connection: On Death and the Continuity of Life* (New York, 1979). For a briefer introduction to Lifton's ideas, see his 'The Sense of Immortality: On Death and the Continuity of Life', *American Journal of Psychoanalysis*, XXXIII (1973), pp. 3–15.

30 John Bond, spy for Elizabeth I and assistant to Sir Francis Drake, decided to 'borrow' Philip's motto for his own coat of arms while on a raid in the Azores (newly acquired by Spain) in 1586. The motto crops up in Ian Fleming's novel *On His Majesty's Secret Service* (1963), where the fictional James Bond is introduced to the coat of arms of his supposed ancestor, the real life Sir Thomas Bond (*c.* 1620–1675). In turn it became the title of the Bond film *The World is Not Enough* (1999), the theme of which is unrelated to that of the aforementioned novel.

31 A medal of Francis I of France struck in 1515 bears the motto *unus non sufficit orbis* (One World is Not Enough), and a Neapolitan dollar of Charles II of Spain dated 1684 the similarly intended *unus non sufficit*. See W. S. Appleton, 'The Inscription Unus Non Sufficit Orbis and Geographical Medals in General', *American Journal of Numismatics, and Bulletin of the American Numismatic and Archaeological Society*, V (1871), pp. 49–50.

32 Juvenal, *Satire X*, 168–73; *Juvenal and Persius*, trans. G. G. Ramsay (Cambridge, MA, and London, 1940), p. 207.

I MINDING MORTALITY

1 The English verb 'to mind' has varied uses in many contexts. There are two quite distinct senses in which people 'mind' children, for example; we can be 'mindful' of something, and also 're-minded' of it; we can be 'minded' to do something; and we can be told to 'mind out'.

2 Note that the verb here in Dickinson's poem is 'could not stop', not 'would not stop'.

3 See, for example, Diana Fuss, 'Corpse Poem', *Critical Inquiry*, XXX (2003), pp. 1–30; and Rodney Stenning Edgecombe, 'Mors Viva: Literary

Renderings of Life-to-death Transitions', *Modern Language Review*,
XCVIII (2003), pp. 11–26.

4 Kenneth Burke, 'Thanatopsis for Critics: A Brief Thesaurus of Deaths
and Dyings', *Essays in Criticism*, II (1952), pp. 369–75 (p. 369).

5 Woody Allen, *Without Feathers* (New York, 1972), p. 99.

6 See, for example, E. Mansell Pattison, *The Experience of Dying*
(Englewood Cliffs, NJ, 1977).

7 Sarah Bakewell, *How to Live: or A Life of Montaigne in One Question and
Twenty Attempts at an Answer* (London, 2010), p. 14.

8 Epicurus, *Letter to Menoeceus*, 125: 'So death, the most terrifying of ills,
is nothing to us, since so long as we exist, death is not with us; but when
death comes, then we do not exist. It does not then concern either the
living or the dead, since for the former it is not, and the latter are no
more.' See Whitney J. Oates, ed., *The Stoic and Epicurean Philosophers*
(New York, 1957), p. 31.

9 *Meditations*, Book IX.3; in C. R. Haines, ed. and trans., *Marcus Aurelius*
(Cambridge, MA, 1930), pp. 234–5.

10 Philip Larkin, 'Aubade' (1977); *Collected Poems* (London, 1988), pp. 208–9.

11 Dylan Thomas, *Deaths and Entrances* (London, 1946). It is believed
that Thomas never showed, or read, this poem to his father. For a more
profound poem on death by Thomas, see his 'A Refusal to Mourn the
Death, by Fire, of a Child in London' (1945).

12 See Diana Fuss, 'Last Words', ELH, LXXVI (2009), pp. 877–910.

13 David Cannadine, 'War and Death, Grief and Mourning in Modern
Britain', in *Mirrors of Mortality: Studies in the Social History of Death*,
ed. J. Whaley (London, 1981), pp. 187–242.

14 The 'five stages' model originates with the work of Elizabeth Kübler-Ross.
See her *On Death and Dying* (London, 1969).

15 Michael P. Katz, ed., *Tolstoy's Short Fiction*, 2nd edn (New York and
London, 1991), p. 110. The translation is that of Louise and Aylmer Maude
(1935).

16 Sigmund Freud, 'Thoughts for the Times on War and Death' [1915],
The Standard Edition of the Complete Psychological Works of Sigmund Freud,
vol. XIV, ed. James Strachey (London, 1957), p. 289.

17 Ernest Becker, *The Denial of Death* (London and New York, 1973).

18 Ernest Becker, *Escape from Evil* (New York, 1975), p. 3.

19 For an overview of TMT, see Sheldon Solomon, Jeff Greenberg and
Tom Pyszczynski, *The Worm at the Core: On the Role of Death in Life*
(New York, 2015).

20 See, for example, Mark R. Leary and Lisa S. Schreindorfer, 'Unresolved
Issues with Terror Management Theory', *Psychological Inquiry*, VIII (1997),
pp. 26–9.

21 A. C. Cowley, ed., *Everyman and Medieval Miracle Plays* (London, 1974),
p. 210. Similar sentiments are found in some of Jean de la Fontaine's
Fables (1668–94), for example, 1.15 ('I'll ask of Death no greater favour /
Than just to stay away for ever.') and 8.1 ('Death never taketh by surprise
/ The well-prepared, to wit, the wise' . . . / "O Death," said he, "d' ye call it
fair, / Without a warning to prepare, / To take a man on lifted leg? /
O, wait a little while, I beg!"') (trans. Elizur Wright, 1841).

22 One should not rule out the possibility that the 'deathbed experience' might also involve supernatural or post-mortem agencies, such as angels or already deceased individuals. See Karlis Osis and Erlendur Haraldsson, *At the Hour of Death*, 3rd edn (Norwalk, CT, 1997).

23 Shai Lavi, 'How Dying Became a "Life Crisis"', *Daedalus*, CXXVII (2008), pp. 57–65; here pp. 58, 62.

24 'Le soleil ni la mort ne se peuvent regarder fixement' (maxim 26).

25 One should, in any case, remember Wittgenstein's dictum that 'death is not an event in life; death is not lived through' (*Tractatus* 6.4311).

26 Kenneth Burke, 'Thanatopsis for Critics: A Brief Thesaurus of Deaths and Dyings', *Essays in Criticism*, II (1952), pp. 269–75.

27 Nancy Lee Beaty, *The Craft of Dying: The Literary Tradition of the 'Ars Moriendi' in England* (New Haven, CT, 1971).

28 'Satipatthana Sutta: The Discourse on the Arousing of Mindfulness' (MN 10), trans. Soma Thera, *Access to Insight*, 13 June 2010, available at www.accesstoinsight.org. For further details, see Soma Thera, *The Way of Mindfulness: The Satipatthana Sutta and its Commentary* (Kandy, 1981).

29 John Keats, *Isabella; or the Pot of Basil* (1818), stanza 45 (lines 353–8).

30 The idea of death as a friend can be represented either mythologically or metaphorically. See, for example, Judith L. Lief, *Making Friends with Death: A Buddhist Guide to Encountering Mortality* (Boston, MA, 2001).

31 On this theme, see Mircea Eliade, *Rites and Symbols of Initiation* (New York, 1965).

32 Bruce Lincoln, 'The Rape of Persephone: A Greek Scenario of Women's Initiation', *Harvard Theological Review*, LXXII (1979), pp. 223–35.

33 See Peter Moore, *Where are the Dead? Exploring the Idea of an Embodied Afterlife* (New York and London, 2017), pp. 78–9.

34 For more on this, see David Kinsley, 'Freedom from Death in the Worship of Kālī', *Numen*, XXII (1975), pp. 183–207.

35 Stanley Brandes, 'Iconography in Mexico's Day of the Dead: Origins and Meaning', *Ethnohistory*, XLV (1998), pp. 181–218. See also Barbara Brodman, *The Mexican Cult of Death in Myth, Art and Literature* (Bloomington, IN, 2011).

36 See R. Andrew Chesnut, *Devoted to Death: Santa Muerte, the Skeleton Saint*, 2nd edn (New York, 2018).

37 Charles Baudelaire, *Les Fleurs du Mal* (1857); translation mine.

38 *Iliad* 16.671.

39 Francis Bacon, 'Of Death' (1612, enlarged 1625).

40 See his *Lectures on Psychical Research* (London, 1962), p. 430.

41 A soteriology is a doctrine or theory of salvation. The soteriological function of religion is not its only function; and some religions are not soteriologies at all.

42 A fairly recent example is the case of Sir Jimmy Savile, the radio and television 'disc jockey' and 'personality' (1934–2011). Lauded in his lifetime and immediately after his death as a tireless worker for charity, he was subsequently revealed to have been a serial sexual predator of the most egregious kind. His ostentatious triple headstone, which bore the inscription 'It Was Good While It Lasted', was broken up and taken to

landfill. Elsewhere, memorial plaques were removed and places named after him renamed. There have been calls for his body (resting, under concrete, in a gold-covered coffin) to be exhumed and cremated. See Dan Davies, *In Plain Sight: The Life and Lies of Jimmy Savile* (London, 2014).

43 Thomas Browne, *Hydriotaphia, Urn Burial; or a Brief Discourse of the Sepulchral Urns lately found in Norfolk* (1658); C. A. Patrides, ed., *Sir Thomas Browne: The Major Works* (Harmondsworth, 1977), pp. 307–8. For a more recent discussion of how archaeological remains fire our imaginations, allowing us to build up a picture of the past sometimes from the most fragmentary material, see Jennifer Wallace, *Digging the Dirt: The Archaeological Imagination* (London, 2004).

44 *Ancient Funeral Monuments of Great Britain, Ireland, and the Islands adjacent* [1631] (London, 1767), 'The Author to the Reader'.

45 'To Bring the Dead to Life'; Beryl Graves and Dunstan Ward, eds, *Robert Graves: The Complete Poems* (London, 2003), p. 363. What others might be making of one's work after one has gone is nicely satirized in Philip Larkin's 'Posterity' (1968); *Collected Poems*, p. 170.

46 Denise Levertov, *Sands of the Well* (New York, 1994), p. 62.

2 STAYING ON

1 This passage is an edited composite of statements made in different publications and interviews.

2 *Six Feet Under*, created by Alan Ball, HBO, series 1–5 (2001–5).

3 'No one thinks he will escape death, so there is no disappointment and, as long as we know neither the when nor the how, the mere fact that we shall one day have to go does not much affect us; we do not care, even though we know vaguely that we have not long to live.' Henry Festing Jones, ed., *The Note-books of Samuel Butler* (New York, 1917), p. 353.

4 Marquis de Condorcet cited in Keith Michael Baker, trans., 'Sketch for a Historical Picture of the Progress of the Human Mind: Tenth Epoch', *Daedalus*, CXXXIII (2004), pp. 65–82; here pp. 80–81.

5 The *OED* has 'longevous' (from the Latin *longaevus*), meaning 'long-lived; living or having lived to a great age. Also: long-lasting, enduring.'

6 See Stephen R. L. Clark, *How to Live Forever: Science Fiction and Philosophy* (London, 1995).

7 Stephen Mitchell, trans., *Gilgamesh* (London, 2004), p. 178.

8 Ronald A. Veenker, 'Gilgamesh and the Magic Plant', *Biblical Archaeologist*, XLIV (1981), pp. 199–205.

9 G. K. Anderson, *The Legend of the Wandering Jew* (Providence, RI, 1965).

10 On the connections between these figures, see Judith Chernaik, 'No Resting Could He Find: The Mariner, the Dutchman and the Wandering Jew', *Times Literary Supplement* (24 January 2003), p. 13.

11 See David Keck, *Angels and Angelology in the Middle Ages* (New York and Oxford, 1998), pp. 22–3.

12 Alfred, Lord Tennyson, 'Tithonus' (1859; first published in the *Cornhill Magazine*, February 1860).

13 Aldous Huxley, *After Many a Summer* (London, 1939).

14 In *Satire X*, Juvenal mocks the decrepitude of the aged: 'Give me length

of days, give me many years, O Jupiter! Such is your one and only prayer, in days of strength or of sickness; yet how great, how unceasing, are the miseries of old age! . . . [O]ld men all look alike. Their voices are as shaky as their limbs, their heads without hair, their noses drivelling as in childhood. Their bread, poor wretches, has to be munched by toothless gums . . .'.

15 Jonathan Swift, *Gulliver's Travels* (1726), Part 3, ch. 10.

16 See Bernard Williams, 'The Makropulos Case: Reflections on the Tedium of Immortality', in *Problems of the Self: Philosophical Papers, 1956–1972* (Cambridge, 1973), pp. 82–100.

17 These words are from Act III of Janáček's libretto for his opera (in the English translation by Norman Tucker).

18 The likely negative consequences of a world inhabited by a multiplicity of human immortals – following an accidental medical discovery that grants people prolonged life and eternal youth – are dramatized in Drew Magary's novel *The Postmortal* (2011).

19 Joseph Needham, *Science and Civilisation in China*, vol. v, part 2 (Cambridge, 1974), pp. xxvii–xxxii, 71–127. On Japanese traditions concerning earthly immortality, see Edward R. Drott, '"To Tread on High Clouds": Dreams of Eternal Youth in Early Japan', *Japanese Journal of Religious Studies*, XLII (2015), pp. 275–317.

20 Burton Watson, trans., *The Complete Works of Chuang Tzu* (New York, 1968), p. 130.

21 *Alciphron, or: The Minute Philosopher*, Dialogue 4; Alexander Campbell Fraser, ed., *The Works of George Berkeley*, vol. II: *Philosophical Works, 1732–33* (Oxford, 1901), p. 190.

22 Mary Y. Hallab, *Vampire God: The Allure of the Undead in Western Culture* (Albany, NY, 2009), p. 9.

23 From Richard Wilbur, 'The Undead' (1961); *Collected Poems, 1953–2004* (Orlando, FL, 2004), pp. 272–3.

24 Bram Stoker, *Dracula*, ed. Maurice Hindle (London, 2003), p. 229.

25 Ibid., p. 401.

26 Anne Rice, *Interview with the Vampire* (New York, 1976), p. 283.

27 In *Blade Runner 2049* (dir. Denis Villeneuve, 2017), the sequel to the original film, androids have been redesigned to be less easily confusable with human beings.

28 On this particular question, see Neal J. Roese and Eyal Amir, 'Human–Android Interaction in the Near and Distant Future', *Perspectives on Psychological Science*, IV (2009), pp. 429–34.

29 European Parliament (Committee on Legal Affairs), 'European Civil Law Rules in Robotics', 2015/2103, www.europarl.europa.eu, 31 May 2016.

30 Philip K. Dick, *Do Androids Dream of Electric Sheep?* (Garden City, NY, 1968), p. 164.

31 Ibid., p. 193.

32 Augustine, *De civitate dei*, 22.20; Henry Bettenson, trans., *Concerning the City of God Against the Pagans* (Harmondsworth, 1972), p. 1062.

33 See *Bhagavad Gita*, 2.22; R. C. Zaehner, trans., *The Bhagavad Gita* (Oxford, 1973), p. 133.

34 See Ian Stevenson, *Where Reincarnation and Biology Intersect* (Westport, CT, 1997).

35 Friedrich Nietzsche, *The Gay Science* [1887], trans. Walter Kaufmann (New York, 1974), p. 273.
36 Philip J. Kain, 'Nietzsche, Eternal Recurrence, and the Horror of Existence', *Journal of Nietzsche Studies*, XXXIII (2007), pp. 49–63.
37 Albert Camus, *The Myth of Sisyphus and Other Essays*, trans. Justin O'Brien (New York, 1955), pp. 119–23.
38 Philip J. Kain, *Nietzsche and the Horror of Existence* (Plymouth, 2009), p. 58.
39 This is opening paragraph of Alan Harrington's *The Immortalist: An Approach to the Engineering of Man's Divinity* (New York, 1969).
40 See his *Methuselah's Children* (1941) and *Between Planets* (1951).
41 The consequences for someone awakening from suspended animation in a future era are explored to comic effect in the film *Sleeper* (dir. Woody Allen, 1973).
42 Ole Martin Moen, 'The Case for Cryonics', *Journal of Medical Ethics*, XLI (2015), pp. 677–81 (p. 677).
43 Blaise Pascal (1623–1662) argued (*Pensées*, 3.233) that it is rationally better to affirm the existence of the Deity (with all the benefits such belief might bring) than to deny it (with all the risks such denial might bring).
44 David Shaw, 'Cryoethics: Seeking Life After Death', *Bioethics*, XXIII (2009), pp. 515–21 (p. 521). For discussion of a far more modest and already realizable use of cryonic techniques for the purpose of 'earthly immortality', see Gillian M. Lockwood, 'Social Egg Freezing: The Prospect of Reproductive "Immortality" or a Dangerous Delusion?', *Reproductive Medicine Online*, XXIII (2011), pp. 334–40.
45 Conceivably, the cloning of a person with some rare and socially beneficial physical characteristic might be deemed ethically acceptable. For example, in a world facing severe global warming, it might be acceptable to clone persons whose constitutions enabled them to cope exceptionally well with very high temperatures.
46 Tim Radford, 'UK Couple Have Dead Dog Cloned in South Korea', *The Guardian*, 24 December 2015.
47 'Virtual Reality for Virtual Eternity', www.newswise.com, 12 March 2007.
48 'Virtual Immortality – How to Live Forever', www.dailygalaxy.com, 13 June 2007.
49 Named after the computer expert Alan Turing, the (or, more accurately, a) 'Turing Test' is one that establishes (in the opinion of its assessors) whether or not the responses to human conversation of a particular unit of artificial intelligence (computer, robot, and so on) are distinguishable from those of a human being.
50 There would very likely also be laws or principles regulating the way in which androids were 'allowed' (that is designed) to behave, along the lines of Isaac Asimov's 'Three Laws of Robotics'. See also Roese and Amir, 'Human–Android Interaction in the Near and Distant Future'.
51 An android could be regarded as an *imitation* human being or even – where the intention was to deceive – as a *fake* human being. It is by the same criterion that we call, say, a modern piece of 'Chippendale' furniture either an imitation or a fake. And yet a modern 'Chippendale' may well be identical to its antique original in substance, function and appearance

alike, similarities which in the case of an android might prompt an altogether different classification – perhaps something like 'alternative' human being.

52 See 'What is Transhumanism?', www.transhumanism.org, accessed 12 January 2018.

53 Peter Harrison and Joseph Wolyniak, 'The History of "Transhumanism"', *Notes and Queries*, LXII (2015), pp. 465–7.

54 James Hughes, 'The Politics of Transhumanism and the Techno-millennial Imagination, 1626–2030', *Zygon*, XLVII (2012), pp. 757–76.

55 Max More, 'The Philosophy of Transhumanism', in *The Transhumanist Reader: Classical and Contemporary Essays on the Science, Technology, and Philosophy of the Human Future*, ed. Max More and Natasha Vita-More (Chichester, 2013), p. 4.

56 This qualification is important because it is conceivable that some external factor would render immortality or even hyperlongevity an unexpected pain or disadvantage. Imagine, for example, the climate on a planet populated by immortals becoming irreversibly and uncontrollably uncomfortable. Or suppose that the post-human immortals imagined by transhumanism were to be enslaved by a race of extraterrestrial beings.

57 Heraclitus, as quoted in Plato, *Cratylus*, 402a.

58 The reference is to Orsino's opening speech in Act 1, Scene 1 of Shakespeare's *Twelfth Night*.

59 According to one interpreter of Swift, the Struldbrugs are a literary device satirizing not the fantasy that one might live forever, or the consequences of such a destiny, but rather the folly of investing hope in the 'metaphorical immortality' created by earthly fame, since this will wither and die as surely as do living bodies themselves. See Robert P. Fitzgerald, 'Swift's Immortals: The Satiric Point', *Studies in English Literature, 1500–1900*, XXIV (1984), pp. 483–95.

3 POSTHUMOUS PERSONHOOD

1 The sixth stanza of 'Hallowed Ground' (1825) by Thomas Campbell (1777–1844).

2 Isabel Allende, *Stories of Eva Luna*, trans. Margaret Sayers (New York, 1992), p. 43.

3 Henry Festing Jones, ed., *The Note-books of Samuel Butler* (New York, 1917), p. 355.

4 First staged in Paris in 1980, the English-language version of *Les Misérables* opened in London in 1985. The music is by Claude-Michel Schönberg, the lyrics of the English version by Herbert Kretzmer.

5 Roland Barthes, *Camera Lucida* (London, 2000), p. 9.

6 Susan Sontag, *On Photography* (New York, 1973), p. 16.

7 See, for example, Avril Maddrell, 'Online Memorials: The Virtual as the New Vernacular', *Bereavement Care*, XXXI (2012), pp. 46–54.

8 See, for example, James Meese et al., 'Posthumous Personhood and the Affordances of Digital Media', *Mortality*, XX (2015), pp. 408–20.

9 See Joanna J. Bryson, 'Internet Memory and Life after Death', *Bereavement Care*, XXXI/2 (2012), pp. 70–72.

10 'Living memorials' are defined by Andrew M. Shanken as 'useful projects such as community centers, libraries, forests, and even highways that were marked in some fashion, usually with plaques, as memorials'. See his 'Planning Memory: Living Memorials in the United States during World War II', *Art Bulletin*, LXXXIV (2002), p. 130.

11 It is possible too that many of the memories one has of one's own life are in fact 'memories of memories' rather than direct memories.

12 John Kotre, *White Gloves: How We Create Ourselves Through Memory* (New York, 1995), p. 231.

13 'Servius Sulpicius to Cicero (At Astura)', in Cicero, *Letters*, trans. E. S. Shuckburgh (New York, 1909–14); The Harvard Classics, vol. IX, Part 3, letter 27.

14 Cicero modelled his orations on those of Demosthenes, who in the fourth century BCE had delivered a fierce attack on Philip II of Macedon. The term 'philippic' came to be used for any forthright speech directed against a particular political party or opponent.

15 C. D. Yonge, *Orations of Marcus Tullius Cicero* (New York, 1900), pp. 351–3.

16 *Symposium* 209; Jowett translation.

17 *Symposium* 29; Jowett translation.

18 See E. E. Pender, 'Spiritual Pregnancy in Plato's *Symposium*', *Classical Quarterly*, XLII (1992), pp. 72–86.

19 Here I follow the interpretation of Socrates' account of Diotima's philosophy given by F. C. White, 'Virtue in Plato's "Symposium"', *Classical Quarterly*, LIV (2004), pp. 366–78.

20 See Tomas Eloy Martinez, *Santa Evita* (London, 1997).

21 Jessica Mitford, *The American Way of Death Revisited* (London, 1998), p. 47.

22 Robert Pogue Harrison, *The Dominion of the Dead* (Chicago, IL, and London, 2003), p. 1.

23 Diane Samuels, *Kindertransport* (London, 1995), p. 46.

24 John Chrysostom, *On Marriage and Family Life*, trans. Catharine P. Roth and David Anderson (Crestwood, NY, 2003), pp. 85–6.

25 Henry Adams Bellows, trans., *The Poetic Edda* (New York, 1923), p. 44.

26 Horace, *Odes* Book III.xxx; Jeffrey H. Kaimowitz, trans., *The Odes of Horace* (Baltimore, MD, 2008), p. 142.

27 Edmund Spenser, *The Ruines of Time* (1590), ll. 400–413; Edwin Greenlaw, Charles Osgood and Frederick Morgan Padelford, eds, *The Works of Edmund Spenser: A Variorum Edition*, vol. II (Baltimore, MD, 1947), pp. 37–65.

28 In the poem's dedication (to the Earl of Leicester's sister, the Countess of Pembroke), Spenser notes that the poem is 'speciallie intended to the renowning of that noble race, from which both you and he sprong, and to the eternizing of some of the chiefe of them late deceased'.

29 Thomas Carlyle, *On Heroes, Hero-worship, and the Heroic in History*, ed. David R. Sorensen and Brent E. Kinser (New Haven, CT, and London, 2013), p. 136.

30 For a study of the immense power of the dead under American law, see Ray D. Madoff, *Immortality and the Law: The Rising Power of the American Dead* (New Haven, CT, 2010).

31 See Judson A. Crane, 'The Uniform Partnership Act and Legal Persons',

Harvard Law Review, XXIX (1916), pp. 838–50. 'A legal person is an entity treated by the law as the subject of rights and obligations. Human beings constitute the numerically largest class of legal persons and have a wider range of interests and powers than other legal persons, such as the state, the city, the university, the business corporation. But not all human beings are legal persons, nor are all legal persons human beings.' (p. 839).

32 Kirsten Rabe Smolensky, 'Rights of the Dead', *Hofstra Law Review*, XXXVII (2009), pp. 763–803; here p. 763.

33 Ibid., p. 764.

34 See, however, Simon Pulleyn, 'The Power of Names in Classical Greek Religion', *Classical Quarterly*, XLIV (1994), pp. 17–25.

35 Rolf von Eckartsberg and Elsa von Eckartsberg, 'Social and Electronic Immortality', *Janus Head*, XII (2011), pp. 9–21 (p. 10).

36 On this theme, see Jerry L. Walls, *Purgatory: The Logic of Total Transformation* (New York, 2012).

37 P. D. James, *Devices and Desires* (London, 1989), p. 249.

38 Joan C. Callahan, 'On Harming the Dead', *Ethics*, XCVII (1987), pp. 341–52 (p. 341).

39 See David Price, *Legal and Ethical Aspects of Organ Transplantation* (Cambridge, 2000), p. 145: 'But even if the dead are themselves beyond harm, what of the ante-mortem person who is now deceased? Can they possess rights and interests which survive death? If not, then on what basis do we permit individuals to leave property by will and authorise the use of their corpse (for example for transplantation) after death? Indeed, many such (autonomous) wishes are only capable of being respected after that person's death.'

40 Callahan, 'On Harming the Dead', p. 347.

41 Palle Yourgrau, 'The Dead', *Journal of Philosophy*, LXXXIV (1987), pp. 84–101; here pp. 97, 93 n.16.

42 Thomas Hardy, 'The to-be-forgotten' (1902); *The Complete Poetical Works of Thomas Hardy*, ed. Samuel Hynes (Oxford, 1982), vol. I, p. 181.

4 ANONYMOUS IMMORTALITY

1 Rainer Maria Rilke, *Duino Elegies*, 'Ninth Elegy' (ll. 11–17); translation mine.

2 Edna St. Vincent Millay, *Collected Poems* (New York, 2011), pp. 240–41.

3 In some cases, an anonymous title itself comes to function as a proper name – a possible example being 'the Unknown Warrior' as the name of the soldier buried in Westminster Abbey.

4 For more on this, see S. J. Tambiah, 'The Magical Power of Words', *Man*, New Series, 3 (1968), pp. 175–208.

5 László Bíró (1899–1985) was the inventor of the ballpoint pen, popularly known as the biro. The history of the term 'hoover' is more complex. In 1908 a janitor named James Murray Spangler, suspecting that his carpet sweeper was the cause of his asthma, invented an electric suction sweeper, later to be known as a vacuum cleaner. He sold the patent to William Henry Hoover, whose company later changed its name to the Hoover Suction Sweeper Company. The word 'hoover' entered American English

usage both as a generic term equivalent to (in current English) vacuum cleaner and as a verb denoting the activity of suction or vacuum cleaning. In this case the inventor's identity was obscured by the name of a businessman, whose own identity was then eclipsed by the machine itself.

6 In 2014 the Brazilian football club Recife created an organ donor card specifically for Recife fans. The card told fans it would ensure that their hearts would keep beating for their team even after death. In the television advert publicizing the campaign, one man awaiting a cornea transplant says 'I promise that your eyes will keep on watching Sport Club Recife.' Over 50,000 fans signed up – more than could fit into the club's stadium. See J. Carneiro, 'How Thousands of Football Fans are Helping to Save Lives', BBC News, www.bbc.co.uk/news/magazine, 1 June 2014.

7 Robert Browning's dramatic monologue 'The Bishop Orders His Tomb at St Praxed's Church' (1845) remains one of the best poetic satires on this theme.

8 See Peter Brown, *The Cult of the Saints: Its Rise and Function in Latin Christianity* (London, 1981).

9 Boris Groys, Elena Sorokina and Emily Speers Mears, 'The Immortal Bodies', RES: *Anthropology and Aesthetics*, LIII (2008), pp. 345–9 (p. 345).

10 WMC Action News 5, 'Family Receives Wrong Ashes for Cremated Mother', www.wmcactionnews5.com, 21 March 2013.

11 See Richard Dawkins, *The Selfish Gene*, 4th edn (Oxford, 1976).

12 Andrea Wulf, *The Invention of Nature: The Adventures of Alexander von Humboldt, The Lost Hero of Science* (London, 2015), p. 336.

13 Whittle (1907–1996) is, of course, far from being an unknown or forgotten figure to anyone who takes even a passing interest in the history of aviation. Information about him is plentiful and readily available. But the fact that he is forgotten by most people shows that one day he could be forgotten by all.

14 The relevant passage is this: 'What odd chaps you painters are! You do anything in the world to gain a reputation. As soon as you have one, you seem to want to throw it away. It is silly of you, for there is only one thing in the world worse than being talked about, and that is not being talked about.' See Russell Jackson and Ian Small, eds, *The Complete Works of Oscar Wilde: The Picture of Dorian Gray: The 1890 and 1891 Texts* (Oxford, 2000), p. 4.

15 Cnut (c. 990–1035) was a king of Denmark (from 1019) and later of Norway (after 1028) who invaded England following the death of the Anglo-Saxon king Ethelred (1016). He was king of England from 1016 until 1035. The first version of the probably apocryphal story of Canute and the waves appears in the *Historia Anglorum* of Henry of Huntingdon (d. 1157).

16 It could be said, of course, that the original legend is already a misrepresentation of historical fact. This may be so, but the legend, whatever its factual basis, is at least likely to be more a representation than a distortion of Canute's reputation as a wise ruler. See Lord Raglan, 'Canute and the Waves', *Man*, LX (1960), pp. 7–8.

17 Rameses II, sometimes known as Rameses the Great, was the third

pharaoh of the Nineteenth Dynasty (of the Old Kingdom), reigning from 1279–1213 BCE. I say 'would have had the last laugh' because the memory and legacy of Rameses II are in fact well secured through a variety of extant monuments and inscriptions. The Ozymandias of Shelley's poem is, in effect, a fictional character whose name alone remains, his works having all but sunk into oblivion: 'Nothing beside remains. Round the decay / Of that colossal Wreck, boundless and bare / The lone and level sands stretch far away.'

18 Ken Warpole, 'Living with the Dead: Burial, Cremation and Memory', *Studies: An Irish Quarterly Review*, XCVIII (2009), pp. 447–56 (p. 450).

19 George Eliot (1871–2); David Carroll, ed., *Middlemarch* (Oxford, 1986), p. 825.

20 Thornton Wilder, *The Bridge of San Luis Rey* (London, 1927), pp. 139–40. Philip Larkin voices a similar idea, tinged with characteristic doubt, in 'An Arundel Tomb' (1956), when he suggests that 'What will survive of us is love.' See *Collected Poems*, pp. 110–11.

21 A. Wolf, trans., *Spinoza's Short Treatise on God, Man, and His Well-being* (London, 1910), pp. 100–101.

22 Bertrand Russell, *The Conquest of Happiness* (London, 1930), p. 198.

23 Karl Marx, *Reflections of a Young Man* (1835); *Karl Marx and Frederick Engels: Collected Works*, vol. 1 (New York, 1975), pp. 8–9.

24 Sam McFarland, 'The Slow Creation of Humanity', *Political Psychology*, XXXII (2011), pp. 1–20.

25 Diogenes Laertius, *Lives of Eminent Philosophers*, 6.63.

26 *Meditations*, 4.4; trans. Gregory Hays (London, 2004). In this case, 'our state must be the world. What other entity could all of humanity belong to? And from it – from this state that we share – come thought and reason and law.'

27 *Meditations*, 3.9. This unitary view of human kind is part of a unitary view of nature as a whole: 'The world as a living being – one nature, one soul. Keep that in mind. And how everything feeds into that single experience, moves with a single motion. And how everything helps produce everything else. Spun and woven together.' (*Meditations*, 4.40).

28 See Martha C. Nussbaum, 'Kant and Stoic Cosmopolitanism', *Journal of Political Philosophy*, V (1997), pp. 1–25.

29 Edmund Bolton, *Hypercritica: or a Rule of Judgement, for Reading or Writing our Histories* (c. 1621), in J. E. Spingarn, ed., *Critical Essays of the Seventeenth Century* vol. 1 (Oxford, 1908), pp. 82–115; here p. 114.

30 Immanuel Kant, *Perpetual Peace: A Philosophical Sketch* (1795).

31 McFarland, 'The Slow Creation of Humanity', p. 14. See also Sam McFarland et al., 'Identification with All Humanity as a Moral Concept and Psychological Construct', *Current Directions in Psychological Science*, XXII (2013), pp. 194–8.

32 See, for example, K. R. Monroe, *The Heart of Altruism: Perception of a Common Humanity* (Princeton, NJ, 1996).

33 Benedetto Croce, *The Conduct of Life*, trans. Arthur Livingston (London, 1915), pp. 37–8.

34 Mark Johnston, *Surviving Death* (Princeton, NJ, and Oxford, 2010), p. 15.

35 Ibid., p. 332.

36 Ibid., p. 236.

37 Ibid., p. 351.

38 Ibid., p. 350.

39 Thomas Nagel, 'My Future Me', *Times Literary Supplement*, 4 June 2010.

40 Lawrence M. Krauss, 'A Universe from Nothing' (2009), a talk sponsored by the Richard Dawkins Foundation for Reason & Science and Atheist Alliance International; quoted in Noel McGivern, *Freedom from Religion* (Bloomington, IN, 2013), p. 139. See also Krauss, *A Universe from Nothing: Why There Is Something Rather Than Nothing* (London, 2012).

41 William Wordsworth, 'A Slumber Did My Spirit Seal', in *Lyrical Ballads* (1800).

42 R.O.C. Winkler, 'Wordsworth's Poetry', in *From Blake to Byron*, ed. Boris Ford (Harmondsworth, 1957), pp. 152–85 (p. 165). See also Warren Stevenson, 'Cosmic Irony in Wordsworth's "A Slumber Did My Spirit Seal"', *The Wordsworth Circle*, VII (1976), pp. 92–4.

43 Larkin, *Collected Poems*, pp. 196–7.

44 Walt Whitman, *Leaves of Grass* (Philadelphia, PA, 1891–2), p. 396.

45 Herbert Read, *The Contrary Experience* (London, 1963), pp. 184–5. This passage is reproduced (often without attribution) in many guides to humanist funerals.

46 Kieron Winn, 'The Poetry of Herbert Read', in *Herbert Read Reassessed*, ed. David Goodway (Liverpool, 1998), pp. 13–29.

47 Mark Johnston, *Surviving Death*, p. 341.

48 Blaise Pascal, *Pensées* (1660), no. 205; trans. W. F. Trotter. This thought is followed by, and explains, one of Pascal's best-known thoughts: 'The eternal silence of these infinite spaces frightens me' (*Le silence éternel des ces espaces infinis m'effraie*).

49 See Brian Cox and Andrew Cohen, *Wonders of the Universe* (London, 2011), p. 136.

50 Stewart Elliott Guthrie, *Faces in the Clouds: A New Theory of Religion* (Oxford, 1995).

51 Mumsnet Talk, www.mumsnet.com, 5 March 2015.

5 DOING WITHOUT AN AFTERLIFE?

1 These lines are from Frost's poem 'Birches' (1915), which refers to his childhood experience of climbing birch trees. The sentiment is reminiscent of Wordsworth's affirmation of 'the very world, which is the world / Of all of us, – the place where, in the end, / We find our happiness, or not at all!' (*The Prelude* 11.142–4).

2 '*sapias, vina liques, et spatio brevi / spem longam reseces. dum loquimur, fugerit invida / aetas: carpe diem, quam minimum credula postero*' (Odes 1.11); translation mine.

3 For more on the *carpe diem* theme, see Fredelle Bruser, 'Comus and the Rose Song', *Studies in Philology*, XLIV (1947), pp. 625–44.

4 Quoted by St Paul: 'If after the manner of men I have fought with beasts at Ephesus, what advantage is there to me, if the dead rise not? "Let us eat and drink, for tomorrow we die!"' (1 Cor. 15:32).

5 Andrew Marvell, 'To His Coy Mistress' (1681).

6 This is borrowed from the Latin *timor mortis conturbat me* (the fear of death disturbs me) which appears as part of the Third Nocturn of Matins in the Office for the Dead. The phrase became well known largely through its use in Scottish and English medieval poetry.

7 Strictly speaking, neither of these two adages is exactly equivalent to the *carpe diem* exhortation. They refer not to doing something while there is still time but to doing something while the circumstances are right – and of course one might have to wait for the right circumstances.

8 Edward Young, *Night-thoughts*, Night First, 394.

9 John Stuart Mill, 'Utility of Religion', in *Collected Works*, ed. John M. Robson (Toronto, 1963–91), vol. x, pp. 427–8.

10 That a lifespan of seventy years is not a fixed or sacrosanct figure is clear from the source text for this phrase: 'The years of our life are threescore and ten, or even by reason of strength fourscore; yet their span is but toil and trouble; they are soon gone, and we fly away' (Psalms 90:10). The point is this: however long you live, it will always seem too short a time.

11 On the other hand, some might want to argue that an *overflowing* cup is a better image of a plentiful life. 'Thou preparest a table before me in the presence of mine enemies: thou anointest my head with oil; my cup runneth over' (Psalms 23:5).

12 Obituary of Enoch Powell, *Daily Telegraph*, 9 February 1998.

13 Laurence Rees, 'I wish I had died in the war', ww2history.com, 28 May 2011.

14 Seneca, *On the Shortness of Life* (De Brevitate Vitae), 7; trans. Gareth D. Williams, in Elaine Fantham et al., *Lucius Annaeus Seneca: Hardship and Happiness* (Chicago, IL, and London, 2014), p. 110.

15 A critic might well say that the different motives make the action itself different in each case. So be it: the parallel survives the criticism, and even benefits from it.

16 Seneca, *On the Shortness of Life*; Fantham, *Lucius Annaeus Seneca*, p. 132.

17 Satipatthāna Sutta, trans. Soma Thera, *Access to Insight*, www.accesstoinsight.org, 13 June 2010.

18 For an overview of the varieties of meditation systems, see Claudio Naranjo and Robert E. Ornstein, *On the Psychology of Meditation* (New York, 1971); and Willard Johnson, *Riding the Ox Home: A History of Meditation from Shamanism to Science* (London, 1982).

19 Cupitt describes his book as 'a purely rational religious book for the era of cultural globalisation, being pitched somewhere between Christianity, Buddhism, and the kind of modern critical secularism that began with young Hegelians like Marx and Feuerbach' ('The Fountain', *Sofia* 100, June 2011, p. 9; www.sofn.org.uk).

20 *Sofia* 100, p. 9.

21 Don Cupitt, *The Fountain* (London, 2010), p. x.

22 *Sofia* 100, p. 9.

23 Don Cupitt, 'The Radical Christian World-view', Sea of Faith Network, 1999, www.sofn.org.uk. This was a plenary talk at the SOF UK national conference, 1999.

24 Cupitt, *The Fountain*, p. 11.

25 My exposition here follows the analysis given by David Cockburn, 'Simone Weil on Death', *Mortality*, II/I (1997), pp. 63–72.

26 The subtly important distinction between the two approaches might also be represented in the difference between 'making the most of' and 'making the best of' something. Although these two phrases can be given exactly the same meaning, they can also be used to contrast a quantitative with a qualitative approach.

27 William Blake, 'Auguries of Innocence' (1863). For a relevant analysis, see John E. Grant, 'Apocalypse in Blake's "Auguries of Innocence"', *Texas Studies in Literature and Language*, V/4 (1964), pp. 489–508.

28 'It is better to be a human being dissatisfied than a pig satisfied; better to be Socrates dissatisfied than a fool satisfied. And if the fool, or the pig, are of a different opinion, it is because they only know their own side of the question. The other party to the comparison knows both sides' (John Stuart Mill, *Utilitarianism*, 1863).

29 Such sentiments may be naive, but they do not approach the inanity of the title, and refrain, of the 1973 pop song 'I Wish It Could Be Christmas Everyday' (recorded by the rock band Wizzard).

30 See Lisl M. Goodman, *Death and the Creative Life: Conversations with Prominent Artists and Scientists* (New York, 1981), pp. 3, 128.

31 Terry Eagleton, *The Meaning of Life: A Very Short Introduction* (Oxford, 2008), p. 91.

32 Carolyn G. Heilbrun, *The Last Gift of Time: Life Beyond Sixty* (New York, 1997).

33 Wallace Stevens, 'Sunday Morning' (1923), *Collected Poems* (New York, 1954), pp. 66–70.

34 'The Poems of Our Climate' (1942), *Collected Poems*, p. 194.

35 Adam Phillips, *Darwin's Worms* (London, 1999), p. 12.

36 See OED under 'dead-line, n.'

37 See Mario Praz, *The Romantic Agony* (London, 1951).

38 For examples, see Garrett Stewart, *Death Sentences: Styles of Dying in British Fiction* (Cambridge, MA, and London, 1984).

39 This stanza became well-known through being quoted by Sir Walter Scott in Chapter Thirteen of his novel *Old Mortality* (1816).

40 A newspaper article about people who have chosen older partners quotes a 33-year-old man as saying: 'I sometimes worry that things will get more difficult as we get older, say in 20 years' time when I'm middle-aged and [she] is nearly in her seventies, but it would be stupid to let something so special go just because of a vague worry about the future. Who knows what it holds anyway?', *The Times*, Weekend Supplement (10 September 2016), p. 3.

41 Pascal, *Pensées* (1660), no. 233; trans. W. F. Trotter (1931). See also Terence Penelhum, 'Pascal's Wager', *Journal of Religion*, XLIV (1964), pp. 201–9.

6 DEATH AND THE END OF THE WORLD

1 *Tractatus Logico-Philosophicus* 6.431; trans. D. S. Pears and B. F. McGuinness (London, 1961).

2 *The Collected Poems* (Manchester, 2012), p. 485.

3 Written by Arthur Kent and Sylvia Dee for the American singer Skeeter Davis (1963).

4 Montaigne, *Essays* 1.19: 'That to Study Philosophy is to Learn to Die'; trans. William Hazlitt.

5 Henri Barbusse, *L'Enfer* (1908), ch. 14; *Inferno* (1918), trans. Edward J. O'Brien. Arguably the 'otherness' of death can never intrude into the world of the true solipsist. See F.C.S. Schiller, 'Solipsism', *Mind*, LXX (1909), pp. 169–83; and Herbert Dingle ,'Solipsism and Related Matters', *Mind*, LXIV (1955), pp. 433–54.

6 Quoted in Lewis Hyde, *The Gift: How the Creative Spirit Transforms the World* (Edinburgh, 2012), p. 45.

7 William Wordsworth, *Essay on Epitaphs* (1810), *The Prose Works of William Wordsworth*, 3 vols (New York, 1974), vol. II, p. 50.

8 Larkin, 'The Old Fools' (1974), in *Collected Poems* (London, 1988), pp. 196–7.

9 Bryan Magee, 'Intimations of Mortality', *Philosophy*, LXXXVI (2011), pp. 31–9; here p. 32.

10 Various aspects of this assumption are discussed in my book *Where are the Dead?: Exploring the Idea of an Embodied Afterlife* (New York and London, 2017).

11 'Because in history there is no equivalent for what for the individual is the absolute discontinuity of death, historical discontinuity is always, I wouldn't say *relative*, but irremediably bound up with continuity.' Eelco Runia, *Moved by the Past: Discontinuity and Historical Mutation* (New York, 2014), p. 57.

12 See J. Logie Robertson, ed., *The Complete Poetical Works of Thomas Campbell* (London, 1907), pp. 232, 234.

13 See Jerome J. McGann, ed., *Lord Byron: The Complete Poetical Works* (Oxford, 1986), pp. 40–43.

14 Mary Shelley, *The Last Man* (London, 2004), pp. 329–30.

15 Ibid., p. 272.

16 Olaf Stapledon, *Last and First Men* (London, 1999), p. 298.

17 Ibid., p. 303.

18 H. G. Wells, *The Discovery of the Future* (New York, 1913), pp. 54–5.

19 'The Star', in *Best Science Fiction Stories of H. G. Wells* (Mineola, NY, 2018), p. 303.

20 See *Roger Ebert's Movie Yearbook 2013: 25th Anniversary Edition* (Kansas City, MO, 2013), pp. 528–9, also available online at www.rogerebert.com, 20 June 2012.

21 This statement was originally made by Boyle Roche (1736–1807) during a debate in the Irish House of Commons after the Chancellor of the Exchequer had described a grant he was proposing as not likely to be felt burdensome for many years to come and an objector had responded that the House had no right to load posterity with such a debt. See Jonah Barrington, *Personal Sketches of His Own Times*, 2 vols (London, 1830), ch. 17.

22 Samuel Scheffler, *Death and the Afterlife* (Oxford, 2013), p. 69.

23 Scheffler refers to a fictional account of such a circumstance, P. D. James's novel *The Children of Men* (1992), subsequently made into a film with

the same title (dir. Alfonso Cuarón, 2006). Earlier novels dealing with extinction through sterility include Brian Aldiss, *Greybeard* (1964), and Frank Herbert, *The White Plague* (1982).

24 Scheffler, *Death and the Afterlife*, p. 136.

25 Ibid., p. 48.

26 Ibid., p. 10.

27 Ibid., p. 17.

28 Ibid., p. 18.

29 Ibid., pp. 48–9.

30 Ibid., pp. 56–7.

31 Ibid., p. 63.

32 Paul Davies, *The Last Three Minutes: Conjectures about the Ultimate Fate of the Universe* (London, 1994), p. 155.

33 Nevil Shute, *On the Beach* (New York, 1957), p. 79.

7 WHAT OF THE WORLD WITHOUT US?

1 That one's own life can be viewed as the end product, or at least as one end product, of all those thousands of lives of one's ancestors might well instil in us a sense of awe and even gratitude – or instead a feeling of one's insignificance within the history of the universe.

2 'Can humanity, in principle, survive forever? Possibly. But we shall see that immortality does not come easily and may yet prove to be impossible. The universe itself is subject to physical laws that impose upon it a life cycle of its own: birth, evolution, and – perhaps – death. Our own fate is entangled inextricably with the fate of the stars' (Paul Davies, *The Last Three Minutes: Conjectures about the Ultimate Fate of the Universe* (London, 1994), p. 7).

3 For a recent technical estimate of the number of galaxies in the universe, see Christopher J. Conselice, et al., 'The Evolution of Galaxy Number Density at z < 8 and Its Implications', *Astrophysical Journal*, DCCCXXX (2016), p. 83.

4 One counter-example is Philip Larkin's description, in 'The Old Fools', of the elderly 'crouching below / Extinction's alp', unaware of its looming proximity.

5 According to the International Union for Conservation of Nature (IUCN), 'A species is considered extinct when there is no reasonable doubt that its last individual has died.' Georgina M. Mace and Elodie J. Hudson, 'Attitudes toward Sustainability and Extinction', *Conservation Biology*, 13 (1999), p. 243.

6 Carl Safina, *Beyond Words: What Animals Think and Feel* (London, 2015).

7 See Frans B. M. de Waal, *Are We Smart Enough to Know How Smart Animals Are?* (New York, 2016).

8 According to recent research, Neanderthals were a distinct species of the genus *Homo*, and not a subspecies of anatomically modern humans (*Homo sapiens neanderthalensis*) as earlier assumed. See Samuel Márquez et al., 'The Nasal Complex of Neanderthals: An Entry Portal to their Place in Human Ancestry', *The Anatomical Record*, CCXCVII (2014), pp. 2121–37.

9 Alan Weisman, *The World Without Us* (London, 2007).

10 Some indication of what would happen is given in descriptions of
the wealth of wildlife now flourishing in the abandoned area around
Chernobyl and in the no-man's-land between the borders of North and
South Korea. See, for example, T. G. Deryabina et al., 'Long-term Census
Data Reveal Abundant Wildlife Populations at Chernobyl', *Current
Biology*, XXV (2015), pp. 824–6.

11 Jan Zalasiewicz, *The Earth After Us: What Legacy Will Humans Leave
in the Rocks?* (Oxford, 2008), pp. 240–41.

12 Ibid., p. 239.

13 There is no consensus among experts as to when the Anthropocene
Age, as a potential geological epoch, should be said to have started.
See, for example, Will Steffen et al., 'The Anthropocene: Conceptual
and Historical Perspectives', *Philosophical Transactions of the Royal Society
of London A: Mathematical, Physical and Engineering Sciences*, 369 (2011),
pp. 842–67.

14 It could be argued that the dinosaurs (or at least the group known as
theropods) secured for themselves a spectacular form of earthly afterlife
– namely, by becoming birds. Despite all the evidence, however, the 'birds
are dinosaurs' hypothesis is still disputed in some quarters. See Richard
O. Prum, 'Why Ornithologists Should Care about the Theropod Origin
of Birds', *The Auk*, CXIX (2002), pp. 1–17.

15 It may well be true that, as Enoch Powell said, 'All political lives, unless
they are cut off in midstream at a happy juncture, end in failure, because
that is the nature of politics and of human affairs' (*Joseph Chamberlain*,
London, 1977, p. 151). But this is not to say that all political careers are
in themselves failures.

16 Olaf Stapledon, *Last and First Men* (London, 1999), pp. 303–4.

17 Particular forms of this 'enrichment' will be regarded by some critics as
morally dubious – for example, enjoying the spectacle of animals at the
circus, or even gazing at animals in the zoo.

18 See the passage quoted in the final paragraph of Chapter Six.

19 Weisman, *The World Without Us*, pp. 246–7.

20 Time capsules have been defined by one historian as 'deliberately sealed
deposits of cultural relics and recorded knowledge that are intended for
retrieval at a given future target date'. See William Jarvis, *Time Capsules:
A Cultural History* (Jefferson, NC, 2003), pp. 1–2.

21 This date, 6,177 years into the future, was chosen because the interval
would be the same as that separating the crypt's inauguration in 1936
from the establishment of the Egyptian calendar in 4241 BCE. See Paul
Stephen Hudson, 'The "Archaeological Duty" of Thornwell Jacobs:
The Oglethorpe Atlanta Crypt of Civilization Time Capsule', *Georgia
Historical Quarterly*, LV (1991), pp. 121–38.

22 David S. Youngholm, 'The Westinghouse Time Capsule', *Science*, LXXXVIII
(1938), p. 327.

23 Timothy Ferris, *Smithsonian Magazine*, www.smithsonianmag.com, May
2012. One reader comments: 'Beautifully written and haunting – suggests
that every space shot is really a kind of futile arrow against our own
solitude and mortality. Loved it.'

24 Timothy Ferris, 'The Mix Tape of the Gods', *New York Times*,

5 September 2007. Elsewhere Ferris notes that 'The technology, though outdated, has the advantage of longevity. As Iron Age cuneiform inscriptions remind us, grooves cut into a stable medium can last a long time. The Voyager records should remain playable for at least a billion years before succumbing to erosion by micrometeorites and cosmic rays. A billion years is 5 times the age of the Atlantic Ocean, 5,000 times longer than *Homo sapiens* have existed.' *Smithsonian Magazine*, May 2012, www.smithsonianmag.com.

25 Gregory L. Matloff, *Deep Space Probes: To the Outer Solar System and Beyond* (New York, 2005), p. 177.

26 Ibid., p. 178.

27 Jonathan Leake, 'Don't Talk to Aliens, Warns Stephen Hawking', *Sunday Times* (25 April 2010). For more optimistic views, see Douglas A. Vakoch, ed., *Extraterrestrial Altruism: Evolution and Ethics in the Cosmos* (2014) and George Basalla, *Civilized Life in the Universe: Scientists on Intelligent Life in the Universe* (Oxford, 2006).

28 Arthur C. Clarke's *2001: A Space Odyssey* (London, 1968), developed from his short story 'The Sentinel' (1951), was published after the release of Stanley Kubrick's film (1968) – the film and novel both products of a close collaboration between Clarke and Kubrick. A sequel, *2010: Odyssey Two* (1982) was the basis of the film *2010: The Year We Make Contact* (dir. Peter Hyams, 1984). Clarke went on to write two further sequels, *2061: Odyssey Three* (1987) and *3001: The Final Odyssey* (1997). For quote, see Clarke, *2001: A Space Odyssey*, p. 215.

29 Steven J. Dick, 'Cultural Evolution, the Postbiological Universe and SETI', *International Journal of Astrobiology*, II (2003), pp. 65–74 (p. 69).

30 Transhumanists and others would do well to bear in mind T. S. Eliot's famous questions (in his verse drama *The Rock*, 1934): 'Where is the wisdom we have lost in knowledge? / Where is the knowledge we have lost in information?'

31 Stapledon, *Last and First Men*, p. 285.

32 See Eric M. Jones, *'Where is Everybody?': An Account of Fermi's Question* (United States Department of Energy, 1985).

33 Glen David Brin, 'The "Great Silence": The Controversy Concerning Extraterrestrial Intelligent Life', *Quarterly Journal of the Royal Astronomical Society*, XXIV (1983), pp. 283–309.

34 See Stephen Webb, *If the Universe Is Teeming with Aliens . . . Where is Everybody? Seventy-five Solutions to the Fermi Paradox and the Problem of Extraterrestrial Life*, 2nd edn (Cham, 2015).

35 It might be suggested that *someone* has to be first, and that this 'someone' is just as likely to ask the question 'where is everybody?' as any latecomer. On the other hand, if conditions are right for multiple extraterrestrial civilizations to arise, it is unlikely that any one of them would be 'first' in any simple sequential way, any more than a particular raindrop, mushroom or fruit fly could be 'first'. By the time a 'first ever' civilization in the universe had got around to asking the question, other civilizations would have started appearing.

36 For a scientific paper touching on the subject, see J. Garriga and A. Vilenkin, 'Prediction and Explanation in the Multiverse', *Physical*

Review D, LXXVII/4 (2008). The authors challenge the argument 'that we should never assume ourselves to be typical representatives of some reference class of observers, unless we have evidence to back up that assumption. We disagree. We would suggest that, on the contrary, we should assume ourselves to be typical in any class that we belong to, unless there is some evidence to the contrary. This is a statement of the principle of mediocrity.'

37 See John Leslie, 'Is the End of the World Nigh?', *Philosophical Quarterly*, XL (1990), pp. 65–72; here p. 66.

38 Freeman J. Dyson, 'Time Without End: Physics and Biology in an Open Universe', *Reviews of Modern Physics*, LI (1979), pp. 447–60; here pp. 454, 459.

39 Roland Puccetti, *Persons: A Study of Possible Moral Agents in the Universe* (London, 1968), p. 118.

8 THIS WORLD IS NOT ENOUGH

1 C. A. Patrides, *Sir Thomas Browne: The Major Works* (Harmondsworth, 1977), pp. 314–15.

2 Stephen Cave, *Immortality: The Quest to Live Forever and How It Drives Civilisation* (London, 2012), p. 2.

3 See Chapter Five, note 10. According to Genesis, Methusaleh lived 969 years, Noah 950 years and Abraham a mere 175 years, for example. On these 'impossible' human lifespans, Donald V. Etz, 'The Numbers of Genesis v 3–31: A Suggested Conversion and Its Implications', *Vetus Testamentum*, XLIII (1993), pp. 171–89.

4 Robert S. Morison, 'Misgivings about Life-extending Technologies', *Daedalus*, CVII (1978), pp. 211–26 (p. 215).

5 Miguel de Unamuno, *The Tragic Sense of Life*, trans. J. E. Crawford Flitch (New York, 2005), p. 45.

6 George Santayana, *The Life of Reason*, vol. III: *Reason in Religion* (London, 1906), p. 240: 'The Greek gods, to be sure, always continued to have genealogies, and the fact of having been born is a bad augury for immortality; but other religions, and finally the Greek philosophers themselves, conceived unbegotten gods, in whom the human rebellion against mutability was expressed absolutely.' For more on Santayana's views on immortality, see Joseph Ratner, 'George Santayana's Theory of Religion', *Journal of Religion*, III (1923), pp. 458–75.

7 'On My Own Friend And My Father's Friend, Wm. Muir In Tarbolton Mill' (1784). Of course, if there were indeed another world after death, the friend's good life in this world would still be worthy of celebration.

8 Francis James Child, ed., *The English and Scottish Popular Ballads*, 10 vols (London, 1882–98). See also Martin Puhvel, 'The Revenants in "The Wife of Usher's Well": A Reconsideration', *Folklore*, LXXXVI (1975), pp. 175–80.

9 Robert Harrison, discussing Benedetto Croce's account of grief as a kind of madness, writes: 'In its insane desire to be reunited with the deceased, grief puts the griever at odds with reality and turns him or her into its helpless antagonist' (*The Dominion of the Dead* (Chicago, IL, and London, 2005), p. 55).

10 David Graeber, 'Dancing with Corpses Reconsidered: An Interpretation of "famadihana" (In Arivonimamo, Madagascar)', *American Ethnologist*, XXII (1995), pp. 258–78.

11 For a useful summary of the Egyptian cult of the dead, see David P. Silverman, ed., *Ancient Egypt* (London, 1997), pp. 132–47.

12 *Ad resurgendum cum Christo*, www.vatican.va, 15 August 2016.

13 David Prendergast, Jenny Hockey and Leonie Kellaher, 'Blowing in the Wind?: Identity, Materiality, and the Destinations of Human Ashes', *Journal of the Royal Anthropological Institute*, XXII (2006), pp. 881–98.

14 Various companies specialize in 'ashes incorporation fireworks' – for example, Heavenly Stars Fireworks Ltd (www.heavenlystarsfireworks. com).

15 One company states that their jewellery 'will remind you that your loved one is with you. In a fleeting thought or a fond memory, a favourite song on the radio or a conversation with a friend. By wearing it or just holding it in your hand, you will connect with your loved one and share these special moments together' (https://ashesintoglass.co.uk). Another offers to create 'stunningly beautiful diamonds from your loved one's hair or ashes so you can hold on to your special memories of them – forever' (www.heart-in-diamond.co.uk). Both sites accessed 12 January 2018.

16 'Ashes to Pottery: How a Designer Makes Dinnerware from the Dead', www.guardian.co.uk, 24 October 2016.

17 In eighteenth-century France, proposals were published to turn the vitrified bones of the dead into glass busts, ornaments and other items which would decorate cemeteries or be cherished by family members. See Philippe Ariès, *The Hour of Our Death*, trans. Helen Weaver (London, 1981), pp. 513–16.

18 W. C. MacLeod, 'The Distribution of Secondary Cremation and of the Drinking of Ashes', *American Anthropologist*, XXXII (1930), pp. 576–7.

19 James Holly Hanford, 'The Temptation Motive in Milton', *Studies in Philology*, XV/2 (1918), pp. 176–94; Andrew Sabl, 'Noble Infirmity: Love of Fame in Hume's Political Theory', XXXIV (2006), pp. 542–68.

20 John Milton, 'Lycidas: A lament for a friend drowned in his passage from Chester on the Irish Seas, 1637' (1638).

21 John Milton, *Areopagitica* (1644).

22 See Sandra M. Gilbert, *Death's Door: Modern Dying and the Ways We Grieve* (New York, 2006), pp. 103–34.

23 Peter Porter, 'An Angel in Blythburgh Church', in *The Rest on the Flight: Selected Poems* (London, 2010), p. 174.

24 For an excellent analysis of the various nuances of these and other terms, see Christopher Cherry, 'Can My Survival Be Subrogated?', *Philosophy*, LIV (1984), pp. 443–56.

25 Paul Badham, 'Religious and Near-death Experience in Relation to Belief in a Future Life', *Mortality*, II (1997), pp. 7–21 (p. 17).

26 Peter Moore, *Where are the Dead?: Exploring the Idea of an Embodied Afterlife* (New York and London, 2017), pp. 72–102.

27 See Howard Gest, 'The Discovery of Microorganisms by Robert Hooke and Antoni Van Leeuwenhoek, Fellows of the Royal Society', *Notes and Records of the Royal Society*, 58 (2004), pp. 187–201.

28 'It must have taken a huge leap of faith for people to accept that tiny, living organisms were responsible for diseases that had hitherto been attributed variously to the will of the gods, the alignment of planets, miasmic vapours emanating from swamps and decomposing organic material' (Dorothy H. Crawford, *Viruses: A Very Short Introduction* (Oxford, 2011), pp. 1–2).

29 See, for example, Penelope Murray, 'Poetic Inspiration in Early Greece', *Journal of Hellenic Studies*, CI (1981), pp. 87–100.

30 'Essay on Epitaphs' (1810), *The Prose Works of William Wordsworth*, 3 vols (New York, 1974), vol. II, p. 50; punctuation as in original text. See also Seymour Lainoff, 'Wordsworth's Final Phase: Glimpses of Eternity', *Studies in English Literature, 1500–1900*, I (1961), pp. 63–79.

31 Lorna Clymer, 'Graved in Tropes: The Figural Logic of Epitaphs and Elegies in Blair, Gray, Cowper, and Wordsworth', *ELH*, 62 (1995), pp. 347–86; esp. p. 348.

32 Ryan Bell, 'You are Stardust and to Stardust you will Return: Lent for Atheists', www.patheos.com/blogs/yearwithoutgod, 5 March 2014.

33 Frank J. Tipler, *The Physics of Immortality: Modern Cosmology, God, and the Resurrection of the Dead* (New York, 1994), p. 1. For a critique of Tipler, Dyson and similar thinkers, see Mary Midgley, *Science as Salvation: A Modern Myth and its Meaning* (London, 1992).

34 Bertrand Russell, *The Conquest of Happiness* (London, 1930), p. 196.

35 See Nyanaponika Thera, *The Heart of Buddhist Meditation* (London, 1969).

SELECT BIBLIOGRAPHY

Appleyard, Bryan, *How to Live Forever or Die Trying* (London, 2007)

Ariès, Philippe, *Western Attitudes to Death: From the Middle Ages to the Present* (London, 1974)

Armstrong, A. Hilary, *Expectations of Immortality in Late Antiquity* (Milwaukee, WI, 1987)

Barmé, Geremie R., *Shades of Mao: The Posthumous Cult of the Great Leader* (New York, 1996)

Bauman, Zygmunt, *Mortality, Immortality and Other Life Strategies* (Oxford, 1992)

Becker, Ernest, *The Denial of Death* (London and New York, 1973)

Belshaw, C., *Annihilation: The Sense and Significance of Death* (Montreal, 2009)

Bennett, Andrew, *Romantic Poets and the Culture of Posterity* (Cambridge, 1999)

Bradley, B., *Well-being and Death* (Oxford, 2009)

Brodman, Barbara, *The Mexican Cult of Death in Myth, Art and Literature* (Bloomington, IN, 2011)

Brown, Guy, *The Living End: The Future of Death, Ageing and Immortality* (London, 2008)

Brown, Peter, *The Cult of the Saints: Its Rise and Function in Latin Christianity* (London, 1981)

Bull, Malcolm, ed., *Apocalypse Theory and the Ends of the World* (Oxford, 1995)

Burdyuzha, Vladimir, ed., *The Future of Life and the Future of Our Civilization* (Dordrecht, 2006)

Cave, Stephen, *Immortality: The Quest to Live Forever and How It Drives Civilisation* (London, 2012)

Cavitch, Max, *American Elegy: The Poetry of Mourning from the Puritans to Whitman* (Minneapolis, MN, 2007)

Clark, Stephen R. L., *How to Live Forever: Science Fiction and Philosophy* (London and New York, 1995)

Conway, Heather, *The Law and the Dead* (London, 2016)

Davies, Douglas J., *Death, Ritual and Belief: The Rhetoric of Funerary Rites* (London, 1997)

Davies, Jeremy, *The Birth of the Anthropocene* (Oakland, CA, 2016)

De Grey, A., and M. Rae, *Ending Aging: The Rejuvenation Breakthroughs That Could Reverse Human Aging in Our Lifetime* (New York, 2007)

De-Shalit, A., *Why Posterity Matters: Environmental Policies and Future Generations* (London, 1995)

Donnelly, John, ed., *Language, Metaphysics, and Death*, 2nd edn (New York, 1994)

Ettinger, Robert C. W., *The Prospect of Immortality* (London, 1965)

Feldman, Fred, *Confrontations with the Reaper: A Philosophical Study of the Nature and Value of Death* (New York and Oxford, 1992)

Gilbert, Sandra M., *Death's Door: Modern Dying and the Ways We Grieve* (New York, 2006)

Gruman, Gerald J., *A History of Ideas about the Prolongation of Life* (Philadelphia, PA, 1966)

Guterl, Fred, *The Fate of the Species: Why the Human Race May Cause Its Own Extinction and How We Can Stop It* (New York, 2012)

Hall, Stephen S., *Merchants of Immortality: Chasing the Dream of Human Life Extension* (New York, 2003)

Harrison, Robert Pogue, *The Dominion of the Dead* (Chicago, IL, and London, 2003)

Killilea, Alfred G., *The Politics of Being Mortal* (Lexington, KY, 1988)

Krznaric, Roman, *Carpe Diem Regained: The Vanishing Art of Seizing the Day* (London, 2017)

Kurzweil, Ray, *The Singularity is Near: When Humans Transcend Biology* (New York, 2006)

Lamont, Corliss, *The Illusion of Immortality* (New York, 1935)

Laqueur, Thomas W., *The Work of the Dead: A Cultural History of Mortal Remains* (Princeton, NJ, 2015)

Leslie, John, *The End of the World: The Science and Ethics of Human Extinction* (London, 1996)

Lifton, Robert Jay, *The Future of Immortality and Other Essays for a Nuclear Age* (New York, 1987)

Maddrell, Avril, and James D. Sidaway, *Deathscapes: Spaces for Death, Dying, Mourning and Remembrance* (Farnham, 2010)

Meilaender, Gilbert, *Should We Live Forever? The Ethical Ambiguities of Aging* (Grand Rapids, MI, 2013)

Miller, Paul, and James Wilsdon, *Better Humans? The Politics of Human Enhancement and Life Extension* (London, 2006)

Misztal, Barbara A., *Theories of Social Remembering* (Maidenhead, 2003)

Mitchell, Margaret, ed., *Remember Me: Constructing Immortality – Beliefs on Immortality, Life, and Death* (New York, 2007)

Monroe, Kristen Renwick, *The Heart of Altruism: Perception of a Common Humanity* (Princeton, NJ, 1996)

Newitz, Annalee, *Scatter, Adapt, and Remember: How Humans Will Survive A Mass Extinction* (New York, 2013)

O'Connell, Mark, *To Be a Machine: Adventures among Cyborgs, Utopians, Hackers, and the Futurists Solving the Modest Problem of Death* (London, 2017)

Olshansky, Stuart Jay, and Bruce A. Carnes, *The Quest for Immortality: Science at the Frontiers of Aging* (New York, 2001)

Purdy, Jedediah, *After Nature: A Politics for the Anthropocene* (Cambridge, MA, and London, 2015)

Quigley, Christine, *The Corpse: A History* (Jefferson, NC, 1996)

Ramazani, Jahan, *Poetry of Mourning: The Modern Elegy from Hardy to Heaney* (Chicago, IL, 1994)

Rumsey, Abby Smith, *When We Are No More: How Digital Memory is Shaping Our Future* (London, 2016)

Sacks, Peter, *The English Elegy: Readings in the Genre from Spenser to Yeats* (Baltimore, MD, 1985)

Scheffler, Samuel, *Death and the Afterlife* (New York, 2013)

Scranton, Roy, *Learning to Die in the Anthropocene: Reflections on the End of a Civilization* (San Francisco, CA, 2015)

Sikora, Richard I., and Brian M. Barry, eds, *Obligations to Future Generations* (Philadelphia, PA, 1978)

Slusser, George Edgar, Gary Westfahl and Eric S. Rabkin, eds, *Immortal Engines: Life Extension and Immortality in Science Fiction and Fantasy* (Athens, GA, 1996)

Smith, George Patrick, *Medical-legal Aspects of Cryonics: Prospects for Immortality* (Port Washington, NY, 1983)

Solomon, Sheldon, Jeff Greenberg and Tom Pyszczynski, *The Worm at the Core: On the Role of Death in Life* (New York, 2015)

Sperling, D., *Posthumous Interests: Legal and Ethical Perspectives* (Cambridge, 2008)

Stafford, Fiona J., *The Last of the Race: The Growth of a Myth from Milton to Darwin* (Oxford, 1994)

Stein, Arnold, *The House of Death: Messages from the English Renaissance* (Baltimore, MD, 1986)

Tumarkin, N., *Lenin Lives! The Lenin Cult in Soviet Russia* (Cambridge, MA, 1983)

Verdery, Katherine, *The Political Lives of Dead Bodies: Reburial and Postsocialist Change* (New York and Chichester, 1999)

Wagar, W. Warren, *Terminal Visions: The Literature of Last Things* (Bloomington, IN, 1982)

Walliss, John, and Kenneth G. C. Newport, eds, *The End All Around Us: Apocalyptic Texts and Popular Culture* (London and Oakville, 2009)

Watkins, Carl, *The Undiscovered Country: Journeys among the Dead* (London, 2013)

Weiner, Jonathan, *Long for This World: The Strange Science of Immortality* (New York, 2011)

Weisman, Alan, *The World Without Us* (London, 2007)

Zalasiewicz, Jan, *The Earth After Us: What Legacy Will Humans Leave in the Rocks?* (Oxford, 2008)

Zey, Michael G., *Ageless Nation: The Quest for Superlongevity and Physical Perfection* (Piscataway, NJ, 2014)

ACKNOWLEDGEMENTS

The writing of a book, although a peculiarly solitary activity, depends in no small measure on the interest and support of those around one, and this goes well beyond the purely intellectual. I must first express my gratitude to Michael Leaman, of Reaktion Books, for his willingness to take on *Earthly Immortalities*. I owe special thanks to David McLellan and Christopher Cherry, friends and former colleagues at the University of Kent, for their willingness to read and comment on draft material as it appeared; to Theresa Grant who, in very kindly undertaking to read through the penultimate draft of the manuscript, helped save the text from a number of errors; to Alex Wright for his interest in and encouragement of the project from an early stage; and to Amy Salter, editor at Reaktion Books, for the friendly and reassuring efficiency she demonstrated at all stages of preparing the text for publication. But it has been my wife, Maria Moore, who has been the greatest source of support and encouragement. In this, as in so many other ways, what I owe her is beyond evaluation. The book itself I dedicate to the memory of my parents, lovers of books and ideas into their very last years. In so doing, I demonstrate in a very small way the main theme of the book itself.

Permissions

Edna St. Vincent Millay, excerpt from 'Dirge without Music', from *Collected Poems* © 1928, © 1955 by Edna St. Vincent Millay and Norma Millay Ellis. Reprinted with the permission of The Permissions Company, Inc., on behalf of Holly Peppe, Literary Executor, The Millay Society.

INDEX